WHEN THE STORM BROKE

Also by Ethel Shapiro-Bertolini

AND MY HEART WAS
AT HOME

*a semi-documentary novel
dealing with the McCarthy
Era of the 50's*

"I NEVER DIED," SAID HE

*dedication to Dr. Martin
Luther King*

THE SWINDLE

*and other
short stories*

WHEN THE STORM BROKE

A Novel of the Great Depression
1929-1933

By
ETHEL SHAPIRO-BERTOLINI

arti et veritati

Boston
BRANDEN PRESS
Publishers

Standard Book Number 8283-1307-5
© Copyright, 1971, by Branden Press, Inc.
Printed in the United States of America
Library of Congress Catalog Card No. 72-133831

To honor the memory of our humble parents

FEIGA AND USHER SHAPIRO

in whose orthodox home we enjoyed love and respect for
each other. They left us a heritage of dedication to all
who strive for the progress of mankind.

Acknowledgments

With deepest gratitude to my husband, Angelo, for making it
possible for me to work uninterruptedly on this story.

Special thanks, of course, to the friends and relatives—too
many to list—who have studied the manuscript and have contributed numerous ideas for improvements.

Sincere appreciation to the Southern California Library for
Social Studies and Research, and to its director, Emil Freed, for
allowing me full use of the rare books and files.

To Donald C. Wheeldin, teacher of black history at Fresno
State College, and former editor of the L. A. Black Voice, special
acknowledgment for the many hours he spent reading, and
discussing with me, the manuscript.

CONTENTS

Introduction

WHY THIS NOVEL? was the perplexing question that pursued the author much of the time while researching the material for this story. It was necessary frequently to redefine the purpose of adding another book to the many already written about the Great Depression. The need for an objective answer became especially urgent as the events of the 30s unfolded, and the desire to *TELL IT ALL*, to gush forth with expansive scenes of the unbelievable destruction of human and material values, became real.

All the facts, and personal experiences of "the heroes of the 30s", however, continued to point to the yet unwritten story—the danger that faced this nation in the first three years of the crisis, of becoming so demoralized, and so prostrate, as to be incapable of coping with the nightmarish effects of that disaster. The answer, then was summarized in a letter to the publisher:

My novel, therefore, attempts to tell in fiction form, how the American people dug themselves out of the greatest catastrophe of our time.

In the four years of research and writing, I have become convinced even more than before I began this major work, that we do not have available in the English language, any one single book of fiction, which tells the story of the first three years of the Great Depression. Yet, those were the years which had laid the basis for much that followed in that memorable decade: the great social advances, the unprecedented unity and solidarity of blacks and whites, social security, the cultural upheaval, the formation of the large trade union center, the C.I.O.

I have interviewed many people who had participated in those gigantic movements, and became fascinated with those true patriots, who had led a large scale resistance movement against hunger and demoralization. I found them to be wonderful, heroic, stupid, imaginative, fanatic people, who had succeeded in staving off even greater tragedy than history now records.

And that is what the novel is all about, and why it had to be written.

E. S. B.

Los Angeles, California

7

CHAPTER I

God Enters the Basement

I

The deep inner joy shared by the three girls as they prepared
for the last day of school was so tangibly real that they imagined
the entire City of Chicago was anxiously awaiting their graduation. This feeling had been built up for some time; it was
cumulative, it was part of the general atmosphere of confidence
and trust in the future which prevailed all around them. The
three agreed that the year 1929 would remain the happiest in
their memory, as they pledged each other eternal friendship.

Betty Dunhill, who had spent a full school year in the Windy
City, sharing her cousin Molly's home, would soon return to
Southern Illinois, to the Dunhill farm; Molly, too, had made
plans to leave Chicago immediately after her marriage to the
young reporter—who was already in Washington. Only Sylvia
Kanofsky would remain behind, where the three had walked
to Humboldt Park, and had done their homework, and shared
their many secrets. Sylvia, they decided, would initiate reunions
of the three, while Betty, who owned a typewriter, would copy
Molly's letters from other cities, and from abroad, and send
them on to Sylvia.

It was during that last week before graduation, however, that
Betty had suddenly become very quarrelsome and irritable,
arguing frequently over the most trivial matters. There were
moments when Molly even overheard her cousin mumble to
herself, when she thought she was alone in the house.

Betty Dunhill was never much of a talker. When she first
arrived, to do her last year of high school in Chicago, it seemed
to the others that she behaved peculiarly, sulking frequently,

9

incommunicative for days. When Molly or Sylvia attempted to engage her in a discussion, Betty would tell them in a dull voice:

"Listen more if you want to learn more."

"But somebody has to talk if you're going to learn so much," Sylvia told her.

"Sometimes it's better to be seen than heard, like the old folks say," she answered in the same detached voice.

"You mean you learn from the silence around you?" Sylvia asked.

"Well, yes. On the farm you get to hear all kinds of sounds, and it's important to understand what they all mean."

That is how it came about that Molly and Sylvia had gotten used to doing the talking and Betty the listening.

This Saturday, as the three were helping each other with the sewing of their graduation dresses, Betty startled the others when she asked, "You ever stop to think that we're living in unusual times?" She looked at them as if she had just made a most significant discovery.

"What's so unusual about getting married, or returning to a farm, or Sylvia's . . ." Molly began, but was interrupted by her cousin.

"Yeah, Sylvia, what are you gonna be doing? You gonna make a revolution?"

"Maybe," Sylvia snapped, turning red in the face. "You said yourself we're living in unusual times, didn't you?"

"Well, you know what I mean. Ouch!" Betty shrieked. "I betcha you did that on purpose!" Jerking herself loose from Sylvia, she shouted sharply, "You stuck that pin all the way in my behind!"

"I didn't do that on purpose; I pricked you by accident, so what?"

"So what? I betcha my behind is bleeding and my dress is ruined!" Betty twisted her upper part of the body sideways and backwards, in search of a nonexistent spot on her white dress.

They continued pinning each other's dresses and basting the seams in silence, each with her own thoughts. Molly was confused over what was happening to Betty and began to wonder why her natural, soft voice, would so suddenly become flat, and with a nasal twang she'd shout insults at Sylvia.

"I don't know why you have to make your sister Helen's

10

nightgown into a graduation dress. I could have bought you a couple of yards of material like mine," Betty said, infuriating Sylvia.

All three knew that it was not a nightgown; it was Helen's white satin dress which she had outgrown. All knew that the Kanofskys were poor, but proud people and would have refused such a gift. Betty was just being spiteful.

During her year's stay with her uncle and aunt, and Cousin Molly, she had spent most of her free time across the street, with Sylvia. It was Sylvia to whom she confided that her father's real motive in sending her up to Chicago was to get her out of the way, so he'd have more freedom with their new housekeeper. It was to Sylvia that she once opened her mouth and stretching the lips with both hands, told her, "Look, go ahead, see for yourself," explaining that she never had a cavity, and had been chosen as the farm girl with the most perfect teeth. Her clear blue eyes looked directly into Sylvia's, her finger still pointing to her open mouth and the small upturned nose towards the ceiling, as the chubby Sylvia stared at her long blond hair, and shining country skin, and responded with genuine admiration:

"Gee, but you're pretty, Betty."

"Oh, go on! It's on account of my teeth that people think I'm pretty."

"No, honestly, it's your whole face that looks so pretty," Sylvia said with a slight lisp.

Perhaps Betty had become so spiteful these last few days because she was angry at having to part with Sylvia, who had shown her all the beautiful sights of the Windy City, and had explained to her why the downtown area was called the Loop. She remembered their walks on Michigan Avenue, Sylvia leading her towards the Tribune Tower, and asking her:

"You ever read the Chicago *Tribune?*"

"Of course we read the *Tribune* on the farm. Dad clipped the same portrait of President Hoover that you see hanging in cousin Molly's home."

Perhaps it was the lake front, the sandy beaches on the edge of Lake Michigan that Sylvia had pointed out to her, which now made Betty feel so sad to part with. She seemed to draw on many recollections which she associated with Sylvia . . . once having asked her with alarm, as if something ominous was about

11

to happen to both of them, "What is that? That awful smell? What is it?" And Sylvia explained that the foul smells from the stockyards could bring no harm to them. "You get used to that after a while and don't even notice it."

Now as the time for returning to the farm approached, Betty's sadness and irritability had increased, and had broken into the open in odd ways. She wanted to say many things that were crowding her inside. She wanted to tell Sylvia that she really didn't mean to ridicule her for worshipping her older sister, Helen; that she, too, thought Helen was very beautiful and very brave, and interesting. She wanted to tell her not to be angry with her for refusing to read all that stuff about the Russian Revolution, and what they were doing over there for the farmers.

Then she broke the silence again. "I probably won't see you ole girls for many years. Look what happened to me: two years ago Ma dies and I'm only sixteen, and everybody's all messed up. Grandma moves in to take over till I finish high school, and she reminds us over and over again that the Dunhills came to this country from the Palatinate in 1710, and with her odd Amish ways insists that nice people like us just don't leave their household slovenly; and from then on we never enter the house in regular shoes, we wear carpet slippers."

Betty continued without once looking up. "Every weekend one of us has to scour all the pots and pans and that doesn't preclude the everyday cleaning that they got after each use." She looked at Sylvia for approval of the use of the word "preclude." It was Sylvia who had taught her to use many new words, which they called Big City Words.

"Did you ever wash your shoestrings once a week? Well, we did. The one unforgivable sin in Grandma's household is the use of a mop—horror of horrors! that any dirty old mop should ever touch a floor of hers, and she's right! They push dirt in corners and muck up the baseboards."

Never before had they heard Betty Dunhill talk that long— as if wanting to get it all out now, so they would understand her better. They already knew that Betty had to return to the farm and take over the running of that household exactly as Grandma had set it up, and she resented it all.

"What about Lucy?" Sylvia asked. "She's older than you, why can't she take over?"

12

"Lucy's getting married as soon as I come back. She'll be moving to East St. Louis with her husband."

"What about the boys?" Sylvia continued. "Pennsylvania-Dutch are like the Orthodox Jews, ah? The women have to do all . . ."

"There you go again. You want my brothers to quit the navy and . . ."

"That wouldn't be a bad idea," Sylvia stopped her. "They enlisted, like you said yourself, to get away from that farm of yours. But they don't care what happens to you girls."

"Well, wouldn't you have done that if you were a man, and had an opportunity to see parts of the world you'd never be able to get to on your own?" Betty said in defense of her kin.

"I sure wouldn't enlist if I was a man; I'd rather become like one of those four cocoanuts than . . ."

"Caught you! See! You did go to that moving picture last night, instead of seeing *The Jazz Singer*. That Al Jolson is the greatest! I tell you! But you went to see the *Four Cocoanuts* with those zany Marx brothers. I can tell by the way you just said it—you always do it." They all laughed aloud. Sylvia could never keep a secret from them. Her brother, Louie, ushered at the State-Lake Theater, and let her in free.

"You know what Grandma would have done to you for lying like you did last night? She would have spanked you so hard you wouldn't have been able to sit on your 'tooches' for weeks," Betty said, and pretended to be washing off her tongue. "Excuse me, ole girl, I shouldn't use those words, I know. But then you shouldn't teach 'em to me in the first place. Anyway, excuse me!"

She was sincere in apologizing for using words that Sylvia did not approve. Twice before Sylvia checked her. "Helen says that a great man once wrote 'If you go to the gutter for your words, your thoughts belong there, too.'"

The second time she said it, Betty asked her, "Who's that great man your sister Helen is quoting?"

"Lenin. Nicolai Lenin. You'll have to admit he was a great man."

"I admit nothing, but show me where Lenin said it. Prove it," Betty challenged.

"I'll prove it, sure I'll prove it. It's in Helen's books, and I'll find it, and prove that Lenin once said it."

13

The two cousins often teased Sylvia about the quotations she used; she, in turn, retaliated by throwing all kinds of statistics at them, and by asking embarrassing questions.

"Do you know how many unions there are in the automobile industry?" she sprang on them the day after Helen Kanofsky had brought home reams of information about the status of the American labor movement.

"Why do you ask such stupid questions? I don't intend to go to work in an automobile shop, so who cares?" Betty answered.

"But why do you always think just about yourself? There are many thousands of people working in those shops. It's one of the biggest industries in the country, right?"

"Right!" the girls answered in unison, as if playing her game.

"If those men want good conditions, they have to have a union. Do you agree to that?"

"I agree," Molly answered.

Sylvia repeated, "Well, do you or don't you know how many unions there are in the automobile industry?"

"Two," Molly said quickly.

Sylvia sat back, paused long enough for the two Dunhill cousins to notice the wise look in her eye, then shared her wisdom. "Helen says there are seventeen craft unions in the automobile industry, and what they need is just one, big industrial union."

"Hooray for one big industrial union!" Betty shouted, and saw Sylvia close her mouth tight in anger. Again there was frozen silence in the room.

After a while Betty said calmly: "You're not really Jewish, are you, Sylvia? I'll betcha there was an Amish man in the woodpile when your folks landed here." They all laughed, and Betty now insisted that Sylvia give a better account for going to see the *Four Cocoanuts* instead of accompanying her to the Biltmore Theatre.

"Louie told me if I came after nine o'clock he'd let me go in for nothing. I didn't lie to you, Betty."

"I think you're fibbing again. You just don't want to see a minstrel show, and you should have owned up to it," Betty was admonishing her. "You're real gone on this subject, as Grandma would say."

14

"So I'm real gone. Maybe that's why. I don't care for minstrel shows. They make me sick to my stomach! To think that people would . . ."

"Hold it, hold it!" Molly stopped them. "Let's not go spoil our day and argue about all that stuff. Let's forget that business just till Betty leaves, all right?"

"I don't have to forget it. I'm going to live with it the rest of my life," Sylvia answered, a hint of offense in her voice.

"I know, I know. You're going to be a g-r-e-a-t revolutionist," Betty tossed in quickly. "But let's finish our dresses first. It's Saturday already, and we better shake a leg and start stitching on your sewing machine."

"That's out!" Sylvia snapped. "We can't sew in our house on a Saturday."

"Why not? Your mother doesn't mind if we use her sewing machine."

"Not on a Saturday! In our home we don't sew or cook on Saturday. You've never seen us do that, have you? And Orthodox Jews, like my parents, don't even like to see me spend so much time with Christians like you two."

"You must be kidding," Betty said, genuinely taken aback.

"No, I'm not kidding. They don't stop me from doing whatever I want to do outside our home, but in our home, that's different." She sounded as if she was talking about a holy place.

"They don't have to know that we've been sewing while they were away in church," Betty suggested.

"You know it's called a synagogue," Molly corrected her, adding, "We can stitch up all those seams and come back here before they return from the synagogue, and do the hand sewing here."

Sylvia was amazed at her suggestion. "I wouldn't do that! I don't lie to my parents. I wouldn't be sewing at home on a Saturday, and my parents know I wouldn't be doing such a thing." There was finality in her tone.

"What about this fellow Helen's going with? He's not Jewish. Have they met him yet?"

"No. Helen never told them about Art Walton."

"Isn't that being dishonest with your folks?" Betty pursued.

The mention of Helen's name seemed to cast a spell of some kind upon the three school girls. They had long ago agreed that her dreamy hazel-blue eyes were very romantic, and that her wavy brunette hair, parted on the side, and combed loosely, made this petite and trim sister of Sylvia's the most attractive girl on the block.

They now welcomed a discussion about Helen, having become restless and fidgety over their inability to proceed with the sewing until the following morning. For Sylvia, however, the very idea that anyone could refer to Helen as being dishonest was upsetting. The walls of the Dunhill living room suddenly seemed to be crowding her, as Betty's and Molly's eyes were demanding more explanation about Helen's dating a Christian man without telling the elder Kanofskys about it.

"She has nothing to tell. Just because she sees Art once in a while doesn't mean she's dishonest. She's twenty-one and free to do whatever she wants," Sylvia said and broke away from the other two girls who remained sitting on the floor with their garments on their laps. "I've been with Helen to some of her club meetings and have met Art Walton. He's a very nice man."

"Does Helen like poetry?" Betty asked to the surprise of the others.

"Why poetry?" Sylvia inquired.

"People who like poetry like to read it out loud, and eventually they develop a good voice and good diction. Helen has very good diction."

That smoothed things over for a while and reminded the others that Betty Dunhill knew something about poetry.

But Betty was not through yet. "Our neighbors, the Moffetts, have eleven children, and Mrs. M. is only a few years older than Helen."

"Maybe that's why Helen isn't in a hurry to get married," Sylvia said in defense of her sister's marital status. "She doesn't want to have many children and have to give up her activities."

It was impossible for anyone closely associated with Helen to think of her other than as a pretty girl in perpetual motion. She had been trapped in her own enthusiasm for several years, and she continued to respond more than the other young militants—to calls for picket duty, for distribution of anti-war leaflets, and recently, for setting up a neighborhood children's club.

Yet Helen Kanofsky made no allowances for involvement in the theoretical debate that was raging among the radicals on social and political issues. "Let the intellectuals of our movement figure that one out," she said when questioned about her position on the American Negro Liberation Movement. Helen barely grasped the meaning of the new demand for the right of self-determination for the American Negroes—up to and including separation from the United States of America—if they so desired.

The other sweeping debates about the significance of the Russian Revolution, and its meaning to the future of mankind, also seemed to pass over her head, and even threatened to drown her. Helen kept rescuing herself through still deeper involvement in routine commitments. Her enthusiasm and self-propelled busy life were contagious, and tended to infect the others in the club, as well as her followers in the shop where she was employed.

To the Dunhills across the street, and especially to Betty, this beautiful activist appeared to be so different from any girls she had ever met that she frequently plied Sylvia with questions about Helen's personal life.

"That Art, what is he really like?" Betty asked, stretching herself full on her back, ready to give her undivided attention.

"Oh, he's real nice! If I ever met a man like him . . ." Sylvia said and blushed lightly. She just hadn't grown up yet, where boys were concerned. When confused, she somehow managed to quickly change the subject of the conversation. But the two cousins didn't allow Sylvia to sidetrack them this time.

"Well, he teaches high school, and he met my sister only a few months ago, but I think they're in love with each other. I can tell. He's very smart, and very good looking. Helen says he's talking about going South, to the Black Belt, she calls it, to work among the Negroes," she added with admiration.

"What if they should get married, he wouldn't go then, would he?" Betty inquired.

"Helen would go with him. She, too, wants to work among the Negroes."

"Honey chile, you just got to be teasing me," Betty said as she sat up straight again on the floor and and leaned against Molly's back. "You can't be for real."

Noticing the stricken look on Sylvia's face, she asked meekly, "What kind of work would she be doing among the colored folks of the South?"

"I don't know myself too much about what revolutionists

from the North, like Art and Helen, could be doing down there. But Art said that in the South it's still like it was during the slavery days, and in some cases even worse. He attends open-air meetings in Washington Park, where many Negroes gather and talk about the South, and about their conditions up here. Art said that everybody should go to that park if they want to get better acquainted with the problems of the oppressed Negroes. I've been thinking about going there some Sunday. Next week Art is lecturing in the club again but it's about something else, about the coming crisis."

"What kind of a crisis is this Art churning up?" Betty mocked.

"He warned that a big economic crisis is in the making," Sylvia said, hinting that she knew more than she was willing to reveal at the moment.

"You're a real worrier, aren't you, honey?" Betty said flashing her beautiful even teeth.

"I'm glad Helen is buying all that material for me to read because if I ever become a teacher I'll know what the real truth is."

Sylvia was so serious in her new pledge to teach the truth in the future that the others giggled, and soon tried to get her mind back on the sewing.

But the comfortable world had suddenly collapsed when Sylvia advised them that they couldn't use her sewing machine. "We can sew tomorrow morning, before we go on the hike," Sylvia consoled them.

"I'm not going with you, Syl. I have too much to do tomorrow," Molly said casually.

"Neither am I," Betty said and paused to see the reaction.

"Afraid you'll be called Reds if you go hiking with us? Why don't you say so? Don't go! I don't care what you do! I'm gonna stitch up my dress as soon as Ma gets up, then Helen and I will go hiking with the club," Sylvia answered angrily.

She realized, however, that she had acted childishly in admonishing her friends, and attempted to correct herself.

"You can come and do your sewing later, if you want. Ma doesn't mind if you use her machine. She likes you both, especially you, Betty. Ma said she doesn't care if you're Amish—that means 'friendly' in Jewish. And she thinks you're like any

18

other Jewish girl, because you're really 'haimish' or is it Amish?"

They had become accustomed to Sylvia talking like that once in a while. She sounded so very much like her mother who frequently coined puns and witty sayings.

Molly understood Sylvia's peculiar ways better than Betty, having been born and raised almost next door to the Kanofsky home, on the northwest side of Chicago. They attended Wicker Park school together, later Tuly High, and during the hot summer months they'd go swimming at the Oak Street beach, and play "Games of Phantasy" about lost swimmers. They'd sit there on the sand and watch a swimmer go way out into Lake Michigan, beyond the horizon, and after disappearing from their sight, they'd give him up for lost. Then they would weave their imaginary stories: Molly describing him in detail, giving him a name and an age, while Sylvia would put the finishing touches with words she had recently acquired. "His proficiency is suspect," she'd say and smack her lips. When at last the swimmer returned to shore, they'd laugh heartily in relief.

Other times Molly and Sylvia would climb up high on the rocks, away from the other bathers, and exchange secrets. It was there that Sylvia first shared with Molly a cluster of new ideas that had intrigued her.

"Helen once pointed to that tall new building—over there —turn around and you'll see it for yourself, and said that the rooms in there are very large, and they're able to have suppers and parties for as many as thirty or forty guests. From their living rooms they can see Lake Michigan almost half way across." Sylvia waited for a response from Molly.

"Who lives in there?' she asked.

"That's exactly what I asked Helen, too. And you know what she said?"

"What?"

"Helen said to me: 'At the present time the very rich live in there, but in the future it'll be occupied by the very poor.' And I asked her how could the poor people afford to live in such expensive homes. Then Helen told me: 'When the poor move into that building they won't have to pay a lot of money for rent; they might even get their rent free altogether, like they did in Russia, right after the revolution, because,' Helen told me, 'when we'll have socialism in this country, all the best homes and best things will go to the poor people who produce everything.' "

"The working people aren't so poor," Molly commented meditatively.

"No, not all of them, but most of them are, if you count everybody who works for a living," Sylvia answered, expecting more questioning. But Molly's silence indicated that she wasn't going to challenge her further.

Sylvia continued, "Then I looked at the other buildings facing the Lake and picked one out. 'That one will go to the teachers of Chicago, they work harder than anybody else,' I told Helen. I put in a bid for it in case what Helen was telling me would come true some day. But Helen did not agree."

"Why not? The teachers do work very hard!" Molly confirmed.

"Helen was very serious. She asked me: 'Have you ever seen the stockyard workers or the steel workers after a day's work? If you did you'd change your mind. They should get that building.' Then she laughed so loud that people began to stare at us. She wasn't serious any more. But I thought there was something wrong with that whole setup, so I asked her: 'If all the poor people will move into these beautiful buildings, who's going to live where the poor live now, like the Negroes of the south side?' "

"That's a good question," Molly conceded.

"Not so good; wait till you hear this. She made me feel ashamed for asking it. She said: 'There won't be no slums under socialism.' What do you think about that, ah?"

"I don't know, Syl. I really don't care about these things that Helen is telling you, and the books she's buying for you. I can't read that stuff."

By the time the two friends had climbed off the rocks and raced each other to the water, they had forgotten Helen's ideas, and swam far out into the Lake.

On return to the warm, sandy beach, they talked slowly as they always did while drying themselves.

"Dad is getting on my nerves, Syl. I'm going to leave home next year, as soon as we graduate. Leave it for good."

"Where you gonna go?"

"Any place. I don't care."

The Dunhill home was the noisiest in the block. Molly's

20

three younger sisters and their nervous, worn-out mother could be heard screaming and fighting all the way to Robey Street. Molly's father had no influence on his women. Upon return from work each day, his voice, too, merged in the general turmoil; and Betty's arrival from the farm only added to the confusion.

Sylvia's house had become a frequent refuge for the two Dunhill cousins, but especially for Betty, who thought she had seen similarity between the orderly Amish household which her grandmother had installed, and the orthodox home of the Kanofskys.

The first time Sylvia's father, Mendel Kanofsky, offered her to taste something, he told her: "This is a real 'machl', I make it myself."

Betty looked at Sylvia, who nodded her head to go ahead and taste it. "It's real good, just like Pa says. A machl means something very good."

From that moment on Betty admired Pa Kanofsky an awful lot. He was a kind man, she thought, and whenever he spoke, which was not very often, it was almost like in a whisper, but clear. She could understand him well even when he threw in a few Hebrew and Jewish words; and he always answered her questions simply, like the one about his "machl".

"It's chopped herring. You bone it, then grate a piece of onion and two apples," Mendel told her.

"But what makes it so good, Mr. Kanofsky? Did you put something real kosher in it that makes it so different?" They all laughed. She was using a new word for the first time.

"Everything in it is kosher; but you have to chop the herring a long time, and keep adding a few drops of water," Mendel told her, smiling.

Betty had eaten other foods at the Kanofskys, which she knew were inexpensive, and could be stretched when a stranger joined Pa Kanofsky "accidentally" as he left the synagogue, to go home for his supper. She also found out that if not for Mr. Tuckerman, who rented a bedroom from them, they might have lost their home.

"We couldn't have met our payments," Sylvia explained to her.

"Your dad is working, and Louie and Helen are working;

21

why do you have to give up a bedroom to that old man?" Betty asked sincerely.

"Louie isn't giving Ma even one red cent. He's saving everything so that he and Sophiele could get married next year, and Pa lost four months' work on account of his infected index finger. He had blood poisoning."

"What'll happen after Louie gets married and moves out?"

"Nothing will happen. That'll make it better for Mr. Tuckerman."

"Why him?"

"Because Louie shares that bedroom with him. Helen and I have the other bedroom."

"And your Ma and Pa?" Betty asked.

"Ma sleeps on the sofa in the front room, and Pa on the cot in the dining room," Sylvia said softly. "Some day when the house is all paid for, and Mr. Tuckerman moves out, they'll go back to their bedroom."

"Maybe that's the reason Helen stays out so much?" Betty asked.

"What do you mean?"

"Because she has no room for herself, no privacy. And I could see that she doesn't like that old man," Betty told her, reminding Sylvia that she was in their home when Helen ran out of the house with tears in her eyes, shouting to Tuckerman, "You're a dirty, old man, that's what you are!"

"No, that has nothing to do with Helen being away from home so much. She's busy with her union activities, and after she joined the Hersh Leckert Club, I think she had a crush on the chairman, Chuck Lamson. And she's busy there, too."

Sylvia took her into their bedroom and showed her the unpainted shelves with Helen's books and magazines lined up against the wall. The bedroom was totally dark, with a small window set close to a blocked staircase that led to another flat, where the Gould family resided. Minnie Gould, she already knew, was Helen's best girlfriend.

"Where do you do your home work? And where does Helen read her stuff?" Betty asked, feeling completely cramped in, with no air or light.

"I do my homework in the dining room, and Helen doesn't have much time for reading, except on Sunday sometimes, when she sits out in the back yard, or porch. She says that some

22

day she'd like to buy us a swing, like the kind she sews canvasses for. You know what kind I mean, one of those outdoor
swings?"

"Sure I know what you mean; I'm not dumb."

"Well, you said nothing. I thought maybe you never seen
one of the large outdoor swings. They ship them to the big
estates of the rich, Helen says."

Betty's frequent escapes to the Kanofsky home from her
uncle's madhouse weren't of much help. After being let in by
Sylvia, she wanted to go right back into the street, into the light
and open spaces. They'd take walks to the park, or to Division
Street, and Sylvia would try out some of Helen's new ideas.
Betty seemed to listen attentively and to ask questions, hardly
ever arguing. Yet, when the three girls were together, she'd
make fun of Sylvia, as she was doing this very Saturday, while
they were getting ready for their graduation, when she asked
her sarcastically if she was "gonna make a revolution soon."

Angered, Sylvia answered, "Well, you said yourself that these
are unusual times. But I bet Molly doesn't think there's anything unusual about 1929, except her getting married, and
getting away from Potomac Avenue for good."

"You sure can read my mind," Molly said calmly.

"The way you two talk, one would think that everyone's
prosperous. Sure 1929 is an unusual year, but not because Betty
has to go back to that Dunhill farm, or because you'll be getting
married soon, and park yourself in Washington, D.C."

"So help me, Sylvia! If you're going to tell us again that
Russia is the only place in the world where no one goes hungry
any more, I'm going to say my goodbyes right now, instead of
next week," Betty said, and all three knew that Sylvia had to
be careful what she said next.

"All right, I'll shut up, and don't you start mailing me Special Delivery letters either, asking me how we got into such a
crisis, like Art is warning. When I become a teacher, I'm going
to tell the kids before their minds get poisoned, how they're
cheated out of their surplus value . . ." Betty and Molly burst
out laughing, and tears were soon rolling down Molly's cheeks
because it was the funniest thing she had yet heard her say.
Then Sylvia joined in the laughter, having realized that she
had said something awful silly: children getting cheated out
of their surplus value!

"Look, Syl," Molly said soothingly, "don't try to make a Red out of her this last week."

"I'm not trying to make a Red of anyone. But you ask her yourself—no, I'll ask her: Betty, have you ever heard about Sacco and Vanzetti?[1] Do you know if it's a place, a river, or people?" Sylvia's immobile face was staring at Betty for an answer.

Both cousins resented her uppishness—to ask a question like that! Molly could have pulled her hair out for acting like she knew everything.

"Of course I've heard about Sacco and Vanzetti," Betty replied indignantly. "Everybody knows those two names." With true native shrewdness she sensed that if she kept quiet long enough she would hear from Sylvia all she wanted to know about Sacco and Vanzetti.

Molly, however, came out bluntly, "You aren't fooling anyone. You know all about the case, and you've probably saved every scrap of paper, and every magazine that Helen brought you. Why don't you get it off your chest and stop looking so worried? I'll listen, I don't mind. Do you mind, Betty?"

"No, I don't care either way. We might just as well get a lecture from Sylvia. How about it, ole girl? You want to practice being a soapboxer?" Betty's voice was derisive, as if getting back at Sylvia.

"To hell with both of you! You make me sick to my stomach," Sylvia shouted, and ran out of the house, her face crimson red.

"Don't worry, she'll be back soon," Molly told her cousin. "She's either running around the block, working off steam, or she went across the street to check the fire in the oven. She's already sorry she talked like this. She told me many times that Helen thinks a revolutionist should never lose her patience, or temper."

"What fire are you talking about? My goodness! You think she left something on the stove all this time, since we've been here?" Betty asked with concern.

"No, it's not that. Her mother leaves a small fire in the oven overnight, and Sylvia checks it during the day. That's how they get to eat a hot meal," Molly explained. "They're not supposed to light a fire on Saturday."

Minutes later, on returning, Sylvia said, "I'm sorry."

24

"Go ahead, why don't you bawl us out, and tell us we don't care . . ." Betty began.

"Oh, come off it!" Molly cut in. "I want to hear about Sacco and Vanzetti."

"I had to check the fire in the oven, so I picked up this piece. I'm going to read it to you, but you both be quiet till I finish." She looked at them and began to read evenly.

THE SACCO-VANZETTI LEGEND: A year has passed since the murder of the two immortal workingmen, but their cause burns strongly in the hearts of the thousands of Americans. *The Outlook,* a semi-liberal weekly, has just published the confession of Frank Silva, an underworld character who says he committed the Bridgewater crime for which Vanzetti was first indicted.

. . . Upton Sinclair's novel, *Boston,* which is a faithful and complete fictional summary of the case, has just been published in two volumes. It had an advance sale of 24,000 copies, which really means 48,000 copies, the largest advance sale, perhaps, any novel has ever had in America. The legend grows, it will not die.

. . . This month there appeared on the Broadway stage, a play called "Gods of the Lightning," by Maxwell Anderson and Harold Hickerson, based on the Sacco-Vanzetti case . . . it becomes a study in the whole American frameup system of labor radicals, instead of a single case. Harold Hickerson is a Marxian, and he knew all the values involved . . . it was he who was responsible for lines like the following:

DISTRICT ATTORNEY: So you don't think the workers get justice in this country?

MACREADY: No, do you? Did you ever hear of a policeman hitting a capitalist over the head?

DISTRICT ATTORNEY: You admit you are an I.W.W. What are the principles of the I.W.W.?

MACREADY: One big union, organized to break the capitalist stranglehold on natural resources.

DISTRICT ATTORNEY: Do you believe in our constitution?

MACREADY: I believe it was made by a little group of hogs to protect their own trough.

JUDGE VAIL (*his gavel falls*): Have you no respect for the courts, sir?

MACREADY: Certainly not. The courts are the flunkies of the rich.

JUDGE: You realize that you are on trial in this court for your life?

MACREADY: Do you think you can scare me into respecting you?

DISTRICT ATTORNEY: You were a pacifist and agitator during the war?

MACREADY: I was, and I am proud of it. What were you in the war?

When a play like this is produced on shallow Broadway, one feels as if a miracle had taken place. There simply is no serious drama

being written in America. Broadway is a glittering river of futility,
and gilded amusements.

After Sylvia finished reading the piece from the *New Masses*,
Betty reached for the magazine and flipped through the pages
casually.

Seconds later she asked in a hurt voice, "Why does the editor
allow junk like this poem? He calls it poetry?" In a mocking
rhythm she read aloud:

INTERVAL: GEORGIA

By Norman MacLeod

the negro has left is leaving
but he will come back.
sit on your haunches of prejudice
and deride the progress of the world
and the advancing negro.
people so stalemate are the fungus decadent
and gone.

"That's no poetry!" she now shouted, as if personally offended. Returning the magazine to Sylvia, she said with disgust,
"You can have it!"

"I don't know anything about poetry like you, Betty, so I
skip it. But I read what Bernard Smith has to say—he's good.
If you're honest with yourself, you'll admit it. All right, you
don't have to turn up your nose," Sylvia said, looking directly
at Molly. "I know you're not a bookworm. But this piece tells
you what's going on in the country."

Without waiting to see if either of them cared to listen, she
read again:

Almost without exception the writers identified with the modern
schools exhibit moods of despondency and melancholy . . . these
sad young men are "intuitive." They feel, they do not think.
Something is wrong? Something is evil? Let's have a drink. That's
the state of mind current in the studios. The intellectual expression
is a refusal to take anything seriously but their own spiritual
impotency; denial of values, denial of humanity, denial of historical
destiny . . .

"If you read it to yourselves you'd get it better," Sylvia said,
pushing the magazine back towards Betty, who picked it up
again reluctantly.

"My God! Did you see the list of contributors: Upton Sinclair, Eugene O'Neill, Sherwood Anderson, John Dos Passos, John Howard Lawson, Edmund Wilson . . ."

"Oh, quit it, Betty, will you!" Molly scolded her. "Most of those names mean nothing to you, or to me, so don't pretend."

They returned to the subject of moving pictures, Betty telling them that she didn't care about John Barrymore at all because he was too sweet, and that Janet Gaynor was her favorite star. Sylvia agreed, but said nothing more until it was time for her to go home and check the oven again.

After Betty's departure to the Dunhill farm, it seemed that the two old girlfriends were constantly together again. When a trip to the Loop had to be made by either one, Sylvia and Molly rode the El together, crowding each minute with plans for the future, and with talk about Molly's forthcoming wedding. Sylvia shared her worry about her sister's late peculiar behavior, but Molly consoled her.

"Maybe Helen is acting the way you say because she's in love?"

"Maybe. You can tell better than I. Listen to this," she whispered. "I first noticed it right after Louie got married and moved out his personal things. Helen asked Ma if she'd mind much giving Louie's blanket and pillow to the Kowalski family. You remember the fire? The Kowalski's lost everything that night. Well, Ma agreed, and Pa said it would be a real 'mitzvah' to give to those who need it more than us. But we had nothing to carry it in. I told Helen we should wrap it up in newspapers; but she rushed me out of the house, telling me, 'Don't worry about things like that. Let's hurry,' like she always does; she's always in a hurry. Well, we walked to the North Avenue El, and carried the pillow and blanket for everybody to see."

"Just like that?" Molly asked, as she turned her surprised face to Sylvia.

"Just like that. People on the street stared at us and maybe thought we were running away with stolen goods. I was so embarrassed when I saw that couple on the El giggle right into our faces. I asked Helen quietly, 'What do you think they're saying about us?' You'd never believe the answer she gave me."

"Well?" Molly asked impatiently.

"Without even looking at me, she answered, 'They're saying

that those two girls are carrying a pillow and a blanket.' And her mind seemed to be a long distance off. I could tell, she's been like that ever since she first met Art. Something serious must have happened to Helen."

II

Many things had, indeed, begun to happen to Helen Kanofsky since meeting Art Walton. It was difficult to understand her strange behavior because until recently she had followed in the footsteps of her orthodox parents, and had built her scroll of heroes from their ancient prayer books. But slowly, imperceptibly, a new set of Gods and Goddesses had begun to replace them. Several of her new acquaintances had climbed high onto her list of modern, living heroes—Art Walton was one of them. Like her ancient heroes, she expected him, too, to perform great deeds of valor.

Helen shared her intimate thoughts only with Minnie Gould. Only with her did she begin to question the wisdom of having taken up with Art altogether. Everything seemed to have been happening too fast to her, and even the way she had met him was unusual.

She told Minnie that she would never forget the day she telephoned Chuck Lamson and asked him to send someone to help her with the first meeting of a group of children, which she volunteered to set up on the northwest side.

"Do you know Art Walton?" Chuck asked her.

"Art Walton? Never heard the name, but I don't care who you send, just make sure someone comes," Helen pleaded, and answered his other questions. "Yes, I have a place for the kids. Yes, the kids will be here for sure, at ten in the morning. It's this coming Sunday, in the basement. Tell this fellow to come directly to the basement," and gave the address.

Helen had no difficulty gathering up some forty children from the neighborhood, but she had no idea how she'd keep them busy or sustain their interest beyond the first meeting. She often took on work far above her capacity, feeling a need to see things done quickly, with herself involved in all the doings. Her militant activities in her canvass shop had spilled over into evening commitments, at union caucuses, and at the neighborhood club.

It would appear that Helen had a phobia about being left behind, and she constantly wanted to be with others, with groups of people. She did not wish to be alone, by herself, as if fearing an inner emptiness. Her involvement in the numerous activities of the movement had brought her high praise, as well as rescue from that threatening feeling of inner loneliness. Now this fellow Art Walton would bail her out; he would tell her how to proceed.

In the shadow of her own body, and having difficulty with the rusty key, unable to unlock the basement door after several attempts, she suddenly heard a deep, masculine voice ask, "Are you Helen?"

With her back still to the voice, she replied, "Yes, I'm Helen. Am I glad someone came! Gosh, am I worried about this thing I started here! Soon the basement will be full of kids, and the only thing I have for them are some ties which my club told me to sew up for them. I haven't the slightest idea what to do with them, will you tell them what to . . ." she slowed down as they entered the dim basement, and now looking at this man directly, became embarrassed. She now realized that she had talked on and on, without having asked his name.

But that didn't disturb her as much as the peculiar smile on his face, and the twinkle in the large, black eyes of this handsome man—the smile of one who was agreeing with her, and even admiring her unashamedly.

This couldn't be the young fellow that Chuck told her would come. This one was tall, athletically built, clean shaven with a closely trimmed crewcut—she took quick inventory and returned his stare. He was still holding the large paper portfolio away from his body, ready to put it down on the floor, but hesitated to disturb her long speech.

As the two continued staring at each other, with obvious mutual admiration, they both burst out laughing, and Helen asked, "Are you Art Walton?"

"Yes, I am. Chuck said he received a desperate call for help, and that the caller would have a fit if someone didn't show up. He insisted I go and stop you from having a fit." Again they laughed.

"Oh, my gosh!" was all she could say now. She was so relieved, so happy, so grateful to this wonderful man, that she would have kissed him, or at least hugged him, but she feared

29

he'd misunderstand such behavior. Instead she gave him her hand and said, "Gosh! Am I glad to see you!"

"And I'm glad to have found you and this basement. I don't know this part of the city too well. You're not far from the club, are you?" Art asked.

"No, only about six or seven blocks going that way, towards Humboldt Park," she pointed westward. Her rich soprano voice echoed like a bell, and he asked her other questions so as to hear her talk some more.

As they looked around the empty basement, both realized that they were alone in a dimly lit place, and somehow the thought flashed through Helen's mind that it was like being on a date, in a secluded place, alone with this man. She must have communicated something to Art, because he, too, felt the uniqueness of their situation, and was about to verbalize it when they heard children's voices shouting through the open door.

"Anybody there? Can we come in?"

"Come in, children! Let's open the back door and the windows on the side, and get some light in here," Helen said nonchalantly, as if she had been accustomed to spending every Sunday morning with the handsomest man in the city.

Soon more children arrived, and soon Art Walton revealed that he knew how to handle them and how to make them laugh, and keep them busy singing in unison from the song sheets of his portfolio. He was in full command, the master of the first "funfest", as he called it.

The joy that Helen Kanofsky felt during those hours with Art Walton and the thirty-eight children she thought she would never forget in her entire life; she had to share it with Minnie.

"He's such an educated man, not just because he's a teacher, but I think he knows even more than other teachers; he's like an orator, you know what I mean? You should have heard him talk to those kids! Gosh! Then in the next minute he'd make jokes and have them all laugh until he had to stop them. He's so different, Minnie—I tell you I think I could fall in love with him!" As she said it, she looked at her friend quizzically, as if that couldn't really be possible, or ever happen to her.

Then she added, "Gosh, Minnie, what if I did fall in love with him?"

30

"You're nuts! You meet this man once and you think you're falling in love."

"But that's possible, isn't it? They say when you fall in love you know it because it's so different! The way he looked at me, and when we closed the windows and locked up the basement, he asked if he could drive me home," Helen told her.

"Oh, no!" Minnie responded with some alarm.

"Of course not! I couldn't let him drive me home. I knew right away that he wasn't Jewish, and that I couldn't invite him into the house without first telling them. I think it would have looked bad not to ask him in, you know what I mean?"

"Sure! That wouldn't be good. What did you tell him?"

"I told him it was only three blocks to my home, and I would rather walk because I had to stop at the bakery to pick up the bread for our supper."

"What did he say then?"

"He said nothing. He's different. He must be good or Chuck wouldn't have asked him to help me. You know the way Chuck looks after me. But I think he's like—oh, what would you call it? He's like a gentleman. You know what I mean? He has different ways than our boys in the shop, or in the club."

"Do you think you'll see him again?"

"He said Chuck had asked him a long time ago to come to our club to give a talk, but he was too busy. He also told me that he visits Washington Park, which isn't far from where he lives, he said, and that he's learned many new ideas about the Negro Question from the speakers over there, and from the colored people. He hinted that it would be good for me to come to the park, too. Then he said, 'I hope I'll see you soon, Helen. Maybe some Friday I'll come to your club.'"

Slowly she added, "I know he'll come."

"Maybe," Minnie answered. "But I'm not even sure that there was anybody at your meeting with the kids. I think you're making it all up, like you always do. You're a romantic! Come on, you can tell me the truth; I tell you everything."

"You'll see. He'll come," Helen answered, and immediately resolved never to talk about this man again to anyone, not even to Minnie. A feeling of complete reticence, and a need to keep that strange sensation completely to herself, had suddenly set in. Helen kept her promise and Minnie actually began to doubt that there ever was such a man—until that Friday evening, when Art Walton walked into the club headquarters, and Helen, who had turned ashen white, nudged her, and whispered, "That's him!"

The club room was crowded, all seats already occupied. There was excitement in the air. Chuck Lamson had just announced that he'd report on several actions the club had carried through during the week. This would be followed by a talk from Art Walton, a guest speaker who had already arrived. Art was standing near the table, conversing with Kikki in a most animated and jovial fashion. All eyes were glued on Art and Kikki, as it became apparent that they were old friends, and extremely delighted over their unexpected reunion. Kikki was one of the most sophisticated of the girls in the club, and probably the most attractive. Her face glowed now, her mild blue eyes laughing constantly into Art's.

Helen, who showed strain and tiredness from the week's work, sat back in the chair, and leaned lightly on Minnie's shoulder to get a better view of Art Walton, when she first saw him walk in. A shade of a flush soon appeared on her cheeks, and in that exciting moment, her hazel eyes blended completely with her long eyelashes, and her nose, for some reason pale and resembling a tiny button, seemed to accentuate her full lips. But then she saw Kikki rise up quickly to meet Art's near-embrace, and standing next to him, was now comparing notes on what had happened to them both since they last saw each other, while studying each other intensely and with complete absorption. They both seemed to be telling everybody—especially Helen—that their friendship had somehow been interrupted, but now, now that they had met again, it would be resumed with great delight.

It was time to start the meeting and Art quickly scribbled something on a piece of paper and handed it to Kikki, while Helen, in her sad silence, concluded that they were making arrangements for a more private, more interesting, reunion some other time. Kikki sat down in the front row, all her attention on Art, while Helen was at that moment dying an agonizing, painful death, so severe, so real, that she hadn't heard Minnie whisper to her.

"I don't blame you. It's easy to fall for him. Now I'll always believe you what you tell me, I will, Helen!"

But Helen's eyes were lowered towards the floor, as if in shame. Yet, like a powerful magnet, they kept returning to Art and Kikki.

Art had not seen Helen yet; only now, some minutes after order was established, he heard Chuck say, "Under the first point of our agenda—*Activities of the Week*—I'd like to ask Helen Kanofsky to report on our anti-war leaflet distribution to the soldiers."

There was a hush, as nothing had been mentioned before about this to anybody. This was evidently arranged in secret, for security reasons, by the leaders of the club. Admiration was now centered on the petite and ever-active Helen. But Helen, so completely distraught by the scene she had just witnessed between Kikki and Art, automatically turned her back to the speakers' table, when she approached it, and in a whisper said:

"We held a special executive meeting and decided to distribute an appeal to the soldiers, telling them that it would be better to become deserters than killers of innocent people in foreign lands. Minnie and I distributed the leaflets, while Chuck and Sylvia were watching us, in case we got arrested."

She returned to her seat amidst the same hushed silence, but Chuck, sensing that something had gone wrong with Helen that evening, quickly filled the gap.

"Helen is too modest. She isn't giving us the full picture of this very important assignment that she, Minnie and Sylvia carried out."

He told the eager listeners that they had obtained information that on Wednesday, at three in the morning, a large contingent of soldiers would be passing through Chicago for special military maneuvers. To reach the men with this leaflet, it was necessary to be at the LaSalle Street Depot at 2:45 A.M. and to pass it out as quickly as possible and then disappear as quickly as possible, without getting arrested.

"There was the danger of getting beat up by the soldiers, or by the dicks at the station. Girls could get away better than fellows. In case of trouble one of us would then inform the I.L.D."[2]

However, Chuck did not report several other important details: that the depot was completely deserted at that hour, as no other trains were scheduled to arrive or depart; the moment Helen and Minnie appeared in their leather jackets and berets, they became conspicuous targets for the secret police, who were studying every move of the two radicals. These plainclothesmen were waiting for Helen and Minnie to reveal their purpose for being there. It was a waiting game as long as Helen and Minnie were pacing nonchalantly up and down on the platform, their hands in their sleeves, as if protecting themselves from the cold night air, but actually holding tight, under their jackets, several hundred leaflets.

They waited until large groups of soldiers came out on the platform and quickly handed them copies, hollering simultaneously, "Don't become a killer! Don't go to war!" when they heard a loud, shrill whistle and realized that they had been spotted. They threw the remaining batch of appeals high up into the air and ran, with two plainclothesmen in pursuit of them. Chuck and Sylvia followed unnoticed, and in the street, in the semi-darkness, saw Helen and Minnie disappear somewhere beyond the El station. Several blocks away they heard rapid footsteps behind them. The two girls joined them, as planned.

"We got rid of all the leaflets," Minnie said.

"But I'm not sure that the boys got them, somebody else might have picked up the ones we had to throw in the air," Helen explained apologetically.

Chuck drove them home and parked at the long fence of the LeMoyne Church, a block away. "The car makes too much noise. I'll wake the whole block if I get much closer," he told them. As an afterthought, he added, "Wait a second, Helen. You'll be going to work in a couple of hours and you've hardly had any sleep tonight. Let's skip the meeting we scheduled for tonight. We can make it some other time. Maybe you should catch some sleep instead."

"I can come to the meeting," Helen replied.

"Then let me pick you up."

"That would be nice, Chuck. I'll see you tomorrow, after work, I mean today—it's a new day already."

Sylvia couldn't resist noting the time mixup. "Tomorrow has already arrived and become today. She'll see you today instead of tomorrow."

As they walked towards their back porch to let themselves in, Minnie took Helen under the arm and pinched her.

34

"Why did you do that?" Helen asked. "You better stop it, Minnie. Sometimes you hurt, like you just did."

"Haven't you noticed the way Chuck Lamson is looking out for you?"

"So what? He's looking out for everybody," Helen answered with annoyance.

She refused to admit even to herself that she enjoyed Chuck's attentions. Everything had taken on new meaning and new excitement when she first joined the Hersh Leckert Club—having committed herself to work for a socialist America. Finding herself almost every evening in the company of the admiring Chuck Lamson helped considerably to work for that commitment. He was Jewish, and Helen could invite him inside her home—even as Ma Kanofsky had begun to hint that a girl her age ought to be thinking more seriously about boys and about marriage.

Helen had, in fact, begun to think quite seriously about Chuck Lamson, and it was mostly on his account that she had volunteered to set up a children's club. But how could she, or anyone else, predict that her entire life would take on a peculiar twist upon meeting Art Walton.

As Chuck was still filling in other details about the anti-war leaflet distribution to the soldiers, Art Walton sought Helen with his eyes. But she was not looking in his direction, neither was she listening to the report. Helen was in total emotional disarray and grief, after having felt the shattering effects of a fleeting dream.

For days she had carried an intuitive conviction that Art would show up at the club, and believed all along that he, too, was impatient for a reunion with her. Appearing now in full life, with the same boyish smile spread on a face she had seen day and night in her thoughts, with that provocative twinkle in the eye that lingered in her memory, Helen reacted as if she had seen a vision and had turned ashen pale, when Art walked in.

The split second during which the real and the imaginary merged caused her blood to drain, and her speech to falter. She whispered to Minnie, "That's him!" as she continued to watch his every gesture and movement. The real and unreal kept alternating: the dream world and the actual world were

35

now merging rapidly into a new reality. That man came to-night on account of her; the odd sensation she had felt was related to him—who had just walked in. He is real! He is here!

But as this same Art Walton embraced Kikki in a joyous reunion within the view of all, there was a sudden shattering feeling of total loss: the loss of the dream and of the real Art, and a revulsion—something similar to nausea—had overcome her; then emptiness.

To fill that void she now wished she could weep inside, in silence, unseen by anyone; or run out of this club room, away from the sight of all these people. That emptiness and confusion seemed to have brought on a totally alien sensation: she felt as if she had been drifting into a hazy, unclean atmosphere, which had contaminated her body, her mind and her soul. She wanted to separate herself from that situation, and run, so as to shed all identity with that man, known as Art Walton.

She could not walk out of the club room while Chuck was talking, she reasoned mechanically. Deliberately diverting her eyes away from Art, and from Kikki, she now became impatient for the meeting to end, so she could get far away from both of them and forget them, as if they had never touched her life.

Art Walton, of course, was completely unaware of the deep inner upheaval that was jolting the girl whom he came to see for the second time. His admiration for this rank-and-file leader of militant trade unionists had increased during their separation. And now that he had just learned more about this coura-geous girl, who had risked her life, and . . . he kept staring at her during those precious minutes that Chuck was describing the depot scene, and thought that Helen was not only the beautiful shop girl who had accepted a revolutionary solution to society's ills, but also a true, modern goddess. After being introduced, Art Walton addressed himself first to his goddess.

"I'm sure that Helen Kanofsky will agree with me that Lenin is entirely right when he says (he opened one of the books he had brought with him, and read):

. . . capitalism has developed the productive forces to such an extent that humanity must either pass over to socialism, or for years, nay, decades, witness the armed conflicts of the "great" nations for an artificial maintenance of capitalism by means of colonies, monopolies, privileges, and all sorts of national oppression.

Several club members turned their smiling faces toward Helen. This was a rare honor. For a guest speaker to single out Helen when quoting from Lenin was almost making them synonymous.

"That is why, as you can see for yourselves, the Russian Revolution assumes such tremendous significance in the history of mankind. But as a teacher I must caution you not to limit yourselves to the study of the Russian Revolution," and he held up several other books which he picked up from the table.

"Here we have a new biography of Emile Zola, which is a praiseworthy piece of work. Although it is Matthew Josephson's first book, he succeeded in drawing more than a portrait of Zola. He created a record of a great period in French history, and we should read that, also." Art developed his lecture in great detail, referring to his notes several times. Then his eyes twinkled with his boyish smile, and in a light air added:

"As a captive audience of mine, I ought to warn you also *against* another biography—of a contemporary of ours—the biography of William Randolph Hearst, by John K. Winkler. Here we have an example of the very opposite, a presentation of Hearst as an American phenomenon; but I would consider this kind of writing, in our jazzy age, as the American phenomenon. It has become very profitable to create books of good showmanship. Any writer with a scrap of talent can get rich quick—some magazines pay a thousand dollars for a single short story; one weekly magazine pays five hundred dollars for each five-hundred-word story—a dollar a word. These high-priced words are naturally calculated to thrill, but not to disturb the reader. They are as false as the movies of our time and the programs we hear on the radio or see on the stage—with the possible exception of this." Art now displayed a thin book by John Dos Passos.

"This is now playing the second season, and I'd recommend that you read his *Airways, Inc.* But I believe I've talked too much already for one evening," he laughed aloud and sat down to the spontaneous outburst of applause. Several people, including Kikki, reached over to the table and shook Art's hand.

Helen, however, had already moved towards the rear door, and was quickly walking out of the club room, while Minnie and Sylvia were protesting to her not to be in such a hurry.

But suddenly Art Walton dashed by with lightning speed towards the back door, after Helen.

Minnie and Sylvia followed him to the street, and heard him say, "I'll take you home, if you can wait a few minutes, Helen."

"I'll walk, thanks!" she responded in a strange, distant voice.

"I'd rather ride home," Sylvia interjected, but Minnie was pinching her arm, and added, "It's up to Helen."

"We'll all walk home. Thank you again," Helen said, and began walking away from them. The two girls followed her. At the corner Sylvia looked back and saw Art returning to the club.

"What's the matter with you, anyway?" Minnie now shouted at Helen. "First you tell me how wonderful he was helping you get the kids lined up, then you look like a ghost when he walks in, and now you're not even civil to him."

"You mean that's the same fellow who . . . ?" Sylvia asked with surprise. "You mean Art Walton came to help you organize the kids of our neighborhood? I don't believe it! Honestly, I think that's great, just great! Are you mad at him, Helen? You act so funny."

"Why should I be mad at him?"

"Then why didn't you let him take us home?"

"Because we always walk home after our meetings, and we always talk on the way about the meeting and what took place, and we can do the same tonight," Helen answered.

"Well, have it your way. What took place?" Minnie asked.

"He's a fake!" Helen said and bit her bottom lip. "He talks nice, and makes jokes about everything. Did you see how he and Kikki carried on? They were 'kutzeeniu-mutzeeniu' like they had known each other all their life."

"What's wrong with that?" Sylvia asked. "I thought you liked her."

"Yes, but in front of everybody he acts like an old boyfriend of hers, and maybe he's taking her home now, to her apartment. You know where she lives? Near the Lake. They will get along nicely together. He's a fake! He learned something from books, then he comes here and reads from those books, but he doesn't know a thing he's talking about."

"And I'll betcha you haven't even heard what he was talking about," Minnie said angrily. "I was watching you. You didn't even listen to him. You sat there like you was sick."

"I was sick! He made me sick all evening. I felt like throwing up. Talk, talk, talk! That's easy for him!"

The three continued walking in silence for almost a block. Then Sylvia started slowly. "I don't care what you think of him, but I made up my mind to go to Washington Park next Sunday, like he asked all who can to do so. I want to hear him talk to the Negro people, and I want to see what goes on there. You know anything about the Negro Question?" She now turned suddenly on Helen, accusingly.

"You buy pamphlets but you don't even open them up. You tell me to go ahead and read everything, study everything. You spend all your money buying stuff for me, but you'll never understand what is happening in our society unless you start reading some of those books and magazines. But no! You run to meetings every night after work, meetings, meetings. Sunday you organize kids, and when you get a chance to hear a good lecture, you act like a prima donna."

"There you go with your big words and your big talk," Minnie said. "I'll go with you to Washington Park. I want to hear a good speaker like Art Walton, and I don't care if Helen comes along or not. This man will probably never again come to our club."

"Why not?" Sylvia asked.

"Because tonight he came on account of your dear sister, your nutty sister, and not because he wanted to lecture about the Russian Revolution. You ask her if that isn't the truth."

"I don't want to ask her anything. I think she must have had a stomachache, or something. Maybe by Sunday she'll feel better and come with us."

III

Washington Park was noisy, buzzing with talk and argument. The chilly May air was tense with nervousness. New jobs were opening up near Cottage Grove, and other parts of the ghetto, but black people were not being hired. Hunger was on the increase, and the park was filling up daily with the jobless and destitute.

Hundreds of Negroes and a few whites, scattered on the damp grounds, were standing in tight clusters, listening to speakers harangue them to change their ways, to stop sinning, to save their souls. Others, among them Art Walton and his two buddies, Mirko Yanich and Fred Heller, were gathered closely around the tall, slender Negro, known to many as Isaac, who was explaining calmly:

"As an American Red, a black Red, I see no other way out: Negroes make up a majority in hundreds of counties, in several states of the south. In this Black Belt my people must have the right to self-determination, and if they want to set up their own form of government, that's their business. We are an oppressed nation within a nation, and this black nation must have the same rights as others."

Mirko Yanich disagreed instantly, recalling vaguely another black man saying almost the same thing.

"You sound like Marcus Garvey did about a decade ago, only he proposed that the Negroes return to Africa and build their own governments there, while you want the American Negroes to have their own government, or what you call self-determination, in the Black Belt. But if the Negroes and whites of this country don't stick together, we're all doomed!" There was a light ripple of applause, and a voice in the back repeating, "you're right, brother; you're right!"

Art, too, was about to get into the discussion, realizing that Mirko was misinterpreting Isaac's ideas, when he noticed two white girls walking hesitantly from group to group, as if in search of someone. Believing that Helen was one of them, Art smiled softly, joyously, his eyes following the two figures, who at that moment were moving farther away from him. Quickly he dashed over towards them, and saw that he had mistaken Sylvia for her sister.

"Where's Helen?" he asked with obvious disappointment.

"She didn't want to come with us," Sylvia explained. "She said she had too many other things to do this afternoon; but Minnie and I wanted to familiarize ourselves with the Negro Question; that's what you're going to talk about today, right?"

"No, I don't take the soapbox," Art answered, his natural, playful smile reappearing. "But we have good discussions going on over there, where Isaac conducts his meetings. He'll be starting soon."

As they walked towards Isaac's soapbox, Art made a quick mental summary: how different and yet how alike these two sisters look; it's their eyes, he concluded. Although different in color—he well remembered Helen's dreamy hazel-blue eyes, while Sylvia's were sharp brown—yet both girls seemed to have an inquisitive, wide open, almost naive look, as if anticipating to hear or see the new, the unknown. He noticed Sylvia's dark brown hair, and her irregular left eyebrow. In height she stood a little taller than her older sister. Helen was slim, petite, while this girl was still in her gawky age, slightly chubby, with a hint of a second chin.

They were hurrying towards the crowd that was waiting for Isaac to begin.

"Isaac's the best-known Red here," Art advised them.

"I'd like to hear him talk," Minnie replied softly.

One hardly ever noticed Minnie Gould's presence. She was very quiet and self-effacing. The dark dress and small pocketbook she clutched against her body made her seem deliberately inconspicuous, and in sharp contrast to Sylvia's flamboyancy, whose knickers and cotton stockings were tucked under the knee cuff. But Minnie was a stubborn girl; it was because of her insistence that Sylvia agreed to make the trip to Washington Park.

"Isaac's starting," Art said. "Fred and Mirko are over there but I'll introduce you to them later. You probably know Fred Heller, Kikki's fiancé—excuse the expression," Art laughed heartily. "Sounds so bourgeois, ah? But Kikki insists on referring to him as her fiancé, instead of boyfriend. She's formal in many ways," and he laughed again.

In her own silent study of Art Walton, Sylvia observed that he dressed so differently from the others—in comfortable, warm clothes. His brown corduroy slacks were of a good quality, she thought, and his matching vest had gold buttons. The sport shirt, too, was of expensive material. Only his high tennis shoes seemed to be the same as those worn by the others in the park.

Art pursued the subject of Kikki and her fiancé, as Minnie continued to pinch Sylvia's arm. Now he pointed to a tall, blond man: "I think you'll like Mirko Yanich, from Swift Packing. There's a real blue-blooded proletarian for you! He comes here almost every Sunday afternoon."

Isaac had already begun his speech with his customary: "My name is Isaac, an American Red. . ." They stopped in the rear of the swelling crowd, and listened to this hatless Negro, with the light complexion and curly hair. Soon he began to quote

41

from newspaper clippings a set of statistics, to prove his point. Isaac was talking about danger signals, about bad times lying ahead and threatening the prosperity of the country; he was talking about an economic storm that was coming which would shake up the entire country. He spoke slowly, convincingly, and as usual, asked: "Anybody here disagree with what I've just said is welcome to come up here to say your piece."

A smooth tenor voice replied: "I'll tell you why I disagree with you, old feller," and the speaker belonging to that colorful voice mounted the soapbox. Before them stood now a husky young man, of medium height, with considerable self-assurance, mimicking faintly the venerable Isaac:

"My name is Willie Rivers. I'm an American black; no mistake about my color, ah? but I had a white grandmother."

There was a light ripple of laughter. Art and the two girls were also laughing softly, as they looked up towards the face of this dark black youth.

Although his hair was closely shorn, the small ears pressed close to his head barely showed. Willie Rivers' eyes were full of hidden laughter, showing satisfaction in having anchored the crowd's attention. He seemed to be playing with the audience, accenting his brief, staccato phrases with an occasional wink.

"Should have had a pulpit of my own instead of a soapbox."

Several times he stretched his upper lip, in an attempt to cover the wide space between his front teeth. Suddenly, in a voice that boomed to the farthest end of the speaking area, causing a minor stampede towards this part of the park, he directed himself to Isaac.

"I speak with no disrespect to you, Mr. Isaac. You're old enough to be my father. But you read newspapers to us that write about the markets being glutted; you said we're heading for a big crisis that'll shake the foundation of our society. That's what you said! Whose society you talking about? Whose foundation you got in mind, Mr. Isaac? I've been in a crisis for twenty years—ever since I was born. And you've been in a crisis, and you, and you," he pointed his outstretched hand to the people in front of him.

Some replied, "That's right, that's right!"

Willie told them that he hadn't been able to find regular work in almost two years, and was compelled to take odd jobs,

42

earning a dollar or two a week. He knew that there were thousands like him in the ghetto, he said, and continued:

"Willie Rivers can't get those good things on the market on account of Willie Rivers can't get a job. Prosperity don't mean a damn thing to me, or to most Negro folk! Black boys like me don't get good jobs, or good homes to live in, or expensive clothes to wear. I don't know what you mean when you say these are prosperity years which will come to an end with a big bust. Whose prosperity you talking about? You prosperous, Mr. Isaac? You folks prosperous?" He paused, deliberately enveloping the entire crowd with a sweeping glance, holding their attention in his grip. He hesitated a moment, as if undecided whether to continue.

All mischief in the face and voice were gone. Another Willie Rivers—the orator, the angry young man who had dropped out of school—was now before this silent audience. "Black men fought in the last war and gave their lives. The heroes came back home, to Chicago, to a race riot! I seen that riot. Took thirty-eight black lives and five hundred lay wounded. Race riots in Nebraska, in Texas, in Washington, D.C., in twenty other cities. During that war they sent labor agents down south to bring people here because they needed laborers, and Negroes came here by the thousand. Now they don't need us. They don't know what to do with us. Now white men are taking the jobs away from Negroes, and are getting hired instead of us. But we're here to stay! We're here for good, and we got to fight for jobs! That's what we got to do: fight for jobs!"

Looking directly into the drawn, black faces before him, he asked, "You men working over there, in the slaughter houses, you got prosperity?" and slowly dismounted, as if to let everyone answer for himself.

They understood him: some were probably thinking about their wives, who had been working as domestics to help meet the high ghetto rents for their rat-infested flats; others were thinking about this strange type of Black Belt they found themselves in now, in this northern city of Chicago, with segregation in employment, in churches, in social life. The people responded to this natural-born young orator with handshakes as he rejoined their midst.

"He can sway the crowd against Isaac any time he wants,"

Art Walton said to himself. "That wasn't what Isaac was talking about, and this kid knows it."

Isaac, on the contrary, was quite pleased with Willie Rivers' speech. He shook his hand, telling him, "You come back, son. We need speakers like you in this park."

Isaac was not fooled by the superficial arrogance displayed by this young man. He reminded him of himself, some ten years ago, when he, too, substituted cockiness for lack of knowledge. To him it seemed that this fellow was seeking solutions for himself and for his people, and relied only on his own spontaneous notions to relieve his frustrations. Isaac was sincere in inviting Willie Rivers to return to his soapbox.

Art whispered to the two girls, "Wait and see what happens after the crowd thins out. That's when the real discussion gets under way."

A small group remained behind. Hesitantly Art addressed himself to Willie Rivers, "Isaac's been telling us something new today, but it seems you paid no attention to those figures he read from the newspapers."

As he said it, Art immediately sensed Willie's animosity, as if telling him that he was an outsider and that he didn't care to argue with a white man. His eyes were narrowed as he spit out angrily, "You got prosperity? You got a job? You making good money? And wearing fine clothes? Then you worry about that crisis. I got nothing to lose!"

"Son, that isn't what he means," Isaac intervened softly. "I've been saying all the things you're talking about for a long time. But today I was telling my people that this country's heading for a big catastrophe that'll make things a thousand times worse for everybody, for you and me, and for these here fellows, too," Isaac nodded his head towards the few whites.

"All Isaac was driving at today was that something should be done to warn the people," Mirko added.

Like Isaac, Mirko Yanich also took an interest in this black fellow with the natural gift for oratory. But it wasn't the rhetoric nor the keen look in his mischievous eyes that appealed so much to him. To Mirko this new soapbox speaker seemed to say that he was a rebel, like himself; that he refused to continue living the life he had until now.

44

Again Isaac took Willie's arm gently, and said, "Why don't you come back and we'll talk some more about this."

"Come back next Sunday, if you can," Mirko urged, and in a friendly gesture, extended his hand to him, his blue eyes smiling warmly. "My name's Mirko Yanich. What about that white grandmother that you ain't got? Why did you bring her up?" The small group laughed animatedly.

Willie took the calloused white hand into his own, as he looked at the blond man, and smiled back with eyes full of deviltry. "Some other time I'll tell you all about her," he said and walked away.

The discussion continued. Some argued among themselves, or with Art, who answered many questions. The two girls listened attentively to Isaac, who seemed to be talking mainly to Mirko.

"I'm not proposing that the Negro nation, living in the Black Belt, should separate itself from the rest; I'm proposing that as a nation we should have the *right* to do whatever we think is good for us. There's a big difference, Mirko. A married couple has the right to divorce—that doesn't mean that all couples who get married exercise that right and get divorced. Think about this. If conditions in this country change, we may not want to have a separate government of our own; but only we, the blacks of this country, should be able to decide that; that's what self-determination means also." He ended with newly gained pride, as if he had already achieved that goal.

New vistas had opened up to Sylvia and Minnie, who had never before seen such large gatherings of Negroes nor heard such debate.

Later, on their way out of the park, Sylvia said, "Helen missed something very, very important today. This was a very important afternoon. Honestly, it was great! Helen should have come."

On return home the two girls repeated, and embellished, the many details Art had recited to them about Kikki and Fred Heller, and about their forthcoming elaborate wedding. They admonished her for missing an important discussion on the Negro Question, and made her feel delinquent in her responsibilities as a member of the club.

45

Helen's subdued response was, "How was I to know that she was this fellow's girlfriend. The way she carried on when she saw Art, everybody must have thought . . ."

Sylvia interrupted, "Everybody thought nothing! Only you thought that, just because he once helped you with a meeting of children, Art Walton belonged to you. You're too possessive, Helen. You have to change!"

CHAPTER II
A Piece of Nigger

The summer weeks unfolded uneventfully. Outwardly life appeared unchanged. Washington Park also continued as before to give refuge to hundreds of distraught residents, and to serve as a public arena for discussions. Willie Rivers had already returned several times to Isaac's soapbox where he argued, and made new friends.

Once he asked Mirko, "You play basketball?"

"Not much. I play volley ball sometimes, in back of our house."

"I'll take you with me to the gym and show you real basketball playing," Willie said, communicating that they could be friends.

"That suits me fine. And I'll show you what good volley ball playing is like," and they shook hands on that, laughing warmly. The next few times they met again they behaved as if they had known each other a long time.

"How come you're out here so much? No girlfriend?" Mirko asked.

"No, not interested in girls. More important things bother me," he answered without conviction. Mirko sensed that he was not getting a good answer but let it go.

Willie was a handsome fellow, built like an athlete, muscular, strong. His sharp eyes seemed to penetrate a person deeply, making one recall stories of others who had led rebellions against slavery, whose eyes were keen and alert, like Willie Rivers' were now as he looked at Mirko.

"That ain't true what I told you about girls, I had a girlfriend till a couple years back, when she was still in high school, and . . ." Hesitantly he admitted that he had been a very shy young fellow, yet both were getting too serious about each other.

"Her father is a minister, a good man. I think he liked me because Hattie—Hattie Green," Willie pronounced her name

47

slowly, wishing to hear it aloud again, "Hattie told her father everything about us, and he knew that I been talking about a church of my own some day. But instead I became a dropout, and things ended between me and Hattie."

Willie kept Hattie at a distance when drawing on his memory. "She got into a white school in a crazy way," he said and laughed.

Hattie Green was born on the south side, where she grew up and from where she seldom ventured into the white world. She had seen the white men who owned the stores in the black community and the white policeman on the beat, and once a month a white man came to collect their rent. The Reverend Green never told his children about the insults he had taken each time he had stepped into that other world, and their mother never said anything bad about the people in the hotel where she worked as a maid, except ridiculing some of them, once in a while, for being so spoiled.

When Hattie started going to that white school, she didn't know yet that things were different if one was black.

In the ghetto people talked about their South Side High being overcrowded, with hundreds of uncontrollable kids. Those who didn't do well in the other elementary schools were sent to the South Side High, and Hattie had seen those kids on the street, at all hours, while their parents were at work, or taking care of somebody else's children. She and her two girl-friends dreaded the idea of having to enroll in the South Side High, but they saw no other way out. There was no other place to go. Their graduation slips said to report there. The three girls walked to see how long it would take them each day to get to that high school but somehow they blundered into the gymnasium, having lost their way from the main entrance. It was in the gymnasium where they saw groups of boys and girls sitting on the floor, empty bottles lying in the corners, cigarette butts strewn all over. She recognized two girls, but she had never spoken to them or played with them because they were smokers.

Never would she enroll there! Never, never! she vowed at that moment. Pulling her friends by their hands, she said, "Let's go to the Reese High and see what happens. Let's give our slips to someone there and see what they'll do about it."

"But the slips say to report to the South Side High."

"We did. We just reported, didn't we?" Hattie said seriously, "and we don't like it here. That's what we'll tell them over there, in the white school."

In the ghetto people also talked a lot about that white school. It was new, not crowded at all, with all kinds of outdoor sports facilities, and grounds that looked spacious, well cared for. As the girls approached the white school, walking in silence for nearly two blocks, each felt as if she were entering a strange land—each astonished by the contrast with the school they had just run away from. They found their way to the Dean of Girls, whom they told politely, "We want to come to your school, Ma'm. We have good grades."

The greying, heavy-set woman looked at the Negro children, smiled to them, and wondered what had motivated these ghetto girls—the first blacks to come to her. She said nothing for several moments, lost in her silent thoughts, then asked softly, "Who has your records?"

"The other school, the South Side High."

"Do you know to which class you belong?"

"Yes, we do, we do," the girls replied simultaneously, and sat back stiffly. Their eyes lit up, smiles spread on their happy faces as the Dean began to write a note for them. She then told them to go to Miss Harrington and ask her to send for their records.

"I think you'll do well here," the Dean said, her kind smile inflaming the girls with such joyous feelings that they shouted loudly, "Thank you, thank you," and ran out of her office to look for Miss Harrington. Later they ran all the way to their homes to tell of the miracle. They described the white school in exaggerated detail and each built her own story about the way the Dean had personally welcomed her into the Reese High, as if she had been waiting for her. Hattie, a quiet, reserved girl with a hushed voice, had never been so excited, nor talked so loudly, before her father calmed her down.

"It's too far to walk twice a day, my child; and will cost fourteen cents carfare, times five. You'll also need better clothes and shoes."

He studied the sad face of his oldest daughter, deflated like a busted balloon, tears beginning to gather.

"We'll talk to your Uncle Franklin about this," he said.

Hattie's eyes now filled to overflow with happy tears. She knew that her Uncle Franklin would back her up, if asked.

She cried softly, quietly, her face away from her father, as she heard him leave the room.

But the joys of this young black girl lasted only a few weeks. It was late Thursday afternoon, when she returned home from school, and found a white man sitting with her father, waiting for her. It was the first time they ever had a white man sit in their home. He asked her father, "Is this Hattie?"

"Yes, I'm Hattie Green," she replied, offended that he hadn't asked her directly.

"You haven't been to school for over three weeks, Hattie," the white man said.

She looked at her father, trying to read his face, and asked, "Who is he, Dad?"

"A truant officer. He says you haven't reported to school."

"But you know that isn't true, Dad. I just came from school, like I do every day," she said and for the first time in Hattie's life she felt she was black—Negro: the white man didn't want her in the good school, where only whites attend; this white man came to bring trouble to her and to her family; he showed no respect for her father, or for her; he was shouting.

"You're lying, Hattie Green. The records show that you haven't reported to school this semester. Where have you been going every day? to the moving pictures, with other hoodlums?"

The Reverend Green jumped up, his lips tight, anger on his face and in his voice. "You can't talk to my child like that," he said and turning to his daughter asked, in a controlled, calm voice:

"Hattie, tell us what happened. You know you don't have to lie about anything."

"But, Daddy, you know that I go to school every morning, that I haven't missed a day. I haven't been late or absent since I started at Reese." And pointing to the white man, who was now also on his feet, she continued, "If he asks Miss Harrington, she'll tell him that I've never missed a day in class."

"What school did you say?" the white man asked, his eyes screwed with suspicion.

"The Reese High."

"They didn't tell me that. They gave me the record at South High and said 'go find her,' " the white man said, pointing to Hattie.

The Reverend Green moved towards the door, slowly pulled

it wide open, and stood there stiffly, without looking at the white man cross the threshold. He then banged it shut, and walking over to his daughter, embraced her tenderly, and kissed the top of her head.

Nostalgically Willie continued to tell Mirko how he used to wait for Hattie and protect her from the vile remarks the boys on the street made when they saw a pretty girl like her. Some had a healthy respect for Willie's fists, and when an insulting remark would reach Hattie's ear, Willie would stop abruptly, grab the offender by the arm or collar, say nothing, just look with his fierce eyes directly into the other black boy's, and instantly hear the apology: "Sorry, Hattie."

Hattie's big, round eyes, shining with pride, would light up, and her head would seem to lift up just a trifle higher in the air, as she would walk away with Willie like a conquering queen. Willie thought of her that way—and when he dreamed about her, as he had done many times after they broke up—he would somehow see her fading into the distance, disappearing, with her head high, always out of his reach at the very moment he was about to kiss her, and then, then . . . he would wake up, half-believing that he was holding Hattie's tiny waist between his two big hands.

"That father of hers—great guy! Hattie used to talk a lot about him. She told me once that one hot summer evening when she and her sister, Ella Mae, were alone in the kitchen . . ."

They were near the stove, close to the open window. Ella Mae was sitting on a stool, and Hattie, facing her, was holding a hot pressing comb, ready to apply to Ella Mae's hair, when suddenly she saw a huge rat—both its size and sudden appearance shocked her so that she lost her voice. Still holding the hot comb in midair, she saw the rat crawling down the sill, in her direction, and she let out a wild, inhuman scream of terror. Her sister also saw it now, and both girls were screaming and running towards the hallway, as their father, hearing those frightful cries, ran into the kitchen, where the rat was in full sight in bold command of the situation, not fearing anything or anybody. Quickly picking up the broom, the Reverend began to fight that monster, cornering it, losing it, again almost hitting it on the head, maneuvering for the kill, while the two girls, still paralyzed with terror, heard the pounding and beating, and at last saw their father straighten himself up, meet their terrorized glance with his own feigned smile.

As he guided them to the dining room, without letting them turn their heads to the bloody mess in the corner, he said, "Come girls, your brother will be home soon, he'll clean it up. Come here." And they began to cry on the chest of their tall, kind father, who was embracing them with his long arms, holding them tight, saying softly, "They won't bother us any more; Martin will take care from here on," kissing them on their heads, and disentangling them from his protective fold.

Their brother Martin did, indeed, take care from then on: his beebee shot gun was put to work the next night, and other nights. After everybody had gone to sleep, he'd tiptoe quietly into the kitchen, sit himself down near the electric switch, and wait—wait in silence—and as he'd hear the scurrying around in the walls or sills, he'd hold his breath, and wait just a while longer, thinking, "Give them time, a few more seconds." And then, then, suddenly he'd turn on the light, and fast, fast, fast he'd shoot his beebee gun at the rat that was coming in from the window, and the one from the open space near the sink; he'd shoot fast, fast, in all directions, into the corner, under the sink, and the house would awaken, the Reverend Green coming in now, while Mrs. Green and the girls stayed out, but at last, the two men would return from the kitchen, say nothing to each other, as they'd wash their hands quietly; and all would return to complete their sleep, without fear, without hearing any scurrying noises.

Willie said very little to Mirko about his love for that girl. Instead he often brought up her father's name. "Great talker, always was, and liked to read to us about black people. You know anything about Toussaint? Forgot his first name! You know anything about Nat Turner? No? George Washington Carver?" he continued testing his friend.

"No," Mirko answered.

Willie was a perceptive young man, and sensed that he might have put Mirko on the spot with those questions about black heroes.

"Not married, like me? ah?" he changed the subject.

"No, not married, like you," Mirko replied, relieved not to

have to give an account of Madeline, his girlfriend. He felt more comfortable to talk to Willie again about his old chum, Al Ross, from whom he had been getting an occasional letter or postcard from different parts of the world.

"Got a good one this time," he told Willie.

"Where's he now? Still shipping out?"

"He's in New York, maybe for good. I don't know."

They somehow lingered on Al Ross' image for their escapades into the world of make-believe, wishing to separate themselves mentally from their ugly reality and pretending that they, too, were away from the slaughter houses and the ghetto, and together with Al were doing important, worldly things.

"Al's a union organizer now," Mirko volunteered the last information. He touched his pocket, to reassure himself that the letter was there, as he was about to parcel out samples of "that other world."

I was a volunteer for six months. Walked from Staten Island Ferry Bldg. all the way to 96th St. distributing union leaflets. At night I return to the union, where I sleep. But then I got blood poisoning (on account of my bad shoes) and had to go to the hospital for three weeks. That's when Jackson, the sec. called a membership meeting and proposed that I be put on the payroll for twenty-five cents a day. The proudest day in my life, Mirko, when the Marine Industrial Union made me a fulltime organizer.

It was a sad moment for both Mirko and Willie. Their imaginary, picturesque world-traveler had revealed himself with his own reality: Al Ross, a poor merchant seaman, sleeping on the floor of the union, walking in the cold and slush.

I was assigned to cover the barges which took the garbage out to sea. They dock on 96th St. I liked my union assignment because I got there about noon and the captain would invite me for lunch as soon as he seen me.

"Why don't you go see Al sometime?" Willie asked.

"If I ever got to New York and saw Al again, I think I'd ship out, and wouldn't come back to that joint," Mirko said pointing to the stockyards. They both knew that such a step would spell disaster for Ma Yanich and sister Kata, who depended on him.

Mirko Yanich often felt like a prisoner, doomed to remain

the rest of his natural life in that jungle. His frustrations sometimes reached the breaking point, and he'd quarrel and shout
in wild, beastly sounds at his brother, who refused to share with
him responsibilities for maintaining the Yanich home. Now as
he was talking about his school chum, Al Ross, who broke away
from it all, who was able to spend his life as he wished, shipping
out, or organizing a union, those frustrating feelings started
creeping up and engulfing him again. He had to get off that
subject. It made him ill to even think about New York or other
parts of the world.

"What's the matter with you, Willie? No girlfriend since
you dropped that school kid, what was her name?" Mirko asked
sharply.

Willie could not quite understand why such a change of
tone, why such a rapid shift from one subject to another. He
sat back on the park bench and looked closely at the profile of
his pale, blond friend. Calmly, trying to soothe the pain that he
saw on his face, Willie answered, "I got another girl, but we're
not very serious. She's too tall, real tall."

Willie Rivers enjoyed the company of this young packinghouse worker with the gentle blue eyes, but he'd rather talk of
other matters than girls. They couldn't stay on any one subject
for too long. Their mood kept changing.

"When I left Coleman School, a bunch of us boys would go
up to the viaduct, where the railroad train passageway separated
the Negroes from the white blocks, and we had Mickey fights;
the other side had Nigger fights, and we'd throw bricks at each
other until someone was hurt and then we'd go home," Willie
told him. "Sometimes young white gangs would raid us, in the
black neighborhood, and attack the people, calling them 'jigs',
'niggers', and other such names, and there would be many
bloody faces, black and white. Times sure have changed; you
asking me now if I know anybody on the 'killer floors.' " Willie
laughed to himself. They had just talked about how the stockyards could never be organized into a union unless some way
was found of bringing the Negroes from "the killer floors" into
it, together with the whites from the other floors. Soon they
drifted into a discussion about their families.

"Was that a gag about your white grandmother," Mirko
asked, "to get a laugh out of that crowd? Or was she real?"

"That was no gag. I really had a white grandmother. During the Civil War Grandpappy Buck was working for the Confederate Army soldiers, hauling whiskey in big barrels. He made himself a small auger, and during those long trips with the soldiers, he'd bore a hole in a barrel, and with a little rubber tube would siphon off a couple of gallons of whiskey. Then he'd sell this whiskey and get paid in Federal money. When the war was over, he had a good bit of money stashed away. Some of the poor whites began marrying colored fellows, like it happened to Grandpappy Buck. But she got killed in a bad accident. Grandpa must have loved her a lot; liked to tell us how pretty she was."

"No children?"

"No children. When he got over it, he moved to Texas and met Grandma Rachel there. She was as black as me."

"Your parents there now?" Mirko asked.

"They're still there. They have a large yard of their own, and I send them packages of seed—you seen them in the store —corn, okry, squash, green beans. They plant it in their yard. They get by."

He wasn't complaining, he wasn't looking for sympathy. Willie was sharing a serious matter with Mirko—he had trouble buying those packages of seed for his folks. Willie had trouble getting nickles together lately.

The friendship between the two young men was unique: they seemed to have had a great urge to talk to each other about things they could not tell others. But they also respected the long silences between them. Mirko's mind now drifted back to the day his father got killed, at Swift's.

"I never said this to anybody—but when my dad was brought home from the plant, his eyes were still open, still alive. I looked at him for a long time and made a pledge 'cause I knew he was going to die soon. I didn't want anybody except him to hear my thoughts. I bent down and promised him, 'I'll become a cooper just like you, Pa; I'll take care of Ma and Kata.' "

He was only fifteen, going on sixteen, but a big boy, and before that fatal accident, his father used to let him sit in at the Sunday afternoon meetings in their living room where some ten or twelve men would come regularly, drink red wine, sing songs in their native tongue, and then they'd talk seriously

55

about needing a union in there, to protect themselves from the abuses and insecurities.

Mirko knew all along, soon after he had made that pledge, that there was another element that had bound him to his dying father—an element that he couldn't at first spell out—but he knew that it was there. "I had to go on meeting with those men, like Dad had been doing," he revealed to Willie.

After learning the cooper's skills, after working in his father's place for several years, he became restless, inquisitive, and bold. "It was only a couple years ago I got to understand that all the others in there were just like me. We'd all have to do something together if we're going to change things in there." He turned full face towards Willie, sat up straight, and said: "It came to me just like that," and he snapped his fingers loudly. "Without those black men on the 'killer floors' we'll never get a real union in there, or anywhere in packing."

Willie smiled without commenting. He was wondering why Mirko had been pushing the discussion lately about the "killer floors." Mirko often sought Willie's opinions about how the black men could be won to unionism.

"Why are you laughing? You don't think I'm right, that without the 'killer floors' and the other departments where Negroes are in the majority . . ."

"I'm not laughing at what you're saying. But I know lots of Negroes who won't join unions. They came here years ago, and they scabbed because there wasn't any union that would give a black man an even break."

Mirko had heard his dad and the other men talk about those strikes in packing and steel in 1919, where almost forty thousand black men were brought in to scab. He knew that bit of labor history well.

"But every man in this town can tell you that the companies didn't give them any breaks either; when the strike was over pretty near all the black strike-breakers lost their jobs. The whole business of scabbing to get into industry didn't hold up. It never worked."

They were silent again for some time. "We have no union in the plant even now, ten years after they broke that strike," Mirko continued. "The company unions in there don't mean a thing to either black or white. We need different kinds of unions, like the ones they're setting up in other trades, with the militants on the ground floor," Mirko explained.

But Willie didn't see it that way at all. Times were getting worse for Negroes; inside the plants, too. The ghetto life was oppressive, dehumanizing. Willie kept telling him that things were coming to a head soon because the people couldn't take it much longer.

"Race riots won't solve anything," Mirko said.

"No, they won't. But sometimes I wonder how much longer things can go on like this, without some break-through for us." He said no more. There were thoughts in his mind that he wasn't ready to share with Mirko. He had to try them first on others—on blacks.

Willie returned to Isaac's soapbox several times during that week. "The Orator," as he had been dubbed, came this particular sunny day, and as he mounted the box, his eyes slowly combed through the crowd. He paid no heed to Mirko. Willie's tense eyes were looking past his white friend, deliberately skimming over the faces near Mirko, and roving on to other parts of the crowd.

Then in a strangely pitched, nervous voice, he began, "The City Council gave the Traction Company the franchise. Fine! That's good! The street car lines will soon be extended from South Parkway to Cottage Grove. But you and I expected to get those jobs, ah! We expected to lay those lines, right?"

And it seemed to Mirko that he heard a million voices respond, "That's right!"

"When the work on the car lines got rolling, the Irish got the jobs, the Eyetalians got the jobs. Why? Because they're white, that's why. We, born here, can't get work even in our own neighborhood."

"No, we can't!" came a massive reply.

"They say six hundred jobs opened up. Six hundred of us should be working on the car lines right now; six hundred Negro families should be getting food on their tables and clothes on their backs, from those jobs that opened up here!"

"That's right! That's right!"

"But we didn't get any of them, not one, not a solitary one! We'll see . . ." Willie said, and abruptly dropped his sentence.

57

Observing intently, Mirko became convinced that his friend had some premeditated scheme in his mind but wasn't sharing it yet with the people. He was wondering also why Willie hadn't even glanced at him, or shown some sign of recognition. A dozen husky fellows now crowded around Willie, whispered something among themselves and walked out of the park, quickly disappearing from view.

People questioned Isaac about that maneuvering, but he was as ignorant about it as the rest.

"I'll be damned if I can figure him out," Mirko told Isaac. "Where the devil was he taking all those men with him? And why was he acting like he didn't want to look me in the eye?"

"He sure acted strange today, that boy did!" Isaac said sincerely. "Very strange."

Mirko read and reread the story in the papers, and each time he came across Willie Rivers' name he became more infuriated. "That sonofagun! He planned it all! The bastard!" he kept saying to himself, snapping his fingers repeatedly. As he reread the news about a group of black youths who had beaten up several Irish and Italian men near Cottage Grove and taken away their tools, Mirko felt as if Willie had committed a crime against him, personally; not to have mentioned it to him! He was outraged!

Although seething with anger and revulsion, he held himself in check. He had to sort out the important facts and arrange them in a logical sequence before fully condemning his friend. At first he doubted that the papers had told the whole truth, or had listed the relevant information that he had to have before passing final judgment. He was a slow thinker and slow in making decisions, but at last, after piecing together the details involved in the fracas, he became convinced that it was Willie who had planned and directed that assault.

"I must talk to him; must ask him to his face if this is the way he expects to improve the life of the people," he mumbled to himself. "That sonofagun! Planned it all behind my back!" And that, Mirko decided, was as big as offence as the action itself.

His friendship with Willie Rivers now flashed through his mind with panoramic sweep, and a sad feeling of regret over its termination overcame him. When his anger and bitterness had subsided, and when he had dried his damp face and neck with his big bare hands, he walked out of his house and trudged his way towards Willie's place.

"Glad you came," Willie said, opening the door to Mirko. "I see you have the papers," and looked into the pale face, sapped of life, and eyes that were empty and sad.

"Was this your idea?" Mirko asked quietly.

"Well, yes. Mine and the other fellows, too," Willie answered cautiously—a strange thought suddenly flashing through his mind—what if Mirko is armed?

Mirko continued, "You want us to remain in the jungle, kill each other for a job?" In a flat monotone, free of emotion, he added, "Isaac's ideas, my ideas, that workingmen should stick together, don't mean a thing to you! Not a goddamn thing!" He plunked his tired body into the corner chair and looked away from Willie.

He didn't see the newspapers scattered on the shaky card table, nor the disorderly sleeping cot, with the sheet halfway on the floor, and the pillow, as if thrown in anger; he didn't see the tired, strained face of his friend, who had spent a restless, sleepless night. Mirko seemed to have shrunk into a world of his own.

"What did you expect to gain from that kind of stuff? You think it'll be easier now for me to ask whites to cooperate with the Negro men? Or what? What did you expect?" he asked, talking to himself, assessing aloud the results of yesterday's action.

"It's easy for you to talk like this. You're white."

"Sure, sure, I'm white! And where does that get me? You know damned well that didn't stop the company from canning me," Mirko said, snapping his fingers.

"They didn't fire you because you're white," Willie answered quickly, offensively.

"No, not because I'm white, but because I've listened to Isaac, and became a Red—that's what you mean? All right! So I get canned because I want to see an honest union in the yards, in place of that goddamned company union."

Mirko was wondering whether he should tell him that he had been turned back by every employment agency in the stockyards, that he was blacklisted by all packing houses, large and small. Should he tell him that things were rough at home, nothing to fall back on? Maybe he should tell him that he almost went along with the Irish crew on that track-laying job, then Willie Rivers could have beat the hell out of Mirko Yanich, too.

Looking sternly at Willie, he said, "You think you're smart because you beat them up and took their tools away, and their jobs. Now they'll be coming back the next day to beat up the black men. That's the way you want things done, ah?" His color was beginning to return to his drawn face as he paced the floor, angry that Willie hadn't given him any new facts to add to his own calculations.

"They're workers like you and me. They've got families to feed, too!" he almost shouted.

"That's the whole trouble with you. White people can't understand us. The guys were stealing the bread out of our mouths. They don't care what happens to the people in this part of the city. You say they're just like us? I say, no! No, no! A million times no! They're not like us blacks! They can get work and we can't—that's the big difference! They'll live— we won't. We'll starve and die young!"

"But that isn't their fault any more than it's my fault," Mirko shouted back, surprised at Willie's line of reasoning.

"The hell it ain't their fault!" he answered, his lips tight and narrow.

"You can't blame those Irish or Italian fellows, or me, when the City Hall refuses to hire Negroes."

"Why not? You all know my people is hungry; my people lives here, right here, and should get those jobs. 'Don't blame us, blame City Hall,' " Willie mimicked. "I say all whites are alike: they keep the colored men out of the unions, out of City Hall, keep him out of everything, and then you come here to argue with me when we get a break-through! The hell with you and the rest of your white comrades, as you call them. We'll have to do things by ourselves; no one ever gave us anything, and never will, without us fighting for it," he shouted again, in an ugly voice, his eyes piercing Mirko with their open hatred.

Astonished, his own anger risen to a high pitch, fearing if he stayed on in that small room, they'd come to blows, Mirko swung the door wide open and shouted, "Isaac's right! You'll

60

never make a revolutionist! Acting like an anarchist! Better get yourself a church, and start preaching pie in the sky when you die! You won't get it here putting Irish and Italian workers in the hospitals!" and he flung his newspaper into the air, scattering it loose all over the small room. Slamming the door in Willie's face, he raced down the steps to the street, trotting away fast, cursing and spitting on the sidewalk, saying aloud, "That goddamned bastard! Can't build a movement with anarchists and nationalists."

He continued walking rapidly, snapping his fingers repeatedly, unaware of the people staring at him, turning their heads to this white fellow in the neighborhood who was acting like a madman. He tried to hold fresh in his mind the argument he just had, deliberately clinging to his anger and his bitterness, to justify the things he had said to Willie. However, the farther away he paced, the calmer he became, and soon he found himself on the green grass, a few steps from Isaac.

"Nice seeing you, Mirko. You want to take the box and say a few words?" he asked sincerely, noting the agitated flushed face.

"You want me to talk? Today? Are you off your mind, or what? I want to hear what you and Willie's going to tell the people. I'm gonna stand right here, close by, and hear everything you and he have to say. Everything!"

The usual crowd was there already, others were coming into the park through the connecting streets. Soon Willie, too, arrived and began to study the expressions on the black faces. He was sensitive to audience response; he understood the people's moods. Willie had thought a great deal about what he ought to be telling the people today. He mounted the soapbox and stood in silence for several moments, as if praying. Choosing his words carefully, he intimated that he was about to bring very important news to them and that he wanted everybody to move in close and hear him out well. He waited, as others were still swelling the ranks. Slowly, deliberately, he began in a slightly hushed voice.

"City Hall has just announced it will hire Negroes." A deafening cheer went up instantaneously.

He continued, his rich natural voice loud and firm, "Over a hundred of our men got jobs on the car lines early this morn-

61

ing. Their families will now have food on their tables for a while," and again he waited for the applause and "amens" to subside.

"This is the big breakthrough for us. When we talk the way we did the other day, City Hall hears us. Now they know that we mean to get other jobs opening up in other places. Now they know we'll be watching and we'll be doing it again and again, unless they continue hiring black men from here on!"

Waves of joy flowing from "the Orator" and engulfing his listeners could almost be touched in the charged atmosphere. They shared their pride in this black young leader, and beamed back to him with broad smiles, responding to his every gesture. Willie Rivers had spoken many times to these people, ridiculing others, laughing at himself, then lifting the crowd to the skies, with promises of a better future. Now "the Orator" had brought a down payment on that future. He was promising them that if the people stayed together, worked together, fought together, "The Negro will come into his own. Sometimes we will have to do it the way we did it with the carline trackmen, and sometimes we will have to do it the way Isaac tells us." He talked with assurance, returning frequently to the "most important breakthrough for us in a long, long time."

Slowly turning his head towards Mirko, Willie noticed that his eyes were free of bitterness or anger; his hands were hanging loose, disarmed, and relaxed. He felt the time had come to reestablish communication with his friend. After urging the crowd to stay close together and to come back to Isaac's corner regularly for more news on the job situation, Willie dismounted and stopped near Mirko. The two walked away together, leaving the throng far behind them.

"It's bad to leave things this way between us," Willie began.

"Sure, sure. I know that," Mirko replied sulkily.

"Things would be different if all whites thought like you do, Mirko."

"Lots of whites are like me," he answered in the same tone.

What Mirko really wanted to talk about was that question which had been annoying him all morning; however, the wrong answer could set them apart again. He hesitated, then looking at Willie for the first time since they left the soapbox, he blurted out, "Why didn't you go to work on those tracks, like the other men?"

To Mirko's amazement a broad smile began to spread on Willie's face, a smile that told him they were good friends again. With the breakup of the track gangs, something new had awakened in Willie: it was a turning point of some kind in his young life which he did not fully understand himself. For hours he, too, had been thinking about the very question Mirko just asked him. Willie Rivers seemed to have discovered during that trying period a new quality within himself: he now trusted himself as a leader of men! To continue leading his people, at this moment, appeared to him to be more important than earning the few dollars a week for his maintenance. He could not verbalize his own thinking and his new, strange feelings. He had to return to Isaac's soapbox, to talk to the people, to find out how they would respond to him. The supreme test—the attitude of his people to him—that he had to pass yet. But Willie also wanted to hear what Isaac and Mirko had to say. Now that he saw himself as a man of action who could obtain results for his people, would they accept him as their leader?

And here he was, again by the side of his white friend, being tested by him, as he had tested himself. The man was asking him why he hadn't gone to work on those tracks, like the other men?

This very question had brought on his deeper search for answers to other questions: What next for my people? What next for me? Will I, Williem Rivers, be leading black men the rest of my life in such fights as yesterday, to take jobs away from whites?

Willie Rivers was no longer the clever, the arrogant, and cocky leader of husky black men. He had been examining again and again the most serious question of his entire life: Can all the blacks of the Chicago ghetto, and of the other ghettos, get work by kicking out the whites from their jobs? Is that the only way? Is there no other way? This became so important to him during that sleepless night, because Willie Rivers was the initiator of that idea and the leader of those men who made his idea a reality. He wanted to talk again to Mirko about these matters, but couldn't. Instead he began to think out loud.

63

"I was good with that basketball; could have gone far, but
. . ." he hesitated, thinking to himself: Can this white fellow
really understand what I'm saying? Can anyone who's not black
understand such things? He continued, "But it was futile, futile.
I couldn't expect all my people to become basketball players.
There had to be another way."

He was beginning to feel fatigued, yet he could not stop talking or stop his trend of thought, and asked, "Did you ever think
of becoming a preacher?" and they both laughed heartily.

Willie went on, "My aunt thought I'd make a good preacher,
and she kept telling me all the time 'you know how to talk, boy,
and preachers got to know how to talk.' For a while I thought
she was right. My buddy who was studying down in Virginia
said he could get me in there because of my basketball playing,"
and Mirko heard again about Willie's enrollment in the Richmond University, where he had spent a full year studying and
playing basketball.

"But preaching wasn't for me," he admitted. "We got enough
preachers already. We been preaching for hundreds of years—
that didn't change things for us."

"What will change things for the Negro people of this country?" Mirko asked; and now they were thinking together, slowly,
cautiously, as friends often do.

They both got up, feeling a need for movement. As they
walked away, Willie pulled his own thoughts into the daylight
and began answering Mirko's question.

"I was twice a dropout; didn't care to finish high school because I saw no good of getting more education. Education
wasn't giving work to my people; too many with education
working as janitors, or in the slaughterhouses."

It wasn't lack of education, he told Mirko, that had him
locked up with the roaches and bugs, with the three other families sharing one toilet, one kitchen, and broken-down plumb-
ing. No! It was the color of his skin that had condemned him
to a lifetime of humiliation. But that he couldn't change, he
said; that he didn't want to change. "Then I'll be the best basketball player on the team, best in the city, best anywhere."

After a long pause, he resumed. "I been thinking for a while
that more black men ought to get into business, all kinds of
business, banks, real estate, insurance, everything. My people
ought to be buying only from their own—all that money the

Negroes spend for rent and food, and other things should go back to our own businessmen. But after a while, that didn't add up either. It wouldn't really make that much difference."

Again he became annoyed with himself. His mind was tired. He'd rather listen than talk so much about himself. He asked Mirko, "What about yourself?"

Mirko told him why he became a dropout when "Dad passed away just like that!" he snapped his fingers clearly. "Wished I could have shipped out like Al did." He always seemed to pair himself with Al Ross when referring to the days of his father's accident. They were both born in the slum neighborhood, both became dropouts at the same time. Al, however, was able to run away from home, while Mirko became the provider for the Yanich family. But even from afar, Al succeeded in invading his privacy, and lately had begun to influence his thinking—and Willie's thinking.

In one of Al's undecipherable letters, he wrote: "I've been to many countries since I last seen you, but it seems to be the same all over." He said little more, except for that unusual P.S. "I couldn't get anywhere with a name like mine, that's why I'm now, Your Pal Al Ross," he signed off.

Mirko was confused when he first read that line and was wondering why Alfredo Rossini suddenly had to chop his name down to Al Ross, and what he could have meant by "it seems to be the same all over." But Al gave no return address, and correspondence remained one-way for several more years. He kept sending postcards and brief letters at long intervals, describing life in India, in sea ports of South America, and other countries, and Mirko shared with Willie his thoughts about his invisible Al Ross.

"I've been carrying this thing with me since last Saturday; wanted to show it to you this morning, when I came to your home, but maybe it's better that you read it now to yourself." He gave him Al's last letter.

I landed a job on a ship which was bound for the Black Sea. Aboard this S.S. Yalza there was a son of a well-to-do family who decided to "teach" me a few things. He told me how the Bolsheviks had taken away the property from the rich and denied the existence of God; how plain ignorant workers and poor farmers were put in charge of factories and were running things—and ruining the country.

Our ship spent 23 days in Novorossisk and the Russian workers treated me like a respected person. They worked hard, they were happy, they sang and danced and had confidence in their future. I began to love them as I never thought I would love members of the human race again. For the first time in my life I began to feel self-respect and was sure, deep in my heart, that these people were free people.

"You see, Willie, why sometimes I wish I could have done what Al done, but then there's Mom and Kata."

"What about your brother? You said he's making good money, working at Republic Steel."

"The hell with him! He's a foreman and thinks he's too important or too big for us. Comes home to eat and sleep, gets dressed up in good clothes, and takes off to his girlfriend. Says nothing, nothing, after eating his meals . . ." and Mirko began to laugh.

"That don't sound funny to me. Why are you laughing?"

"My brother reminded me of a story Dad told us about two men who ate together from the same soup bowl. One was a good eater, the other was a good talker. The talker spoke about his grandmother, that she had been ailing for a long time, and how she suffered towards the end with great pains, lasting many months. He noticed, however, that the food was disappearing rapidly and thought he'd ask the other man if he remembered how his grandmother died. 'Sure do; she died suddenly,' he answered and continued eating what was left in the bowl. My brother is something like that good eater; he gets everything for the few dollars he pays Mom; and I had to go to work to take care of Kata and mother." Now he, too, wasn't so sure that there was anything funny in that story. He added, "I'm just like you: not wanted by any of the packing houses, blacklisted because I'm a Red, they say; and you blacklisted because you're black."

"You and Isaac, and that Arthur Walton guy, you all talk of socialism like it was around the corner. All we have to do is join your party and we'll get socialism here, too," Willie said quietly. "But I may not live that long. We have to get jobs and food first, or we may never see that socialism of yours."

"All right, so you get a few hundred jobs for a few hundred Negroes. Now what? Where do you go from here?" Mirko asked.

"That's why you bother me. Even you don't understand the

66

way things are with us. I don't care where we go from here—
and most of us don't care either."

"But I do," Mirko objected.

"Sure you do. Being white makes all the difference; our people get killed just for being black . . ." His voice drifted off.
He was recalling something that had taken place long ago
which had left a scar on his childhood and on his entire life
—when he saw a mob, dressed in its Sunday best, laughing and
joking, and then—as one paper recorded it

. . . the accused Negro was seized by the mob; there quickly
assembled a thousand or more men, women, and children. He was
hung up in a sweet-gum tree by his arms; members of the mob
tortured him for more than an hour. His toes were cut off joint by
joint. His fingers were removed, and members of the mob extracted
his teeth. After further unmentionable mutilation, the Negro's still
living body was saturated with gasoline and a lighted match was
applied. As the flames leaped up, hundreds of shots were fired into
the dying victim. During the day thousands of people from miles
around rode out to see the sight.

What happened to that seven-year-old Willie Rivers, who
had witnessed it all, who saw a man get killed because he was
black? He asked Mirko, "You ever seen a lynching? No, of
course not! But you talk about it in the park and you read
about the five thousand black men and women in this country
who got lynched. I seen one of them."

The silence between the two friends became oppressive, and
somehow made Mirko feel that he, too, had something to do
with those lynchings: he was white, it was whites who did the
lynchings. He had to disassociate himself from those whites,
from those mobs; he had to say something to Willie but didn't
know what.

He asked, "Were you scared when you saw that lynching?"

"I wasn't real scared when I saw that mob. It wasn't something I feared would happen to me at that time. I was just a
kid and my mother was holding my hands tight in hers, and I
could feel her heavy body protecting me. No, that wasn't the
time, as I can remember, being real scared. It was another
time," and he broke into a soft, rolling laughter, as was his
habit when he had something amusing, or serious to tell.

He looked at Mirko and began to give a slow account of that
one time in his life, "About two years ago. Never forget it! For

several minutes I was in the same room with a barbarian." He waited for it to sink in, then repeated, "In the same room with a barbarian—up there, on North Michigan. That was the only time in my life I can remember getting so scared I wetted in my pants. Must have gotten paralyzed with fear: my feet stuck to the floor, couldn't move 'em. 'All right, you bastard, you'll have to come right here, where I'm standing,' I says to myself, and I shake inside of me 'cause I was afraid of what I was thinking of doing to him if he came any closer to me."

Mirko looked into the serious, hard eyes. There was no laughter or mischief in them. Willie continued slowly. "I did odd jobs, here and there. That day I was working at the lake front, in the rich neighborhood, washing windows. I was all through, finished, the last room done, when I seen something there on a table near the window; looked awful strange, I was curious but didn't touch it, just kept staring at that odd thing, when this big, paunchy, red-faced man, this barbarian, comes in from another room and sees me looking at this thing. I could tell he was drinking by the way he walked in, and by the way he was looking at me. He asked, 'You know what this is?' 'No,' I answers him. And he says, looking at me with little piggish eyes, smiling, he says, 'That's a soov'neer, a piece o' nigger,' and he picks up this souvenir and holds it in his fat hand. I says to myself, 'God help me, I'm alone with a barbarian up here on the top floor,' and suddenly he laughs, like he's telling me, 'You're next, nigger,' and that notion gets caught in my mind, trapped right here," Willie pointed to his temple. "That's when I got real scared—thinking what I was about to do to him—but the next second my feet got unfrozen, and I run out of there, down all those floors, and I keep running . . ."

They were both silent. Mirko's mind was still up there, in the room with the barbarian, visualizing it all; but he, too, wanted to run and get away from it.

He asked sincerely, "How's about coming over for supper tonight? You've never met Mom."

"Wished I could, Mirko, but I promised Bernice—she's making my favorite, sweet potato pie."

"Bernice? You never mentioned that name before."

"That's the tall girl I been telling you about," Willie replied. They both smiled and went their own way, after a while.

CHAPTER III

"You Gonna Make a Revolution?"

I

For Art Walton the spring and summer months of 1929 had become most crucial: The time had arrived for a clean break with his mode of life—an exciting, promising future was knocking at his door—but Art was unable to rouse himself and let it in.

Publicly he identified himself with the radical movement which was deeply influenced by the continued survival of the new socialist state—the Union of Soviet Socialist Republics. When alone, in his comfortable, well-furnished bachelor apartment, he studied the events abroad and became a most ardent devotee of the new society. He reread John Reed's *Ten Days That Shook the World*, and argued its merits with all who would listen to him. He agreed fully with Isaac that the readiness to defend the young Soviet Republic was the touchstone of a Marxist's sincerity.

"If they attack and destroy the first workers' republic, humanity will be set back decades and maybe centuries; humanity will be thrown back to the Middle Ages," Art said, and already hinted for the first time that teaching in the South Side High, or any school, was a waste of time; that he, too, was considering a more meaningful way of spending his life.

"You can go to Russia and teach there," Isaac teased him.

"You know yourself they don't need me there. I would be doing them more good by staying here—maybe by going to the south."

"That might not be a bad idea," Isaac replied and dropped the subject, unaware that Art had been considering such a move for some time.

"Too bad you weren't here yesterday. We had visitors from the northwest side."

"The same girls who were here before?" Art asked casually.

69

"The same, only there was three of them this time; they brought a real pretty one with them," Isaac said with satisfaction.

The fleeting thought that Helen Kanofsky might have been to the park had flashed through his mind. "Was the new one the sister of one of the girls?" he asked Isaac.

"I don't know. I don't think so. She was very pretty," he replied.

Art might have forgotten by now the pretty girl whom he once had met in a basement, and whom he came to see a second time at a club lecture; he might have shelved that experience with the others he had accumulated in his bachelorhood. His list of female acquaintances had grown during the years; Helen Kanofsky was on it—the most current one. But learning that there were three girls from the northwest side in the park had suddenly revived his interest in that beautiful shop girl. Could it be that Helen came looking for him?

Meeting her again had become important to the frustrated Art Walton, who was considerably removed from working people's actual life. For some time he seemed to have carried peculiar romantic notions and feelings of glorification of the workers in the industrial plants, especially in the steel mills and packing houses. One would think that Art was attempting to bridge classes—to step out of the established Waltons into the ranks of the unknown, deprived masses—without getting hurt. Helen Kanofsky now loomed again as a person whose hand he might hold on to, as he was crossing over with her. He could talk to her about his decision to give up teaching for good, and perhaps even going to the south, where his break with the Chicago Waltons could be a clean break and an irreversible step. Wasn't Helen a true product of that class of people whom he wished so much to lift up and help liberate? Wasn't Helen the closest to his image of the genuine working-class girl whom he had hoped to meet and to understand, ever since he became interested in the radical movement? Perhaps her behavior at the club meeting, in refusing his offer of a ride home, in refusing to associate with him, was all part of that mysterious and unknown quality of the poor?

He telephoned Helen that same evening and heard the cheerful, soprano voice ask softly, "Who's calling, please?" He felt a slight quiver through his system, making him hesitate a second.

"Helen, this is Art Walton. Isaac said that three girls came yesterday, and if it was you, I'm sorry I missed you."

"Yes, I came with Sylvia and Minnie. I, too, was sorry that you weren't there," Helen answered, her inner excitement and joy restrained outwardly.

"Are you angry at me for something?" Art asked.

"No, why should I be angry at you? I was not feeling well that last time."

"Then I'm very glad, I'm so very glad, Helen, that it wasn't on account of something I said to you that caused you to walk away. Would you like to go for a ride on the Outer Drive? I'll bring you back early, if you wish."

She was waiting in front of the white fence of her home as Art drove up, and quickly opened the door for her. For some moments he sat and stared at her; she seemed so changed, he thought. He saw now a rare beauty, with high natural color on the cheeks and lips, whose thick hair had been cut close to the face, barely covering her ears, yet draping it roundly. Her smile was calm, mature. It seemed to him that she had also aged somehow, but he was unable to explain how. Perhaps it was the dreamy sadness which had filled her eyes that added to the mystery of her transformation.

His delay in driving away from her home embarrassed Helen, as she was quite certain that her mother or Sylvia was in back of that curtain watching their every movement.

"Why don't you drive?" she asked.

"Maybe you'd rather go roller skating first?" Art asked. "We can go on the Drive for a while, if you'd prefer, and then we can spend an hour or so at the rink."

Helen liked that. Sitting at a noisy, large power machine, stitching heavy canvasses without getting up until lunch time, or until she had to, tired her body, and made her wish she had a job which would allow her to be more on her feet, she explained to Art.

"Will you tell me more about your work, Helen?" he almost pleaded. He wanted to hear her talk; her voice was calm and soothing. But most of all he suddenly became consumed with the desire to find out how she was spending the best part of her life, the best hours of the day. What was it like to be sewing heavy canvasses, eight to nine hours a day, in a noisy shop? He

71

had so many questions to ask her, as if she held the secrets to people's lives from another world, and Helen agreed that some other time she would tell him more about the radical caucus in her shop, and about the stoppages they had, to get a half-hour lunch period, instead of the twenty minutes they always had.

But somehow Helen doubted that she would ever be able to tell this man everything, that today the toilet broke down again, and that she had to ask the other girl-operator to go with her to the men's toilet, to stand watch while she went inside. She was sure that she would never tell him that she had spent almost half an hour soaking in the bathtub to get all the lint out of her pores and hair; and that to get the smells of the canvass out of her body, she began using lately that perfumed soap—which made a big difference.

To her Art Walton was the man with the big ideas, with the important talk, the man of books. In her own way she always carried romantic notions towards the intellectuals who could see all the things that were going on everywhere, who could talk about the national or world situation, while she was so occupied with the small things, the everyday items—like that mirror for the ladies' room, and the fight she had with her foreman until she got it. Sylvia, she always thought, would some day be one of those intellectuals, too. She had that special something which made her grasp the lectures and the theories that were so often aired at the club meetings—while she, Helen, was so tired that she wished most of all to take a nap, or just close her eyes. That was probably one of the reasons why she accepted criticism from her younger sister without feeling resentful about it; while the same criticism given her by Minnie would lead to an argument.

But now, riding away with Art Walton from this neighborhood, over to the Outer Drive towards the other side of the city, made her feel that both of them were somehow bound by the same big commitment; both of them were pledged to changing the world, to making it better.

There were other rides with Art, and other evenings at the roller skating rink, and boat rides at Humboldt Park. There was also the first time . . .

She tripped, or fell. "Are you hurt, Helen?" Art asked, rushing to her side. He picked her up as if she were a fragile doll and held her tenderly, close to his body. "Are you hurt?" he kept asking anxiously, not hearing her answer.

"No, I'm fine," she laughed, her color rising, her hair fluffed loosely over her eyes, and Art kissed her—the first time—and then let her down gently.

"Please be careful," he pleaded, but Helen had already skated far away from him, having become lost among a group of other young people, and when at last the two returned to his car, Art made her sit away from him, at some distance.

"Just let me look at you for a few minutes," he said staring at the happy, flushed Helen by his side, her head tilted back on the seat, her eyes closed, as if lost in her own dream world.

"This is just wonderful, Helen. You look so beautiful like this! It's just wonderful," he repeated.

They continued meeting almost daily—near her shop, after work, after meetings. They went for many other rides and walks. Several times they ate at the Japanese restaurant on Wells Street, and Art explained to Helen the meaning of the Oriental names of the various dishes, then ordered for both of them.

Art talked about his plans to go to the south some day and shared his thoughts about wishing to do meaningful work, like she was doing.

"What really matters, Helen, is that we move the people, we influence the people to a point where they themselves will see that change is possible and necessary; that there need not be hunger in the midst of our prosperity."

Once or twice he referred to his parents and to his sister. He explained that while they were all under one roof, they were in two distinct worlds.

"Would you like to meet them some day?" he asked, and when Helen agreed, he rejoiced like a school boy. "That would be just wonderful, Helen!"

But Helen was not acquainted with the social amenities of the middle or upper classes. She should have told Art in advance that she was bringing her friend, Minnie Gould, with her. But how could she if she herself did not know then. It was the very last minute before leaving her home that she began to feel apprehensive about meeting the Waltons, and she decided to ask Minnie to come along.

Had Art known that Helen was thinking of bringing Minnie

with her, he would have discouraged her, because asking Helen to meet his parents was something different, something special —because to Art Walton, Helen Kanofsky had become something very special. Helen was the girl from the other side of the city, from the Division Street neighborhood; the shop girl with little education, yet the accepted rank-and-file leader, with an abundance of physical courage. His parents would not understand these qualities, and Art had no intentions of sharing with them the latest bit of information of considerable importance to him and to Helen: that Helen might soon be going to Cleveland as a delegate to a special convention of union militants, called by the Trade Union Educational League,[3] which could conceivably influence the future of American trade unionism.

Art believed, however, that his kin would be very favorably impressed with Helen's beauty and gentleness, with her softness of speech and genuine modesty. Helen's natural politeness and ability to listen attentively to others, he knew, would impress even his society-minded sister, the "Duchess."

After Helen rang the doorbell of the Walton home, he opened the door and was taken aback—when he saw also Minnie Gould standing there. Politely he invited them in, and asked them to make themselves comfortable.

"Would you like to leave your things here?" he asked Minnie. She declined instantly. She would never have thought of leaving her pocketbook or sweater behind in a totally unfamiliar place. It was her best garment, reaching far below her waist and covering much of her body, like a wrap. Her small pocketbook Minnie clutched—never having let it out of sight. Helen had noticed even before this visit to the Waltons, that Minnie had been acting peculiarly strange since Hymie, the canvass cutter, had left the shop and suddenly disappeared for good. She must have been very much in love with him, Helen often thought, and probably had a picture, or another memento of his, in her small pocketbook.

Art ushered them into the main room and Helen was genuinely, visibly, surprised with its size; she thought the ones she had seen in the moving pictures were only for show, not for real. At the other end, on the long dark-maroon velvet divan, were Fred and Kikki, and next to them, Mrs. Walton, sunk deeply and comfortably into the soft cushions. Art's father, Theodore Walton, stood up quickly, as his son and the two girls entered, and waited for Art to present them to him.

Politely, with an amusing smile, he said, "Very pleased to make your acquaintance, Miss Kanofsky, Miss Gould."

Helen wondered if he was making fun of her name, and her mind lingered on that point for a few seconds. Still holding them both by their arms, Art led them away like small children, to be put on display; he then presented them to his mother:

"Thela, these are my two very good friends," he said, and Helen became confused at hearing him address his mother by a first name. She gave Mrs. Walton her hand, and looking into her sad eyes, wished to say something kind to her; she felt so sorry for this woman.

"You look a little like my Ma; she ought to meet you." But that wasn't at all what she meant; she did not mean that her mother should meet Mrs. Walton, because her mother knew nothing of the existence of the Waltons. Helen only meant to tell her that she liked Mrs. Walton because she felt towards her like towards her own mother, and she continued holding her hand in Mrs. Walton's, until the latter pulled it out gently and walked with Helen towards the grand piano, where the "Duchess" was busily fingering several music sheets.

To Helen, Art's sister also seemed very sad, and she thought that her eyes were like her mother's, but she was not as pretty as Mrs. Walton. The "Duchess" behaved a little peculiar at that moment, Helen thought; she was so very careful not to touch her or Minnie, as if fearing of becoming contaminated with some dread disease.

Later, in the dining room, Thela Walton seated them, and explained apologetically that there was a delay because they had to make last minute changes "when we saw two, instead of you alone, my dear," and Helen was not too certain whether she was being critical for having brought her friend along.

As the various courses of food were being served by the uniformed maid, Helen became more and more uneasy and uncomfortable. She kept thinking that there was something indecent in the critical glances that the Waltons were throwing at her and at Minnie. At one point Helen felt like grabbing Minnie by the hand and running away from them all, without looking back at this group of strangers who were eating without saying a word to each other—afraid to disturb the chewing and the sipping of the wine.

They later moved to the music section of the large room—all except Theodore Walton, who excused himself, and again Helen could not understand why he had to study some important information about the stock market developments, as Art explained to her quietly, instead of doing it later. It made no sense to her at all. Fred and Kikki, too, seemed to have been looking at the two girls in a strange sort of way, like they had been embarrassed all evening.

There were no other visits to the Waltons by Helen. Neither Art nor Helen ever referred to that dinner.

Not being able to share with her parents her new experiences and feelings towards this man who had been pursuing her without letup was very disturbing to Helen. She found herself in a continuous process of review and study of her relationship with Art, and uncovered angles which had been hidden during the first few months of the hectic, intense courtship.

"You treat me like a character out of some book," Helen told him softly as they were walking at the lake front, the cool, fall wind brushing their faces. "Because our movement tries to attract workers from industry, from the shops and unions, I seem to appeal to you like something to toy with. But I feel like I was walking on thin ice, and that any minute I'll go through it and drown, and you'll run back to your own group of educated friends." She dropped his hand, and looked up towards him with an expectant, sad expression.

Art had never seen her like that before; her doubts about his love had added to the innocent, pale face a strange quality of longing beauty. He wanted to reassure her, to tell her what she had meant to him, how much he needed her. They approached a cement stoop, and sat down.

Tenderly he took her face into his hands, and caressed her eyes, and responded gently, "That's why I need you, Helen. With you I feel fully alive, I feel complete. When I'm this close to you I can see the futility of teaching a group of boys and girls the rest of my life; with you by my side I feel like I could go away tomorrow, and throw myself into the work that has meaning in life . . ." His voice trailed off, and as he dried

76

Helen's damp eyes with his handkerchief and pushed back her thick hair behind her ears, he looked admiringly at her in the shadows of the tall buildings lining Lake Michigan.

"Why don't you wear your hair off the face—you look so beautiful like this, Helen; then put a comb, or something, up here, like a tiara, you'd be the prettiest dance partner on the floor. You are coming with me to the dance? You promised, and we'll dance the whole evening, and most of the night, and Helen . . ." again he kissed her tenderly, and looked at her with such intense admiration that she responded trustingly. His moods changed rapidly, his laughter alternating with words of sorrow—laughter and sadness interchanging frequently.

Helen leaned her head back on his supporting shoulder, and looking into the distant waters, said, "You always use the expression 'I need you,' or 'you can help me,' like I was here to help you become a better leader. Forgive me, please, for saying it this way, but I don't feel comfortable when you say those things. I know you mean something good, but . . . it's like I'm somebody to help you, and you love me for that. But where am I? I mean, I get frightened because some day all these things might wear off, when you accomplish what you want. But I'll remain where I am now because I have so little education; and you with your big words, with your smart talk, and easy laughing—there'll be other girls, prettier than me, more educated than me, who can talk music and books with you, like Kikki."

"Why do you keep bringing up her name like this? You know there's nothing between me and Kikki! You know she and Fred are getting married soon! Why do you mention her name again, like you were jealous or something?" There was disappointment and rebuke in his voice. He moved his shoulder from under her head, and rose to his feet. Helen could not understand why he had practically forbidden her to mention Kikki's name; it was like touching an open nerve, she thought.

"I'm not jealous of Kikki, but of others like her. When there's a group of us together, you sit up late, and you talk about philosophy and economics with them and with Sylvia. But some day it won't be my kid sister, but some pretty girl, maybe someone more sophisticated."

"See, see how quickly you picked up this new word! I'm going to write out a few more words for you, and you'll learn their meaning and you'll see how your vocabulary will grow," Art said enthusiastically.

"That's what I mean, Art. Big words are important to you, but I'm not an intellectual, and I'll never be one. Sylvia could become like that. She wants to be a full-time revolutionist. I think she'll become a theoretician some day. I don't care any more if she goes to college or not. But me? I've been working too long in the shops, and I'll remain that way."

Suddenly she realized that Art might interpret her remarks as a rebuff, and she did not want to ever hurt him.

"I, too, love you, Art. This is the biggest thing that ever happened to me. Of all the girls in the club you pick me. I have to pinch myself, like Minnie does to me, to make sure that it's true, that Art Walton—you speak so easily, and you know much . . ."

"Please, Helen, my sweet! Please don't talk like that . . ."

"No, no! I must say it all. I've been so happy ever since you first took me for that ride."

But Art didn't allow her to finish. Again he held her close, and again his sensuous mouth found Helen's warm lips, and she had never before lived through such joyous moments; never before had she experienced such intimacy and tenderness of kissing. But suddenly she felt a sinking fearsome sensation spread over her entire being—a dreadful thought had overtaken her: what if he talks like this to others! She went limp and said nothing more. Again she heard Art's caressing voice.

"I never felt this way towards anybody, either, Helen. I, too, am frightened! I keep asking myself: Is Helen real? Will she always be by my side?"

For some split moment Helen visualized herself back in school, studying and reading from big books and talking with Art like the other educated girls. A new world appeared before her, with Art as her teacher, filling her once more with that strange, joyous feeling he always had when she came so close to him.

Yet the deep conflict within her continued to gnaw: the new reality was there, her newly found desire for learning, and for knowledge, was in stark contradiction with the need to return to the shop early in the morning, and many mornings to follow. Thoughts about the Cleveland conference rushed back and filled her mind. She must go to Cleveland, she must prepare herself immediately. Helen was inextricably tied to the militant, youthful labor movement that had given substance and realism to her life; surely this man by her side must know what Cleveland means to her, surely Art won't try to stop her from going!

But Art was thinking of other matters, and asked: "Is Sophiele planning to remain in the shop?"

"Not after they get married. She and Louie decided that she ought to quit work and raise a family; and they're having a 'choope' and have accepted Pa's recommendation to take the Rabbi from his synagogue to perform the ceremony." She explained to Art what a Jewish wedding was like and why the marriage of the eldest Kanofsky offspring would bring so much happiness to her parents. She held back the important detail that now she, Helen, would be able to get married, too, in accordance with their orthodox tradition. Art interrupted her silent thoughts.

"Have you made up your mind about going to Cleveland?"

"It's not up to me any more. I was elected unanimously. We'll have a car full from our trade."

She answered many other questions. Art's unique ability to obtain information by asking a series of questions in rapid succession compelled one to answer. But she was amazed at his lack of knowledge of the status of the organized labor movement. In answer to one of his questions she found herself lecturing to him. "It isn't enough for the militants to continue working, as some of us are doing, inside the existing American Federation of Labor unions. That's only a small percentage of organized labor. We have to do that, too, but the biggest number of workers are unorganized; the big industries are still open shops, and after this Cleveland conference we'll have to shift our orientation . . ." He smiled, bent down, and kissed her. He had taught her the word "orientation" and she was using it so naturally! Helen was unaware why he looked at her with that familiar twinkle in the eye. She felt uneasy whenever he scrutinized her in silence, as he was doing now, saying nothing, yet transmitting the feeling that she was being observed and studied. She tried to shift her thinking away from herself.

"How soon are you planning to leave for the South?"

Art was surprised to hear her ask so carelessly this most important question in his life.

79

He took her hand and said quietly, "I'll go as soon as you agree to come with me, Helen. Tomorrow, if you say so."

II

"Can't you see, Fred, what I'm driving at? You've said yourself that Helen is not beset by false middle class values; Helen is simple, unsophisticated. When she's close by me, things clear up for me—things that a year ago, or a month ago, confused me begin to make sense," Art said with enthusiasm, his eyes alive with excitement, as he was arranging snacks on a tray for the two of them, and a drink for Fred.

Fred sipped his drink slowly, eyes half-closed, as was his way when relaxing leisurely, comfortably. He continued to listen to Art talk in his intimate tone.

"Let me tell you what Helen said to me. She says that the workers in her shop know that they can obtain many improvements in their working conditions if they fight through a good rank-and-file union, like the one Helen has going in her shop. But some of them go even farther, like herself, and believe that eventually exploitation of man by man will have to be done away with. Do you, Fred Heller, realize what she is telling us? She has grasped the dynamics of our society—that exploitation of man by man will some day have to be done away with! It's the most marvelous thing about her." A smile of deep personal satisfaction had spread over Art's happy face.

"What are you driving at, Art? You've been going around in circles ever since I walked in, instead of coming to the point. You asked me to come over tonight because you said you have something very important to talk over. So why don't you start with that?"

Fred had felt for quite some time that Art was running away from something, but was afraid to run alone, by himself; he had dragged Helen Kanofsky into his scheme of things, and was looking for reassurances. There was also a visible change in Art's appearance. He had become negligent with his dress, rarely wore a tie since he gave up teaching, and had quit shaving every day. It seemed to Fred that his friend was pretending to casualness and indifference, as if he had become detached from his immediate reality and was creating a new reality for himself. Art's moods also kept changing more often lately, his easy, ever-ready laughter harnessed.

In a serious, calm voice, his eyes on his hands, as if they held the secret he was about to share with his closest friend, Art said, "The best contribution that I can make to equal in some degree Helen's sacrifices is to become a full-time educator for the movement. I've thought about this from different angles, Fred, and I've come to the conclusion that I ought to volunteer to go to the Black Belt."

Making his commitment aloud, to someone he trusted and respected, gave him the self-assurance he was seeking to hold himself to that commitment.

Looking now at Fred's confused reaction, Art advanced in rapid succession a multitude of justifications for his drastic decision, adding, "There's no doubt whatsoever in my mind that we'll soon be confronted with an economic catastrophe, which will eventually affect many other countries, too. You said yourself that capitalism cannot control the anarchy of the market which is inherent in this system of production, and that Isaac is telling the people the truth. But in the south the Negroes and the poor whites alike will be caught in this disaster without any recourse whatsoever! They'll be hit the hardest. I'd leave tomorrow, if only Helen would come with me, and help me." Again he looked meditatively at his hands.

Fred wasn't able to follow the logic for such a decision, yet he knew that it was somehow tied up with Helen Kanofsky, but he wondered how.

"What if Helen refused to leave her family? What then? What if she refuses to give up her work in the shop and in the union? Let's say she agrees to become your comrade-in-arms: I'm beginning to think that she is in love with you—I don't know about you, though. Several times before you thought you were in love, and I've seen you get excited like you are now. But I think Helen has fallen for you. I can see that. Still—going off with you to the south! I don't know, Art. She's a disciplined girl, and will do what is best for the movement. You could help her by becoming a fulltime worker for the movement right here, where she—"

"No, no, Fred! You're off on this. I couldn't become a fulltime worker in my own bailiwick: I'll have too many strikes against me trying to organize steel workers, or packinghouse men. Intellectuals don't sit right with them. There's an invisible wall between us. Even Mirko and Willie don't talk to me about the people inside the plants—and sometimes I think they don't trust me. You've seen how Isaac handles his meetings: he asks me to explain the meaning of the heavy Wall Street speculations, and all that, but it seems that he, too, tries to keep me away from the private conversations going on all the time about the progress they're making inside the packing houses—like he doesn't trust me, either."

"Yet you think the share-croppers of the south will accept you with open arms, will respond to you better than the workers from industry?" Fred asked, but didn't wait for a reply.

"If you want to be accepted by working people, you'd do better to go into a shop and stay there; work like all the others do for their living. This isn't old peasant Russia, where political education had to be brought in from the outside, by the intellectuals. This is the most industrialized country in the world, with an educated population."

Fred's mouth was like a long slit under his prominent nose, his thin lips closing tightly after each phrase and sentence. "Radicals like you and me should try to help the workers organize powerful industrial unions, like Helen's been telling you, and in that process they'll learn what this system is really like. I think that's the ABC for a militant of this country at this juncture in our history."

Art listened attentively. Perhaps he had hoped that Fred would discourage him from taking that drastic step he had been considering for months. There was the same indecision and vacillation which had plagued Art all his life whenever he had to make a major departure from the established routine. It was during those moments of doubt that he argued the sharpest with his friend, as if trying to convince himself, more than Fred.

"But it's different in the South. They are in many ways like the peasantry of Czarist Russia: denied education, intimidated, totally unorganized; and I know that I could work more effectively in the Black Belt than here, or anywhere else," Art said.

"You know what I'd call your whole line of reasoning? I'd call it white supremacist, or as we hear it called in our circles —white chauvinism. Because you're educated, and glib, and wear good clothes, you expect to walk into some southern community and tell the black people what is good for them. You look upon yourself like upon a Good White Father who'll rescue the blacks from their centuries of oppression. The white man knows everything: he knows how to keep a whole people down, and now you, the white Messiah, are going to tell them that you know what they should do to liberate themselves because they, the black men, don't have the brains or the courage to figure that out. That's why I don't like your whole approach. You can't even see that the Negroes of the South are fundamentally the same as the Negroes in the steel mills and packing houses—they trust only their own, and they'll accept leadership only from their own midst. Even Mirko couldn't get to first base until he became friends with Willie Rivers and found out a thing or two about how the black people feel about joining labor unions. But you, the northern white intellectual, are going into the Black Belt to—"

"Don't go telling me that we, in the north, can't help the people of the Black Belt—"

"I didn't say that," Fred stopped him short. "You're not interested in how the people of the north can help the people of the Black Belt; you are interested in helping Art Walton run away from something that's been bugging you for a long time, and you're using the South as an excuse."

Fred had disagreed with Art many times before, and had argued with him many times that he was not facing up to the real situation, that he tended to look for ready-made panaceas to solve the difficult, complicated problems in life.

Calmly Fred Heller announced his own plans for the period ahead.

"The movement needs skilled men, Art. Skilled men are respected in the shops and are accepted as leaders. The small craft unions are doing all right for their few men, but what about the others? I'm talking about the big unorganized shops. Some day soon they'll have to come into industrial unions, and I want to be on the ground floor when that shapes up."

Fred was a man of patience and tolerance. He continued, "If I stay long enough in the shop to earn the men's trust and confidence, I'll be able to talk unionism to them, large-scale unionism. There's room for you, too, Art. You can come in with me, instead of going South."

"Helen doesn't put it quite that way, yet she seems to be

saying the same thing. She can't see the idea of my going to the South, but she doesn't try to stop me, instead she talks to me about her own work, and about the Cleveland Conference. She says they'll be shifting their emphasis to the big, unorganized industries, and try to lay the groundwork for the big unions that are bound to come into being; that's why I say you sound like Helen," he said and shook his head as if in disbelief. "And Helen is going to that conference."

"What's wrong with that?"

"Oh, what the hell's the matter with you? Can't you understand what this is leading to? Helen is going one way, and I another. My plans to go to work in the South aren't changed just because you think I'm running away from myself." He waved his hand to indicate that he couldn't treat such criticism seriously.

"You don't seem to realize that we're living in a country in which we, the whites, you and I included, all of us whites, are exploiting another nation, the Negro nation, the black people!" Art continued to elaborate the very themes both of them had heard Isaac speak about before. "We live off the super profits that are extracted from these millions of tenant farmers and share-croppers, as if they were a colonial people. No difference, Fred. None! And we both know that things won't change in this country until the South begins to move, I mean until the Negroes of the South begin to move on a large scale, and I know I can help if I'm right there, in their midst, where the terror is the greatest and where our contribution in such a fight as they're conducting is very valuable."

Pointing to the contents of his affluent surroundings with some contempt in his voice, he said, "Others are fighting for things like these, things I have had all my life and have taken for granted. Take a good look, Fred. This carpet—step on it and see again how soft and thick it is; and the victrola and these records, and the refrigerator in the other room—always full of food, of good things—and these expensive books in this wall of bookcases. Where does it all come from? Who's creating all this wealth? All this comfort I'm living off for twenty-eight years?"

Fred stopped him. "This isn't anything new. Or is it? Are

you first discovering now, now that you've met a working-class girl, that we live in a parasitic society where those who work hard own the least, and people like your family . . ."

Art barely listened to him now. He was occupied with his own thinking. "I've seen those kids blocked from growing up into full manhood; they won't be able to break out of that poverty. You've seen this book by Paul de Kruif? You've read *Hunger Fighters*? Haven't you?"

"No. Haven't had time yet," Fred replied quietly, a thin suggestion of a smile appearing on his long face. He was acquainted with Art's ways. He was expecting something new to be sprung on him, as had happened before when Art took on airs of the hurt man.

"Well, in this book it shows this Jewish doctor from the East Side investigating and doing a lot of research, and he comes up with the idea that the deadly pellagra is not caused by germs at all, but by the absence from the diet of some unknown vitamin. The cause of pellagra, he discovered, is hidden hunger. Among other things leading to this conclusion was the fact that this doctor observed that people whose incomes are above $1000 a year are seldom pellagrins. The destitute, whose diet usually does not include fresh meat and milk, are susceptible to the disease. The cure, then, is plenty of food of the right kind. I see these kids every day with this hidden hunger written on their faces and there's nothing I can do about it, absolutely nothing! I was a carrier of American culture to these boys and girls of the South Side High. I was supposed to have prepared them for the world that they'd be entering as grown-up men and women! But it's all a fraud, and I was part of this fraud! Twenty or thirty years from now I'd still be here, still pretending," Art said with disgust.

"What's eating you, Art?" Fred asked, his eyes turned towards his friend without having moved his face.

Art rose and stretched his athletic, tall body, to its full height. He began pacing the floor as if wanting to push aside the walls and all obstacles hindering him from breaking out of his environment.

"I'm supposed to be a teacher—but what kind of culture was I bringing to my students? Not the kind this magazine speaks about, not—listen to this:

. . . for the working people culture is a matter of struggle, a matter of heroism. Heroism is the driving force of its daily struggles, the sustaining power of the striker, the union builder, the communist, the Negro fighter for freedom . . .

"Where do I fit into this picture of culture being a matter of struggle? For me it had become a matter of escape. I could hide myself in that school, pretend there was no poverty, pretend I didn't see what was going on there among those Negro boys and girls. Then I could come back here and live comfortably under my parents' roof, in this wing of the Walton home, cuddled, protected—I spit on it all!" he finished, exhausted. "Helen is a better carrier of modern culture than I ever was."

Art's involvement with Helen had brought in its trail a new set of concepts about personal conduct and morality. He never referred to her as to a woman with whom he had fallen in love, or as one who would some day become Mrs. Arthur Walton. He picked up his trend of thought.

"What is so beautiful about Helen, and was so difficult for people like me to understand, Fred, is that she knows that she might be victimized again, as in the past. Yet, she pushes ahead, fights like a tiger, dedicates herself completely, I mean completely, to the movement. To Helen the struggle is a natural phenomenon—it's her life. Her courage is spontaneous—that's the essence of her culture. When you get to know her better you first begin to understand our society and that she's a true carrier of the new type of culture."

Art needed to talk, to strip himself emotionally, and let his feelings bounce around, and be seen by himself and by his closest friend. He moved closer to Fred and continued.

"I've been wanting to talk to you about something else, Fred; it's about Helen and her parents. She told me casually—not to impress me, just to inform me—that she and Sylvia often talk to their parents about our movement, about what transpires in the club or in Helen's shop. But listen to this: sometimes these older Kanofskys tell the girls where they make mistakes—incredible, ah? But they do! You know what Yom Kippur means to these religious Kanofskys?" Art asked. "It's their holiest of days: they fast until sunset in atonement, and prayer. Well, this Yom Kippur Helen and Sylvia came to visit their parents in the synagogue—it's customary, I now understand, even for non-believers to spend time with their parents during those holy days. They took their mother out for a little fresh air, for a walk. But they noticed two young fellows from their club, standing nearby the synagogue, eating sandwiches, and demonstratively washing their food down with seltzer water. Mrs. Kanofsky and the girls were stunned—deliberately mocking their traditions, their religion! I asked Helen, 'What did you do? Did you chase them away, or bawl them out?' 'No!' she told me, 'I couldn't do anything. I was so ashamed of those boys that I didn't want Mother to know that we were familiar with them.'"

Fred looked at him in amazement. "You mean members of the Hersh Leckert Club deliberately went to a synagogue to make fun of those religious people?"

"They did, yes, they did! And it was their mother, the girls' mother, who explained what a terrible thing those boys were doing, acting like anti-Semites, and that she believed that they were Jewish boys from the neighborhood, and that it was the most disgraceful thing she had seen. Then Mrs. Kanofsky asked, 'Who could be teaching them to do things like that?'"

"Then what?" Fred asked.

"Then Helen and Sylvia admitted to their mother, as if making their own atonement, that they were acquainted with both boys, that they were members of their club, and that they were going to bring them up on charges of anti-Semitism. Can you imagine me talking to Thela about my activities in the movement? Or to my father? Don't you see what is going on in the Kanofsky family? There's no hostility, no antagonism there —even though they hold different views! It's just amazing! And the club arranged a lecture on the subject of *Religion and Society*. A big debate ensued, and the two boys were admonished for their behavior!" Art was practically smacking his lips in delight. He added, "They even brought in the Red Bishop's books—you've seen Bishop William Montgomery Brown's books on *Christianity and Communism*? Well, they brought them into the club to show other approaches to the study of religion. It was extraordinary! Just marvelous!"

"The Kanofskys are poor people," Fred said. "The poor stay together pretty much. Even when the girls began to follow a different philosophy, they still remained together as a close family unit," and suddenly he started laughing.

"What's funny about that?" Art asked.

"Soon you'll find out for yourself. I bet if Helen ever agrees to go away with you, she'll insist on being called Helen Kanofsky. And you'll have some explaining to do, especially if it's in the Black Belt you wind up," and he laughed again.

"But that isn't funny. I don't see why you make a joke of this. It may become a real problem to convince Helen to use my name," Art said.

"Why don't you marry her? Wouldn't that be much simpler? Ask Helen to become your wife, legally; and if she accepts you as her husband, she'll probably go with you to the South, or any other place."

Fred stretched his legs, sat back, and looked directly at Art. "Isn't that what's really bothering you, Art? You're ready to throw yourself into full-time work for the movement—but then there's Helen, whom you dragged into your plans, so you could lean on her; but Helen has her own ideas, her own moral codes —and it confuses you. Yet, it's all quite simple—if she becomes Mrs. Arthur Walton—officially."

III

For Sylvia Kanofsky the summer and fall months were crowded with events which had quickly pushed her out of the ranks of the adolescents. Only weeks ago, it seemed to her, Betty Dunhill had asked her, "Are you gonna make a revolution?" and already Sylvia was answering that question with her personal freedom.

It all happened suddenly, unexpectedly, on the corner of Division Street and Washtenaw, when she climbed upon the ladder, and in a weak voice said: "Come closer, please; tonight we will discuss the true significance of the American Revolution, and what it meant not only to us, but to the entire world —" and was arrested instantly.

It was Chuck Lamson, the club chairman, who had suggested that she prepare a few minutes' talk on the American Revolution, and Sylvia felt that there was no greater joy in life for any girl than to carry out such a request. She, the newest member of the club, and the youngest, was asked to chair the open-air meeting, on the eve of the July Fourth celebration!

"Can you imagine? They all thought that just because I want to be a history teacher that I'd be able to prepare something important for that open-air meeting. Imagine, asking me to do it!" she told her parents.

For several days she was gushing with excitement and had to share it with her close ones. She did not tell them, however, how flustered she became, her face having turned red, her insignificant lisp had suddenly become a stutter when she rose and said, "I wouldn't know what to s-s-say."

"We're not worried about that, Sylvia. You have a lot to say about the American Revolution, and it's a good idea to break in new speakers."

And there she was, standing on top of a stepladder, looking into the faces of the people who had come to that corner regularly, when she suddenly gets pulled down brusquely, as she hears someone shout authoritatively, *"You're under arrest, miss!"* It all happened so fast that Sylvia had no opportunity to see that the other speakers for the event, who followed her on the ladder, protested the arrest of their chairman, and were also arrested, as well as the three other young men who followed them, and that weekend was the first time in Sylvia Kanofsky's life that she sat all alone in a small cell, with bars in front of her, unable to do anything, except to lie down on the narrow cot with the straw mattress and think. . . .

And Sylvia was thinking about Betty's question, "Are you gonna make a revolution?" "But they didn't even let me tell the people about the American Revolution, and why it was an important step forward for all mankind. . . . I was going to say that the Russian Revolution was another one of those great leaps forward of humanity . . . revolution is an inherent right of all people . . . This cell—what if the mattress catches fire? What if there's a fire in the building? . . . Will they remember that I'm here, alone . . . that I can't open this door . . . Ma and Pa, they'll be so worried . . . will Chuck, or someone else, tell them that I'm all right—but they ought to talk to Pa first, tell him first, he doesn't get excited like Ma . . . He'll tell her not to worry, that I know how to take care of myself."

But Sylvia had never experienced such loneliness, such emptiness. The two other cells, opposite hers, were empty. The light in the corridor was too far away to be able to read; then she remembered that she had nothing to read, they took away her pocketbook, and the magazines she was . . . those loud footsteps? Somebody's coming closer. Quickly she got off the cot and grabbed a hold of the bars. The man just passed the empty cells and didn't even look her way, but she should talk to him, say something, "Officer, officer," she heard her own voice resound like in an empty, hollow barrel. He looked but continued walking, and on his way back he asked, "Whatyawant?" Yes, what do I want? What should I tell him? Got to tell him something. "I want to make a telephone call," Sylvia said, and wondered whom to call. He asked her several questions, some she couldn't answer; the two now walked out and soon she was in front of the desk, speaking clearly, calmly into the telephone:

"Hello, Ma, it's me, Sylvia. Don't worry about me, I'm only a few blocks from home—at the North Avenue Police Station. I'll have to stay here until Monday morning, but tell Helen to call the I.L.D., the secretary, maybe she can take me out before Monday."

"That's all, Sylvia," the man at the desk said, and she didn't hear her mother say anything—but she knew that she was on the other side of the line; she heard her breathing. They returned Sylvia to that lonely cell again, and soon more ideas came and went, and she spent her long night in jail—not falling asleep at all, she thought—when she heard the clanking of keys.

"You're going home, Sylvia," a man said, and there at the desk stood Art and Helen and Lillian Goodman of the I.L.D., all smiling into her face, as they walked out of the station.

"They say you make a good public speaker," Helen said, taking her hand.

"Who says that?" Sylvia asked with anger. "They didn't even let me speak my piece. I prepared myself for a five-minute talk, like Chuck told me to, but they pulled me down before I even introduced the first speaker."

"We know, we know," Art said. "The boys will have to wait until tomorrow."

"What boys?" Sylvia asked.

Lillian told her about the other five arrests on that corner, and on other street corners where open-air meetings were broken up.

"You can come with us to the outing, where everybody will be happy to see you; you can finish your speech in Humboldt Park, on Lenin Hill," Art told her.

"Your coming to Humboldt Park for the outing will be important, Syl," Helen added.

90

Somehow she felt as if something more significant than spending a night in the police station had happened to her. Her own sister and Art and Lillian—they were all treating her so differently now! And why would it be important for her to come to the outing, she wondered.

"Are you going, too?" she asked Art.

"I wouldn't miss it for anything," he answered with a broad smile. "I want to hear your piece about the significance of the American Revolution."

They raced from the outskirts of the park to the famous hill where radicals usually gathered and where many young people were already singing songs and eating the refreshments they had brought with them. When they recognized Sylvia walking towards them, their clenched fists quickly went up into a salute to their young heroine, as they rose on their feet and surrounded her with caressing hands. Art and Helen pulled her away, explaining that Sylvia would join them later, as they wished to eat first and visit with her a while.

They stretched out on the green carpet of freshly cut grass, a distance away from the others, and Art asked, "What are you planning to do now, Sylvia?"

"I don't know yet what I'll be doing," she answered.

"Going to enroll in college?" he pursued.

"Maybe. I'm not sure yet."

"You'd be wasting your time," he said.

"Do you think you wasted your time studying, when you were my age?" Sylvia asked sincerely. Art's opinions rated high on her list of living earthly Gods. Hero-worshipping seemed to come naturally to her, and to so many others her age. Art Walton's opinion on the direction of her future plans was precious to her.

"I think I'd like to become a history teacher. As long as Pa and Helen are working, I could continue in school, and concentrate on American history—I like that best; I'd like to teach it some day, teach it the right way."

"But, Sylvia, supposing you've found out that slavery operates in the South in a new way, do you really believe you'd be able to teach your students that five billion dollars of super profits are extracted from the hides of the American Negroes? I'm not talking of the regular profits that are extracted from all working people—this is super profits because they are black, and oppressed. Do you think you'd be able to tell them that this perpetuates a Jim Crow society which pulls us all down and degrades us all, even you and me? You mean you'll be able to teach history that way?" He watched closely the reaction on her impressionable mind. Her silence was misunderstood; Art pursued.

"Or take a fact of contemporary history: when fourteen foreign armies, including the American, invaded the emerging, young Soviet Republic—could you detail the suffering it had brought to the Russian people, and how it had delayed their recovery for many years?"

The doubts Sylvia had harbored and had debated with herself, were the very ideas that Art Walton was picking apart, and compelling her to reevaluate.

"What would you have me do, go to work in a millinery shop or in the stockyards, instead of becoming a history teacher? You said once that all young revolutionaries should get into the basic industries and help build honest unions—is that what you're driving at?"

"No, Sylvia, but you'd be better equipped some day, if the movement called on you to become a professional revolutionary, a full-time worker, if you picked up speed in typewriting, and perhaps learned some shorthand—maybe you should be thinking about these matters for a while; they might be good tools in your hands for further study of theory—you seem to have inclinations in that area."

Art had mentioned the magic words "professional revolutionary"—words used to describe some of her heroes whom she admired so much. Her rapid political maturation could probably be traced to that very moment—when she began to look upon herself as one who might also become, some day soon, a professional revolutionary, for the movement. She, too, would be brave and dedicated! The very thought made her feel important and courageous. Somehow she began to feel as if she really was a more important person now—as if she possessed new powers. People treated her, she thought, with respect, and listened to her attentively. She began to be more careful about what she said, choosing her words more deliberately.

Helen had also noticed that from the time of her first arrest, Sylvia had begun to change into another person. Her casual movements, the slow speech to cover up the lisp, her participation in the weekly hikes had lost their meaning to the future professional revolutionist. Sylvia Kanofsky seemed now to be in a hurry about everything, and impatient with people who were idling away valuable time.

Soon even her outward appearance became noticeably changed. She was nervous and argumentative, complaining frequently about falling behind in her reading of the important national and international material. She gave up all ideas about becoming a school teacher; the time had arrived for Sylvia to go to work to improve her typewriting speed, and to prepare herself for the day when she would be called upon to dedicate herself completely to the movement.

But she was unfamiliar with the procedures of obtaining employment in the white collar field. She did not know how to dress properly, or how to apply, and was turned down in several places, without having been given an opportunity to prove that she was an accurate typist.

At the Nelson Knitting Company, on Milwaukee Avenue, expecting to be rejected again, she demanded in an arrogant voice, "I want to see Mr. Nelson."

"I'm Mr. Nelson. What can I do for you, Miss?"

"There's a sign in the window that says you need a typist. I'm a good typist and I can prove it, if you give me a typewriting test," Sylvia said.

No one had ever asked Mr. Elmer Nelson for employment in that manner. Sylvia's little speech, as crazy as it was, intrigued him. Mr. Nelson did exactly what she asked him to do. He let her copy a letter that was lying on his desk, and knew immediately that she was telling the truth.

"Is this your first position, Miss — ?"

"Miss Kanofsky is my name. Yes, it's my first position," she replied in a natural voice.

"Do you think you'll be able to handle also the cash which my managers bring here daily from the Nelson stores, for deposit?"

"Of course I can handle it," Sylvia answered firmly.

"If you're ready to go to work, you can start now. First, however, I'll ask you to please fill out some papers, so when our bookkeeper and office manager return from lunch, one of them will be able to bond you."

"Bond me?" Sylvia asked with a hurt look, as if she had been insulted in the worst possible manner.

"All our employees are bonded, Miss Kanofsky," Nelson said calmly. "We handle large sums of money in this office, and we have to protect ourselves."

"What do you mean? I won't run off with your money. We live only ten minutes' walk from here. I can give you our address; my parents are there, and my sister Helen," and Sylvia was getting ready to tell her first employer a few other things.

"This is no reflection on you, or your family, young lady. You appear to me like an honest girl. But what if you're held up on the way to the bank, or right here while you count all that money? Are you going to be able to make it good yourself?" He paused and looked at her flushed face in sheer admiration of her naïveté.

"Bonding our employees is a formality, and means nothing to you; that is, unless you have a police record of some kind," and for the first time he smiled broadly at his own seemingly absurd statement.

"I have no objection to being bonded," she replied calmly.

During that moment of hesitation, she decided that she would not tell this man that she had spent a night at a police station. She was not booked or fingerprinted. There was no record of her arrest, the I.L.D. attorney told her.

For several months Sylvia Kanofsky had deposited large sums of money at the bank near Ashland Avenue—until that one afternoon, when she began to wonder what the movement could do if it possessed those thousands of dollars; how many other people, like Art Walton, could be sent to the South to work in the Black Belt, or for other requirements. The notion that she personally was now responsible for holding back the progress of the movement by not turning over that money began to take root.

She had read about several great revolutionaries who had sacrificed their lives in the effort to obtain funds for the movement, and she began to think that perhaps she was a coward, and was not able to perform such acts of courage.

Perplexed, unable to sleep, unable to discuss such a matter with her parents, she decided, one day, to continue walking the extra few blocks to Chuck's office, near Robey Street, instead of going into the bank. After entering, she closed the door behind her, and whispered:

"This is between you and me. I have to talk to you alone. Do you want $11,012.63 for the movement? I have that much with me. It's right here, in my pocketbook."

At first Chuck did not believe the young girl, with the exciting, brown eyes and slight lisp. But after looking into her pocketbook, he knew she was serious, and that she had come to sacrifice Elmer Nelson's money—and herself.

He was overwhelmed by her sincerity and courage, as well as by her childishness, when she told him that she would need only a few dollars for fare to Canada, or Mexico, so she would not be any trouble to anybody. Gently taking Sylvia's hand into his, and looking her in the eyes, he said,

"You are worth more to us than the eleven thousand dollars, Sylvia. Our movement can't be built here in this way. We need the people, the masses, and when they begin to follow us, they will also donate money to build our movement. We need you to help us reach out to the masses. Some day, I hope soon, you'll be working for the movement—that's where we need you, here, in this country, not as a refugee in some strange land."

They talked in hushed voices. Her girlish body and face somehow began to look tired and aged; the brightness and excitement totally deflated, as Chuck continued to talk.

Sylvia walked out of his office and mechanically moved towards the bank. But it was a different person from the one she had been only hours ago, who now made the deposit to Nelson's account. A total sense of futility had overtaken the disappointed young woman. She could not visualize herself returning to the old routine; it was all so useless, so unimportant, such a waste of her time and her effort. Without waiting for the day to end —to the amazement of her co-workers—she announced, "I'm quitting. Goodbye everybody! I'll come Saturday for my pay," and Sylvia walked into the street, carrying in her heart the secret, the unfulfilled offering, she had shared with Chuck Lamson.

During those eventful summer-fall months, Sylvia had spent several more nights at the North Avenue Police Station, and had lost her shyness and gawkiness, and fears of being alone

95

in a cell with bars in front of her. Division Street and Washtenaw had at last been secured as a free-speech corner on the northwest side of Chicago. Open-air meetings were held unmolested, and Sylvia Kanofsky became a familiar figure on the platform of indoor and outdoor rallies alike. Her time was now fully occupied with activities of her own choosing—until that unforgettable day, when she received a telephone call from Gilbert Burck, Lamson's assistant, requesting to see her in private, if possible at her home. The tone of his voice and the precaution Gil took to assure privacy had quickly filled Sylvia's imaginative mind with a multitude of possibilities for this leader's reasons to seek her out.

She cautioned her parents not to disturb them in the living room, when Gilbert Burck arrived for a serious conference with her. Hurriedly she changed her blouse and combed her hair, wetting down the unruly cowlick, forcing it to lay flat. Her color rose, and she noticed in the mirror, under the bright lights, how unbecoming the uneven left eyebrow was, and for the first time the idea of penciling in that area, so as to make it look even with the good eyebrow, occurred to her. She refrained from doing that, fearing that her parents, especially her mother, might misjudge her motive. She studied herself again and again in the mirror, from different angles, and thought that Sophiele might be telling the truth—she was beginning to look quite pretty.

Walking into the living room to await the arrival of this important visitor, she suddenly began to feel coquettish, womanly—but checked herself quickly, rejecting flirtatious notions as unbecoming to a serious Marxist. Instead she became concerned with the need of saying something pleasant to him, considering that it was his first visit to their home. "Maybe I ought to say, 'Hello there. Glad to see you.' What nonsense!" she scolded herself as the door bell rang.

Gilbert Burck was a busy young organizer, he came directly to the purpose of his visit: she had been considered for full-time work, for an assignment in Gary, Indiana—a heavy industrial community—but totally unorganized. He detailed plans for starting educational-cultural work among the youth of Gary, who were employed in the big steel plant, and transmitted to her the feeling of confidence he and his colleagues had in her.

Her mind began to race; though feeling flattered, and also

so aged suddenly, she knew that she could not accept such an honor now, not when her father had lost his job, and when payments on the house had to be made regularly for some time, or years of hard labor would be lost. If she went to Gary, she calculated in silence, she'd have to send them at least twenty dollars each month for some time to come. She also questioned the wisdom of leaving home at a time when so much depended on her presence.

"Well, what do you think, Sylvia?" Gil asked.

"If there's no one else, and I have to go, I'll go," she told him, but pressing her lips tight, and indicating that she was about to make an important request, added, "But not right away. I can get work in a millinery shop and I think I ought to take that job, and save some money for the remaining payments due, otherwise my parents would be left homeless."

This was yet the most important decision she ever had to make: leave her aging parents, who needed her—or go to work for the movement. "But they are only two, two people," she argued to herself, "and now they'll be like two orphans. Parents-orphans!" the phrase insisted on dangling in her mind, when she heard Gil's voice again.

"Then you'd consider our recommendation?"

She replied with a jerk of her head, as if coming out of a trance, that she would, but a little later.

During this brief, but extraordinary visit of a stranger, on important business with their daughter, the two elder Kanofskys were in the kitchen, in total silence, cautious not to make noises, desirous to hear, however, whatever they could through the closed door to the living room. But soon Frimma broke that stillness and in an exaggerated falsetto voice, deliberately shouted for the others to hear, "Mendel, let's go out on the porch for a while, it's too warm here."

Mendel was completely surprised, after having prepared himself to sit out the full time of this visit by the first male caller on his youngest offspring. And furthermore, it was not too warm at all in the kitchen, and why should he go out on the porch in the chilly air, when the kitchen was so comfortable?

But Frimma motioned urgently with her eyes and hands, and soon she moved herself in the direction of the door, in an attempt to get Mendel to follow her. Reluctantly he got up and followed his wife out, on the dark porch, and asked with annoyance, "What's the matter with you, Frimma? Why do you act so funny?"

"There's nothing the matter with me, but where's your head, Mendel? Why don't you use your head for other things besides wearing the big black hat?"

Mendel realized that she was angry with him for not having followed her quickly enough; he also understood that his wife was telling him that he wasn't the smartest man on Potomac Avenue.

"It isn't nice to sit there, on the other side of the door, snooping. What if that young man should decide that he wants a drink of water, or that he wants to go to the toilet, ah, Mendel, I ask you? He'd have to come into the kitchen first, right? Then he'd see us sitting there like two mice, and . . ."

"All right, all right! So we'll wait here until he leaves."

A few minutes later they heard the front door slam with the familiar loud bang, and Frimma, followed by her husband, walked back into the house. Cautiously they opened the door to the living room and saw their "baby" stand there with the look of a young bride: her eyes shining, her cheeks rosy, and Frimma even thought that she detected lipstick on her daughter's mouth, God forbid, but when she took another look with her eyeglasses on, she realized that it was a natural red, and that Sylvia was just not the same girl.

"A Jewish boy?" she asked, and received a sharp rebuke from Mendel's scolding eyes.

"I don't know, Ma, what nationality Gilbert Burck is. We didn't get around to discussing religious questions," Sylvia said, and to Frimma her daughter's voice sounded joyous, and so happy! But neither asked their daughter what they did discuss; they never pushed themselves into their children's private lives. They always waited for them to volunteer whatever information or ideas they were ready to share with them.

Slowly Sylvia began, "Gil Burck—he's the second most important man in our movement here, in the midwest. He asked me if I'd go to Gary, to help organize a club of young people; most of them are steel workers, now working in the Big Mill, that's one of the largest mills in the whole country. These young people will be very important for the building of a union inside the plant, he explained," tilting her head a little, and looking at both her parents with pride.

"What did you tell him?" Mendel asked quietly, his kind eyes caressing her already, in a sad farewell.

"I told him maybe a little later, that now I want to go to work in a millinery shop for a while, and learn the trade."

For the first time the two Kanofskys felt that they had lost their youngest daughter, that her leaving them was only a matter of time. Yet, they remembered the Gil Burck visit for some time. In their reminiscences, later, when they were alone, they drew on those precious recollections, when their "baby" had at last become interested in boys, too.

CHAPTER IV
When the Storm Broke

I

THE STORM BROKE! Disaster spread with hurricane fury
across the land! Financial and industrial corporations collapse
in ruins! Twenty bankers commit suicide. Theodore Walton,
father of Art Walton, found dead. "The greatest stock market
catastrophe of the ages" drives thousands onto the highways
and roads, as if running from a rumbling, devastating earth-
quake. Life's savings are wiped out—hunger and demoralization sprawl menacingly among the vast multitudes.

Surpluses glutting the production system are deliberately
being destroyed: cattle and hogs killed and buried in ditches;
oranges soaked with kerosene, to prevent being eaten; vast
amounts of corn used to fire furnaces; wheat rotting in crammed
silos.

President Herbert Hoover summons officials of the American Federation of Labor to White House,* who pledge him
they would not seek wage increases or other benefits during the
economic difficulties; while William Z. Foster tells the nation
that "capitalism in the United States of America has become
idiotic in its chaos" and calls on the hungry to take to the
streets, and demand immediate government relief. Over a million people respond (March 6, 1930)[4] in all major cities, at
gigantic rallies and demonstrations, under one banner:

DON'T STARVE, FIGHT!

Soon hunger gathers up the militants of the nation, at Chicago's Carmen's Hall: fourteen hundred blacks and whites

* November 11, 1929

converge on that hot July weekend to place unemployment relief on the agenda of the entire country. They come from rank-and-file trade unions, from all industries, from settlement houses; from all parts of the country they hitch-hike, ride freight cars, or walk.

Willie Rivers and Isaac are in the hall. Sylvia has just arrived with her Gary youth delegation. Mirko Yanich, seated near the platform, befriends another stockyard delegate from Omaha, Nebraska.

To many sitting in Carmen's Hall, hunger had been an old acquaintance, an intimate of long standing. To others, hunger came almost unnoticed, like a thief, when the storm broke, having entered their homes through the empty shelves and empty ice boxes.

To Willie Rivers it seems that he had gone hungry ever since he stopped seeing his girlfriend, the very tall Bernice Washington—weeks and weeks ago. Strange, whenever he gets this hungry, a sweet potato pie appears before his eyes . . . he can't remember the other dishes she used to make for him, and in his mind he keeps calling her "my sweet potato pie."

When Mirko asks him, "How's Bernice, still working in the laundry?" Willie becomes confused. Who's he talking about?

But he recovers from his hungry spell, and answers, "I don't see my sweet po . . . I don't see her any more."

"Broke off?"

"No. Just don't see Bernice any more. Got no time."

Time, time! That is what everybody now has on the south side, and everywhere else. Time! Time to come to the park every day, all day long; time to walk miles and miles, to all parts of the city, to seek a day's work, a few hours' work.

"You got no time to see Bernice?" Mirko asks surprised.

"Nope! No time to see Bernice," and the subject of Bernice Washington is closed for good, for both of them. How could Willie ever tell his white friend when he couldn't tell Bernice, to her face, why he would not see her any more?

It was several weeks back when it all started—for Willie—on the corner of Twelfth Street and Halsted. It was there that large numbers of black women and black girls show up daily, to hire themselves out as domestics, for fifty cents a day plus a meal. The more enterprising ones solicit, and get a little more.

They come to the corner to seek survival. Bernice and her mother were on the corner when Willie walked by, unnoticed by either of the two women. He saw Bernice's tall head, high above all others; he saw the well-dressed white lady talking to her mother. "Three dollars and all meals, for one week," the woman offered loudly. Mrs. Washington accepted and took off with her new employer. Then the white man came, whispered to Bernice, and soon Bernice drove off in his limousine, as Willie walked away hastily, faster, faster, talking to himself, cursing the white man, cursing Bernice and her sweet potato pies, cursing Chicago's Slave Market, where Negro women congregate daily to sell themselves for fifty cents a day and a meal, and more, like my sweet pota . . .

He never called on Bernice again, and it was true that Willie now had very little time, for now he walked every day to the South Side Cafeteria and waited an hour, and sometimes two hours, for the chef to pass some food to him through the rear window. Then Willie would walk back home for his first meal. But this, too, came to an end when the cafeteria closed down.

Now Willie goes daily to the slaughter houses, and picks up the innards of the slaughtered cows: he picks up the hearts, the pieces of stomach, and other parts thrown away. But today Willie came to Carmen's Hall, as did so many others, to see what could be done to stop that hunger that gave him such crazy visions about sweet potato pie.

It was in Gary, at the Zimmermanns', with whom Sylvia Connors resided, where hunger first hit her violently, with severe pain.

It happened a few days before that Chicago conference, at a meeting of young people; they were gathered around Sylvia, on folding chairs, and on the floor, when a boy asked:

"Anybody got a cigarette?"

None answered.

"Anybody have money for a package?" Sylvia asked.

She had never smoked nor tasted tobacco, but she was hungry; she had nothing to eat that day, nor the day before. She was not thinking of a cigarette, but of a glass of milk and a doughnut—a bottle of rich, cool, milk costs the same as a package of cigarettes.

"Yes, let's buy a—" she hesitated, she wouldn't say it.

"Let's get some smokes before we start the meeting," the same boy urged.

They put their pennies together, bought a package, and passed it around. Sylvia also took one, lit it, inhaled deeply—and waited for the hunger inside of her to subside. But suddenly she doubled up with pain, and let out strange screams. They carried her into Mrs. Zimmermann's bedroom, put a cold cloth on her forehead, and covered her up, as she fell into a drowsy slumber, thinking again about rich, cool milk.

Mirko Yanich, sitting near the platform, can hear the speeches clearly, but he can't follow them. Words, words—this young girl with the slight lisp—she's so familiar! Where, where did he meet her?

"My generation is the unwanted generation. We are the surplus youth, looking for work which we know we can't find; looking for food which the government would rather destroy than give us; we're too young to die of hunger!"

Who is she? Mirko wonders.

Mirko's mind keeps pulling back to last night: Why was there so much soup left for him? Is Mother ill? He remembers asking Kate, "Anything wrong with Ma?"

"No."

"What about you? You eat some soup yet?"

"I ate at Mrs. Jergensen's."

"Who's Mrs. Jergensen?"

"Oh, I'll tell you some other time about her."

He remembers everything that happened last night at his home, except that soup. He can't remember eating it. Now his mind turns to his clothes, and he examines his clean shirt and gray summer pants he's wearing. They're all right, he thinks, but the shoes: I must get another pair, soon. I must! Ma never says anything any more. What's the matter with Ma?

Mirko hadn't noticed that hunger had sapped his mother's strength, and had begun to affect her mind. Ma Yanich now retreats to her bedroom often, sits down on the edge of the chair, in front of the mirror, and talks softly to herself. "Today we'll bake the layer cake; get the flour first, add the butter and sugar, and a little salt, Mirko doesn't like salt in his food, the eggs and shortening, add the milk and vanilla . . . wait, wait, double it all, double that shortening, the sugar, make it, make it . . ." and she falls back on her bed and lies exhausted, with her empty eyes staring at the ceiling.

Other days, around noontime, she gets those awful palpitations, but why get scared? It's subsiding. Good! But I can't get up: it's the stomach, pulls like a rock, it's weighing me down, and that pain inside, what is happening? Calm yourself, calm. . .

Then she switches her mind abruptly to an old recipe, that thick soup with beans, and meat, and potatoes, and she tastes it again, and again, and adds, in her mind, another pinch of pepper, a little more stock, and the mouth begins to water, the rock in the stomach isn't pulling any more. Ma Yanich gets off the bed, unsteadily, sways a little, and walks into the kitchen to warm up the water; she adds a few drops of lemon juice, and sits down—until she hears someone come home—then she retreats to her room again.

Sometimes Mirko sees her and says, "Hi, Ma! You O.K.?" and runs off before hearing her answer.

Other times he asks, "Nick still sleeping?" Ma Yanich motions to him to be careful, to speak quietly, and he knows his brother is still asleep. Soon Nick will be getting married, and will move out, and soon he'll stop paying Ma altogether, and then, then . . . where will we all go then? He is interrupted in his thoughts.

"Sorry, brother," the young fellow, who sits down next to him apologizes for having bumped him. He takes a seat without looking at Mirko, his eyes upon the speaker on the platform.

Mirko, too, is now looking at the speaker, trying again to concentrate. He's talking about breadlines and soup kitchens, like the one near his home. Maybe Ma gets the bread over there! Dammit! Dammit all! That's why she cried when I asked her where she got the moldy loaf of bread. Why did I ask her such a stupid question?

The man is now talking about the families that can't pay rent or light and gas bills: "Thousands of families are being evicted; the country is becoming a land of paupers—" He's talking about people moving into shanty towns, near the city dumps, or on abandoned vacant lots, naming them "Hoovervilles." Is that what Kate and Ma will have to do after Nick moves out? But that's impossible! Impossible! I can't take them to a Hooverville! Never, never! Maybe this hurricane will blow itself out, like the President says; maybe prosperity is "just around the corner." That thought has just entered his mind, and he is toying with it, lingering on that idea with some respite, but the man on the platform shatters it.

"President Hoover is lying when he says that the worst will be over in sixty days. We must compel his administration to grant us relief, unemployment relief. The richest land in the world is among the last countries without social security of any kind; neither for the unemployed, the sick, or the aged. This is not an act of God, as some would have us believe."

Mirko looks at his young neighbor, sitting next to him, and whispers: "That's what I've been saying."

"Count me in," he whispers back to Mirko.

"We are dealing with the most far-reaching economic crisis of this century, or of the last century, involving the entire world. It is a manmade catastrophe, and we, the people, have to organize ourselves and dig ourselves and our country out of this mess." The delegates cheer, some are on their feet, applauding loudly.

"We have to set up Unemployed Councils all over the country, in all the neighborhoods, to stop these evictions, and to stop them from shutting off the gas and the light, and from freezing us out of our homes, this coming winter," the speaker shouts through the microphone.

But again Mirko has difficulty following the speaker. His mind is drifting. There is something wrong with him, he thinks. He knows there's something wrong. He has trouble remembering a simple thing like the name of the girl who is registering the people at the door: yet he knows her so well—she's his girlfriend—what's her name?

Hunger had arrived in the Yanich family unannounced, quietly, and had become their daily companion, and had followed Mirko into this large auditorium, and was holding his hand, and making him shiver, making him forget such simple things as Madeline's name.

"Where am I?" he questions himself. "What am I doing in this big place with all these people?" He looks in all directions

105

in an attempt to connect himself with reality, but instead all remains strange and distant to him. Again he turns his head towards the door, where Madeline is helping the late arrivals. Yes, Madeline, of course! Suddenly he wishes the man on the platform would stop talking, then he'd walk over to Madeline and ask her, "Honey, you going home after this meeting is over?" and she'll say, "No, Mirko, I'm taking you to the Village Restaurant, on North State Street. They serve such large portions over there, and we can have second helpings."

He hears loud applause, as the man on the platform sits down; he sees his young neighbor applauding, his hands high in the air.

"He's all right; knows what he's talking about," the stranger says and smiles.

"Sure does," Mirko replies mechanically.

The session is adjourned. For the first time the young stranger and Mirko look at each other. They shake hands.

"I'm Zalman Harris, from Omaha Packing. Zal, for short."

"Well, I'll be switched! I'm Mirko Yanich, also packing. I mean I was packing—Swift's. You people working steady there?" he asks, with some animation.

"A few are working, but they let me out. The Company says that Jews and Reds are messing up this country. They knew I am Jewish, but someone must have stooled on me."

Mirko notices that his new acquaintance is almost a head shorter than himself; and when they shook hands, he felt a hard, vigorous grip.

"Got to sit down a minute," Mirko says, "got a little dizzy before—it's, it's the heat in the hall." He's pleased to have come up with that explanation for his recurring dizziness. "Where you staying tonight?" he asks.

"Don't know yet."

"We can put you up, but maybe they'll have a better place for you at the registration table. Let's ask Madeline."

"Sure be glad to go with you to your home. There was another delegate with me, from Omaha. We had to break up on the road, and I haven't seen her come in yet."

"What happened?"

"We couldn't get a ride together after two hours walking on the highway. We tried it separately. I got picked up right away, but Chris hasn't come in yet," Zal said. His dark smallish eyes became still smaller and sadder. "Hope she makes it here before it's all over."

"Is this her first time away from home?"

"Oh, no! She's hitched rides to different places; made speeches to the farmers and unemployed in other cities besides Omaha."

"Then why worry? She knows how to take care of herself, right? She ain't no kid, is she?" Mirko asked.

"Chris is almost twenty-one, and real pretty. Red hair you can see a mile away," Zal replies, a thin smile reappearing.

"You want to wait a while for her? I'm in no hurry, got to talk to Madeline." Mirko was a sensitive man, and could read trouble on other people's faces.

He was himself in trouble, bringing a stranger for the night into his home. His brother didn't like Mirko's new friends, and he told him so several times.

When Willie Rivers first came to visit, Mirko heard his brother say, under his breath: "Those goddamn niggers coming up here from Georgia and Alabama, taking our jobs away," and Mirko turned deathly white with rage, ready to smack him across the face with his outstretched hand but Willie hadn't heard Nick's insulting remarks, and Mirko put his hand down. Now he was inviting an out-of-town Jewish boy, and Nick could make trouble again, but he said nothing about it to his Omaha guest.

"Let's see if Chris has checked in yet. Let's ask Madeline."

"No point in that. I've been watching all afternoon. Christine Wesly isn't here, in this hall. Could we leave your telephone number for her to call if she comes in later?" Zal suggested.

"We don't have a telephone now. But we can ask Madeline to be on the lookout for her, and later we'll call her and find out where she put her up."

Zalman's eyes glowed with new admiration for this tall, thin man, who seemed to have quick answers and know his way about.

"Say, are you an organizer or something?" he asks Mirko sincerely.

"No organizer, but someone stooled on me, too," he answers with a light snap of his fingers, and the two men laugh heartily as they walk away together.

107

II

"This is Zal, from Omaha. Zalman Harris. He's staying with us for the night. Meet my kid sister, Kata, or Kate to you."

"Hello, Kata. I like that better than Kate." Zal extended his hand clumsily, without knowing what to do or say next. He looked at her admiringly, the light from the floor lamp having cast a soft reflection on her oval adolescent face. The black eyes that met his were clear and steady—the hint of coquettishness confusing him momentarily.

"Are you hungry?" she asked pulling her thin hand away from Zal's grip, already regretting having asked such a question of this healthy-looking boy. "Ma left you some soup. There's enough for both of you," she says in a more natural voice, as they move into the kitchen.

Kate was a most perceptive young girl, frequently amazing the others with her "grown-up ways" and remarks. Aware now that she was being observed by this boy from out of town, she automatically placed the book she had been reading, tightly against her chest, as if attempting to hide her young womanhood that was protruding through her summer blouse.

"Watcha reading?" Zal asked, breaking the silence.

"*Jews Without Money*," she answered and for the first time saw his face in the full bright light, over the kitchen table. "Have you read it yet?"

"No. Who wrote it?"

She looked for the name of the author. "It's by Mike Gold," she said, pushing the book towards him.

Zal fingered the pages without reading any, quickly coming to the end. "Is it good?"

"I don't know yet. Just started it tonight, after Ma went to bed. Madeline likes it. Oh, you don't know Madeline, you're from out of town."

"I met Madeline today; she registered me, and we talked a while," Zal said, feeling part of her world. "What is this book all about?"

"It's about the Jews in New York. You know any Jews?" she asked and again sensed that it was not a very smart question.

"Sure he knows a lot of Jews." Mirko answered for him. "He knows Zalman Harris and other Harrises," and the two men laughed, leaving her out.

108

"You're Jewish?"

"Me, my father and my mother—all Jewish. Maybe this guy is writing about me?" Zal added.

Kate felt totally uncomfortable about that entire discussion, suspecting that Zal and Mirko were making fun of her; and she didn't like the way her brother was looking at her—sideways, through the corner of his eye, studying her.

"But I'd like to read what this guy says about the Jews," Zal said sincerely.

"You can have it next. I'll be through with it by tomorrow."

"I'm leaving tomorrow, right after adjournment; but I'll get a copy in Omaha," he assured her, and Kate suddenly felt sorry that she wouldn't see him again.

She watched them spoon up the soup and dunk the bread in it. Pulling down the coffee mugs from the shelf, she felt all grown up, and anxious to talk about that position as governess she found today, and to tell them that they wouldn't have to live on the stuff her mother brings from the soup kitchen, much longer. Instead she asks abruptly, "Was Willie there today?" as if Willie Rivers was of special interest to her.

"And how he was there! He made a big speech this afternoon," Mirko replied. Turning to Zal, he asked, "Remember that fellow who spoke about the south side? That's Willie Rivers. He comes here once in a while; last time we were talking seriously about setting up a Council in back of the yards."

"Man, can he talk!" Zal said with genuine admiration of Willie's oratory. Zal had never overcome his stage-fright, and had difficulties speaking in public, especially at large gatherings; now he recalled the fluency of Willie Rivers, and seemed to remember every gesture of "the Orator."

Kate was cleaning up and putting away the dinner dishes, when she realized that the two men were not even aware that she was there; Zal was telling Mirko how they had fired him when he refused to become a stool pigeon for the Omaha Packing Company.

"All of a sudden they transfer me to another department and put me next to this guy who talks radical all the time. I wasn't suspicious of him then; every once in a while you see a guy blow his top. But he says to me, 'Buddy, when you work here as long as me you want some vacation, I mean paid vacation.'

That's how he started working on me, talking about himself. You see, we have to have five years' work to get a week's paid vacation, but if you get laid off for sixty days, or more, you lose your standing, your seniority, and you start all over again, like a new employee. Many guys who've worked there ten and fifteen years don't get a paid vacation."

"The same goddam thing's going on here," Mirko interrupted. "Nobody knows who's going to get laid off or fired next."

"You see, they must've been suspecting me for a long time," Zal picked up his story, "but they didn't fire me because they figured that they could get me to work for their company union."

"Why did they pick on you?"

"Just before they kicked me out we distributed a mimeographed song which pokes fun at the company union, and when the men got it, you'd think the whole plant was laughing at the company union. There was six stanzas of it. Here's one of them, wait . . ." Zal lowered his head to concentrate better in recalling the lines.

The Company is good to me, I b'long to the Company Union.
They cut my pay and I agree, I b'long to the Company Union.
My wages, they are up so high; my fam'ly's starving, so am I,
But sooner than complain I'd die; I b'long to the Company Union.

"But what made them suspicious of you?" Mirko insisted.

"You see, I must have been a rebel all my life. When Sacco and Vanzetti were killed the whole neighborhood sat up till it was over, way past midnight. I was still living at home, in Brooklyn, where I was raised. It's been like living in a slum all my life, and I heard Dad use the word 'socialism' ever since I can remember."

A vivid scene had just flashed through Zal's mind. . . they had introduced electricity in the tenements, and the landlords raised everybody's rent; but the people refused to pay the increases, and they had rent strikes and won, and the rent remained the same as when the gas jets were burning . . . and he recalled how all the tenants celebrated that victory with house parties and impromptu parades through the streets.

"You see, if something is invented, for instance, the people ought to benefit from it," he told Mirko, as if confiding in an older brother. "I was just about fifteen years old when I graduated high school. They called me 'a wonder boy,' but you see, it was too much for Dad to pay all the doctor bills, and pay for the medicines for my mother—she was sick, sick all the time—so I went to work."

After both his parents died, he moved to Omaha to live with a relative and there he took a job in a packing plant. "And I made the stupid mistake of shooting off my mouth when I saw what was going on in there." He sat back as if having emptied himself of his entire life history, suddenly feeling self-conscious for having talked so much. But Mirko was attentive, and interested.

"What did they do? Tell you they didn't need trouble-makers, and let you go?" he asked Zal.

"That's just it, you see, they didn't. They let me be for a few months, then they started moving me to other departments, and put me next to this guy, who's telling me that we need a few Reds, and that he wished we had some in the plant. He keeps telling me like it's a big secret he's sharing. He was a company spy, but I didn't know anything about company unions and spies, and I agree with him. Then I get called in and am told that the company knows all about me, and that if I'm interested in a break for the men, why don't I cooperate and become a representative in the union that's already there so I could do some good for the workers. You see, the company union is like a safety valve—many of the real grievances are brought to the meetings, and sometimes the company even makes concessions. The main idea is to keep a genuine union out of the place. This company man who called me in for a talk, leans over and says in confidence, like this," and Zal mimicked him, talking now in a whisper, " 'The higher-ups want me to get rid of you,' he tells me, 'but I think you're a good fellow, you mean well. I'll have to move you around; you'll be able to work all over, and get to know people in the plant—except the killing floors—but I want to keep you in our employ.' You see, they're always worried about the killing floors where the key men are. If you have no killing you have nothing." Zal noticed that they were alone in the kitchen.

"Where's Kate?"

"She's a big reader, stays up late reading everything she can get a hold of."

"She's not angry at us or something?"

"No, no! She's just like that—does whatever she wants. Probably got interested in her book and is reading it." Mirko shook his head approvingly. He urged Zal to continue.

"Well, you see, I talked this thing over with a couple of fellows I like and trust, and they tipped me off that the company was trying to hook me and to find out through me who the other militants were. We had to be very careful because we were doing some work inside the plant—"

"Like what?" Mirko asked.

"Oh, every once in a while we'd receive a bundle of bulletins from Chicago, and we could see that things were the same in Swift's, and Armour, and the other packing houses. They, too, had company unions, the same racket. We passed these bulletins around and the men got a big bang seeing us do it, with all the spies around us—"

Mirko burst out with a loud, rough laugh, and started pacing the kitchen floor. "I help them write those bulletins, and you, guy, was distributing them in Omaha. I'll be switched if this isn't something!" and Zal, too, began to see the coincidence— meeting one who wrote some of those reports for the bulletins he was passing around in the Omaha slaughterhouse.

"We don't always get the postage money to mail them everywhere, but we never miss our Omaha connection," Mirko told him.

"You're kidding me now!"

"No, I ain't kidding anybody," Mirko assured him. "Say, why don't you stay over a few days, and look around here; meet some of the boys from the plant. I'll take you to Washington Park where you'll hear Willie Rivers and Isaac report back about this unemployment conference."

"That's what I got to do myself. We got a big meeting planned in Omaha to hear Chris and me report back. Lots of people depend on us," Zal said slowly, as he was thinking that he, too, depended on Chris to make that report, because she knew how to speak to large crowds. But she had missed a full day already; would she be in the hall for the morning session?

"Say, it's past midnight, we better get some sleep," he said, thinking that the waiting time for Chris' return would be shortened if he went to sleep.

When the lights were turned off for the night, Zalman Harris lay awake, his thoughts with Chris . . . Where are you now, Chris? Are you, too, waiting for the sun to rise? Why do you act like I'm your kid brother, kissing me on the forehead? How pretty your red hair shines, like a halo; your freckles on your nose—where are you, Chris? You'll be in the hall, in the morning. . . . He was dozing off seeing Chris walking into Carmen's Hall, rushing towards him, kissing him in public before all those people, and crying for joy, crying . . . crying.

Kate, too, lay awake long after her light was out. She had waited all evening for Mirko to come home so she'd tell him, "Meet the governess."

"Meet who?" she visualized Mirko's surprised expression on his face.

"The governess."

"Who's that?"

"That's me."

"You gone crazy or something?" Mirko would ask her, and smile in his playful manner, as the two were accustomed to such make-believe. They often played games like that, talking in innuendoes.

"It's true," Kate would tell him, and cross her heart. "Next week I report as the governess for Master Michael Jergensen."

"And who's Master Michael Jergensen, if I may ask?" Mirko would then look up to her with a serious expression.

"That's the young master to whom I have become 'the governess' today."

But when Mirko walked in with that boy from out of town, her entire dramatic scene collapsed, and she decided to skip it all, and get some sleep instead.

Her day had begun as usual. She was telling her mother that she was going to see a very wealthy family, which had a French tutor, and an upstairs maid, and a butler.

"How many people in the family?" Mrs. Yanich asked casually.

"Three. There's Mr. and Mrs. Jergensen, and their boy, Michael," Kate replied.

"And they have a tutor, and a butler, and . . ."

"Oh, Ma, there's a lot of work in that house; its very big. I've seen it from the outside—it's like a castle. They have a gardener, who lives in a small house on the grounds, and there's a chauffeur, and I saw the two automobiles in a big stable, but I know it's not a stable, it's a garage for cars."

"But what do all these people do for the three of them?"

"I don't know too much yet, but I'll tell you after the interview. If they hire me, and I live there a while, I'll be able to answer your questions."

"Live there? You'll have to move there?" Ma Yanich asked with alarm.

"Sure. They'll want me to sleep in, next to Michael's room. There's a nurse who sleeps in, too."

"How come you know so much about them?" the mother was suspicious.

"The principal told me a few things about the Jergensens, and said not to be afraid to go there for the interview, and to act calmly, and speak slowly, and not to show off."

"Why did she say that?" Mrs. Yanich asked. She never considered her daughter a show-off.

"You know how the principal likes me, and thinks I should stay in school and finish the semester, and then she says she could get me a scholarship for college. But I told her that I must go to work. The Jergensens will pay four dollars a week, and all meals, and a room of my own."

III

"*Attention, please, your attention*: Still missing, and unheard from—the entire southern delegation. No word yet from the Omaha young woman; calls from people arrested and released outside the Illinois state line just came in; they are on their way here. The Pennsylvania delegation checked in during this morning session. We'll keep you informed as we . . ."

But Zal Harris hears nothing: he sits through the morning hours of the unemployed convention, immobile, sad and confused, his eyes glued to the doors, in silent vigil for Christine Wesly.

Again the gavel comes down, again he hears meaningless words: "All heads of delegations will meet upstairs, in the balcony, during this lunch hour; heads of delegations proceed immediately to . . ." But Zal does not stir.

"Hey, Zal, let's go upstairs. You're head now of the Nebraska delegation, aren't you?" Mirko shouted to him from another part of the hall where he's talking with Willie Rivers. Mechanically Zal followed Mirko and Willie to the balcony, and mechanically he sat down near the exit, where he continued to stare at the doors of Carmen's Hall.

But suddenly a wild, hysterical scream in another section of the balcony was heard throughout the auditorium, as Sylvia Connors spotted Helen and Art walking up the center staircase, with their small Black Belt contingent behind them. The dramatic reunion of the two sisters and uninhibited flow of joyous tears was watched by hundreds of smiling, understanding, faces. Mirko and Willie barely recognized Art's drawn, lined face and thin figure. Slowly they edged their way to their old acquaintance, and Willie shook hands with the black Southern farmers, informing them that he, too, came originally from the Black Belt, as he introduced himself to them.

"You're not the Willie Rivers that my sister told me all about?" Helen asked, extending her hand to him.

"The very same one, but she didn't tell you *all* about me. She doesn't know me that well!" Willie said, and the people all around them laughed, as the man leaning on the rails of the balcony called the emergency meeting of heads of delegations to order.

Within the brief lunch hour, he said, they have to discuss matters of major importance to the welfare of the entire country. "As leaders and heads of this movement, our big problem is to prevent demoralization from setting in." He reminded them that they had already heard many reports on how the militant Unemployed Councils that were mushrooming everywhere were battling for relief and helping many thousands of impoverished families from dying of hunger.

"But with this national gathering we have to make a drastic turn: we have to broaden this leadership, and make room for other capable, honest people, to come to the fore. This movement is growing to tremendous proportions, and it is up to us, the people sitting right here, to find ways of attracting other forces. We need help from the American Federation of Labor ranks, and from the Railroad Brotherhoods, from the Socialist Party organizations, from the Negro communities, and churches. They should all be involved in the battles that lie ahead, and they should all share leadership with us. Our movement against evictions, and against hunger, and for government responsibilities will grow even faster in the months ahead—if we don't hug the leadership; if we don't think we're the only ones who know how to fight for life in this country."

Those were words they hadn't heard at the regular sessions of the convention. The people were listening attentively.

A man sitting in the center of the balcony was waving his hand persistently, demanding to be recognized. He was given the floor and cautioned to be brief.

"Reverend Norman Vincent Peale says that all we need is a good prayer meeting in Wall Street at which the bankers and corporation executives would freely confess their sins. I tell you, comrades, we have to overcome this kind of propaganda, and we have to explain the real essence of this chaotic system, and tell the millions of unemployed that capitalism is on trial. When thirteen suicides are committed within twenty-four hours in one of the large cities of our country, in Los Angeles, California, then we must say that it's the system that is beginning to smell like a dead corpse, and that this system will eventually have to be changed, and that a prayer isn't going to accomplish that." Loud applause followed.

"I'm almost through, please, just another second. We should also demand that our government recognize the U.S.S.R. because the co-existence of these two governments will benefit us all."

The chairman agreed with the last speaker, and added: "We, the leaders of this big movement, the responsible people, must also recognize that there's an organized terror unleashed against our unemployed movement, and it is spreading rapidly across the country. We have to face up to this terror, and build our defense organization so that this movement doesn't find itself decapitated, without a leadership, with the most militant forces sitting in jail, while the organization of the unemployed gets dispersed by the callous reactionaries who don't give a hoot about the suffering of the millions. These are the two things we want to emphasize here, to you, to the leaders of . . ." The noises from the main downstairs auditorium were getting louder, and were drowning out the comments of other leaders, who rose to speak. Delegates were returning to the hall for the last session. A large group of rank-and-file trade unionists, sitting in the very center, had just begun to sing Hallelujah, as

116

hundreds of others joined them in humming, or singing, of this old hymn: and all over the hall could now be heard

> Oh, why don't you work like other men do?
> How the hell can I work when there's no work to do.
> Hallelujah, I'm a bum, Hallelujah . . . .

The leaders' caucus had adjourned, and as they were walking down the balcony staircases, Mirko's eyes drifted towards the doors, where he saw Madeline motion to him to hurry down. She kept pointing her hand to a girl standing nearby. Somehow he now recalled clearly that last night when he laid awake, unable to fall asleep, he was thinking of Madeline—that she should have invited him out for supper. But she didn't even ask him if he wanted to eat with her. Now as he saw her again motioning to him vigorously, it felt good to ignore her, as she had ignored him last night! He bent his head closer to Willie's, to pick up his confidential remark, that stool pigeons were entering the Unemployed Councils, and that something would have to be done about this soon.

At the foot of the steps Madeline met them and almost shouted, "I've been trying to tell you all along that Christine Wesly is here, but you paid no attention. She's at the table, over there!"

Zal rushed by her, past the others, pushed his way into the main lobby towards the entrance of the auditorium, where he saw Chris talking calmly to another woman, her eyes searching at the same time through the crowd. Mirko fell behind, curious to witness the scene between Zal and the missing delegate from Omaha.

To him the redheaded girl seemed quite ordinary in appearance. True, her hair was a bright red, just like Zal had been telling him, and it fell in a soft wave, parted on the left side, covering her ears and part of the forehead. Her chin was a little too small, Mirko thought, making her nose seem bigger than it really was. He continued studying her changing expressions on her face as she smiled and talked. Mirko was surprised, though, to see her so calm, as Zal approached her. She stretched out her hand to him, as if it were a normal, usual greeting between them.

But Zal saw nothing through his watery eyes, except the tall frame belonging to Christine. She was alive! She was here!

117

Standing in front of him! Ignoring her extended hand, he picked her up, swirled several times a complete circle, until both were dizzy, with Chris begging to be put down.

Mirko could easily tell that she was happy to be in the hall, happy to see Zal—but her cold greeting was a deliberate and calculating mannerism—almost unnatural.

She never once broke into open laughter, he thought, but when she smiled, her face became very interesting. There was fun in her brown-golden eyes, teasing or playing with Zal, like a cat plays with a mouse.

Still unseen by the others, Mirko continued studying the rest of this tall, lanky, almost too-thin girl, with the bright green blouse and brown tie strung through a loop under the collar, her narrow brown skirt matching both the shoes and tie.

Zalman kept staring at her with his broad grin and twinkling, lively eyes, shouting intermittently, "Where the . . . where have you been? My God, we thought you were dead," and Chris heard the "we" and knew that Zal was genuinely worried about her. But still in a teasing mood and inwardly extremely happy to see him and the hundreds of others in the auditorium, asked, "Who's the 'we' that worried about me? Anybody else show up from Omaha?"

"No, nobody else from there, but my friend—hey, where the hell did you disappear to?" he shouted. Mirko was directly behind him, and at that moment he had winked at Chris, communicating to her that he, too, was aware of this young fellow's excitement and confusion.

"I'm right here, behind you. Why don't you introduce us?"

"Introduce you? What the hell! You know this's Chris Wesly from Omaha, who was hiking with me—what the hell?"

"I know all that, but do you remember my name?" he asked, and both Mirko and Chris laughed in unison.

"Oh, what the hell!" Zal repeated. He had, in fact, momentarily forgotten his name, and Mirko knew that he had gone far enough.

"I'm Mirko Yanich, pleased to meet you," he said, giving her his hand. "Zal stayed with us last night and told us about you disappearing on the road. I'll bet you got an interesting story to tell."

"You can bet on that!" Chris replied, paying no attention to Zal.

Her voice had joyous laughter in it, softness and femininity. She seemed to have been aware of its attractive quality and used it coquettishly with Mirko.

There was nothing casual about Christine Wesly. Everything, everything, was there by design: the way she greeted Zal, her hairdo, her clothes; over the right ear she wore a tiny, single, artificial flower, almost totally hidden within the wave of her hair, and pinned down firmly by a tiny matching comb. On the table near where Chris was standing was her large paper portfolio in which she probably carried other personal belongings for the trip; her name and Omaha address printed neatly on the outside, and soon Mirko concluded that this was an organized, disciplined, and meticulous person.

"How come you missed the meeting upstairs?" he asked, to break up his own calculating—and admiring—glances.

"I got here not too long ago," she answered.

"Are you all right, Chris? Is everything really O.K. with you?" Zal asked again.

"Can't you see? Never felt any better. The best rest I've had in months."

"In jail?" Mirko asked with a grin.

"You guessed it, brother."

"All this time?" Zal joined.

"Yes, in Aurora."

"Aurora? How did you get to Aurora?" Zal wondered.

"One question at a time. Take it easy, fellows," she said, waving her hand to slow them down.

"I did O.K. all the way to Illinois and through most of the state. Got rides, good ones, and a few good meals, too. Then two characters pick me up and when I ask them if they're going to Chicago, one replies, 'Almost, close enough.' So I get into their car and ask, 'How far you gentlemen going?' 'To Aurora, just outside Chicago,' the driver answers. This was perfect: timing was good, too; everything added up so far. But then the driver asks me, 'You going to the Convention?' 'Yes, how did you know?' 'We know,' he says and shows me a badge, and tells me that they were from the Sheriff's Office, picking up bums like me. They released me just a few hours ago and I got a ride to Van Buren Street, then I took the street car to the hall, and here I am. They kept me in jail long enough to miss the convention, or almost miss it." Chris finished her account abruptly, biting

119

her bottom lip several times, as if wanting to hold back tears or curses. Mirko saw her anger mounting, the color of her face changing, revealing a coat of freckles underneath her watering eyes.

"Those bastards knew all about this Convention: when it started, and when it was supposed to end, and who was going to make the main report, and who was coming here! They told me more about the convention than I knew when I left Omaha. They were ribbing me all the way into Aurora, telling me that I'd be missing the first session, and not to be too upset because I wasn't the only one being picked up on the highways leading to Chicago! You should have seen those dirty, piggish, faces of theirs, telling me all this, and talking to each other about me, referring to me by my first name, saying: 'Chris needs a little rest, she works too hard, too many meetings lately, getting too thin.' This went on and on till I almost screamed to them to shut up or I'd jump out of their car; they shut up, and said nothing more until they locked me up."

"We had a meeting up there, on the balcony; Madeline should have taken you up there," Mirko said.

"When I registered, the girl who read my name acted like she had seen a ghost, then she tried to catch someone's attention on the balcony. I guess she was looking for you, Zal, when I told her I was the other delegate from Omaha. But she didn't tell me to go up there."

"That's Madeline for you," Mirko said sarcastically. "Should have taken you upstairs; it was a very important meeting," he repeated angrily.

The three walked into the large auditorium together, where the final session was already in progress. They sat down close to the platform, with Chris between the two men. Mirko and Chris were talking softly; Zal was silent—saddened again, as he attempted to follow simultaneously the proceedings of the convention, and the conversation between Chris and Mirko.

His joy at seeing her alive, sitting next to him in the comfort of the large hall, among friends, overshadowed his fleeting jealous thoughts that were disturbing him. Zal leaned over Chris' lap and, motioning to Mirko to bend his head, suggested, "How about asking Madeline if we four can get together after adjournment?" and Mirko's approval of that idea set the young fellow at ease for the remaining hours of the July Fourth week-end of 1930.

IV

The great rejoicing during the sisters' reunion was short-lived; soon they'd have to part again and return with their delegations—Helen to the South, and Sylvia to Gary. They sat in a corner of the large auditorium, clinging to each other, talking in low whispers, in snatches, about their parents and their home.

"You haven't sent me any letters, like you promised you would," Sylvia said, "and you got so thin."

"I don't like to write letters," Helen whispered. She just now realized that she had never before written to anybody.

Her life was so different, and so much had happened to her, that she found it difficult to bridge the gap between herself and Sylvia. She couldn't talk about Art or about herself.

"Our work is moving along pretty good," she said. "There's a union started among the sharecroppers and tenant farmers, and we brought some of those farmers here to the convention; they're sitting over there with Art."

But this wasn't what Sylvia wanted to talk about. She was a well-informed young organizer who read extensively and had kept up with the important developments in the country. She wanted to hear more about Helen.

"You look so different, and Art, too."

"It's not easy to live and work there," Helen said, pretending to be interested in the proceedings of the convention.

"You mean it's not easy to live with Art in the Black Belt?" she asked.

Helen looked at her sister as if she was seeing her for the first time. She was amazed at her astuteness, and wondered if Sylvia had known all along about her difficulties with Art.

"You want to go outside for a few minutes of fresh air?" she asked Sylvia, who rose immediately and followed her out of the hall. They had so little time left, and almost a year's silence between them to fill up. Their minds were crowding rapidly with many thoughts as they walked away from the hall, both aware that there would be no other opportunity to be alone again.

"Art is like a different man from the one I first met in the basement on Evergreen Street. I think it all started when his father died, that's when I think he began to act like he lost his way, you know what I mean?"

She added quickly, "He does his work, all right; he meets with the people, like he's supposed to, and I go along most of the time; but I can see that his heart isn't in the work any more."

"Do you think he'll want to remain here, and not go back?" Sylvia asked.

"Oh, no, no! We talked about it. I suggested that to him, but he wouldn't listen to that! He didn't even want to visit his mother, but I insisted that he must. He promised me that to-night, after the closing of the convention, we'd go there, and maybe stay overnight with her. But he keeps telling me that this is the most significant work he has done in his whole life; regardless what happens, he says, he must return, he must continue working in the South."

"But?"

"But I'm afraid, Syl, that he won't be any good there; he won't be able to work there much longer." Helen lowered her voice, as was her habit when sharing a confidence. "He's de-moralizing."

At first it was difficult for her to formulate into meaningful sentences the many silent thoughts and mixed conclusions she had reached about this man. For months she was reevaluating Art, whom she once told, "If you'd ever leave me, it would be like the sky would fall on top of me, like the world would tumble down, and I'd be buried alive, and there would be no use for me to go on living any longer."

But with those months of suffering, there came objectivity and the sudden awareness that it was Art who needed her and leaned on her.

Opening up a conversation with her sister about Art's de-moralization was like recalling a nightmare that had haunted her for weeks and months. But now that she understood this man better, she would not share with anyone the grief she had suffered—only the conclusions she had reached.

"Art never built his life on his own strength. He always

122

leaned on someone. During his school years he leaned on Fred Heller, I mean he used him. Then it was his family, the Waltons, you know what I mean? When he put one foot into our movement, he never let go of the other foot. It remained there, close to his father's—for his comforts, for his good life. But when his father was wiped out with the big stockmarket crash and committed suicide, Art's foundation crumbled, and he didn't know what to do with that other foot."

Sylvia had never heard her sister talk that way. She had never heard Helen take a situation apart or analyze it in such a manner, and come to a conclusion with such firmness. It was Sylvia, in the past, who often scolded Helen for her indecisions, telling her, "You keep changing your mind all the time. Why don't you stick to what you agreed?" And Helen, somehow aware in that distant past, of inner confusion, and vacillations, but not able to grasp its meaning, would retort then, "You're too rigid, and stubborn. One has to be flexible, and ready to make changes."

Now, however, as they were walking away from the assembly in the auditorium, from Art and the others, Sylvia saw her sister in a new light—she was looking at a mature woman, who was capable of rising above her personal sorrows with brutal objectivity. Helen was talking not about her own involvements and suffering, nor about the man who had completely changed her life, but about a phenomenon operating outside of herself.

"He seemed to have lost his bearings after the news reached us about his father. He was confused, and at first I couldn't understand why he grieved so much; he was never really attached to his father. It's the 'Duchess', his sister, about whom he always talked to me. He felt so sorry for her! She's a sad and unhappy girl, he told me, maybe because she's not very good-looking, I don't know. He doesn't know either. We never went too deeply into that subject. But his father, that's different. He admitted that when he fell in love with me and decided to go away with me, it was on account of his father. He didn't think he could have remained in Chicago, with me as his wife, both of us active in the movement. His father would never have accepted him, or me. There would have been a complete break between them. But away, far away, Art would still be able to remain somehow part of the Waltons. He never said that to me, but that's the way I figured it all out. And after the death of his

123

father, his ties with the Walton family were broken completely, and he needed me even more than before; that's why he clung to me the way he did."

Helen smiled now as she walked on, in step with her sister, looking down towards the pavement and reminiscing. "Those first few days and weeks after the suicide, Art was like a child, not a husband. We cried together, often. He never let me out of his sight. Then it seemed like he suddenly snapped out of it, and the old Art . . ." Sylvia put her arm through Helen's, re-establishing their former intimacy, when they first started going together to the neighborhood club.

"Then he began telling me about that girl he met at the weekend conference; that she recited poetry so beautifully with such depth and meaning, that he had never heard anyone like her before. That she was brilliant . . ."

" . . . and that she was beautiful," Sylvia interrupted sarcastically.

"No, she wasn't. He told me she was very young, but not beautiful. I asked him the same thing, just like you now did, but he said it was her poetry, the way she read it to him that made her beautiful. And then he started staying away from home."

"You mean . . ."

"Yes. He thinks he needs more freedom to find himself, but he doesn't want to let go of me, either. He tells me that I'm the most important person in his life, but I can't understand him half the time, telling me about the women he stays out with, and then acting like a child, like I ought to spank him and forgive him. Then once he was away for nearly a week, and I knew that it wasn't on account of his activities. Someone would have gotten in touch with me if he was in trouble with the law. I knew that it was some one else this time."

"Oh, no! That would make me sick to my stomach," Sylvia said, showing pain on her face.

"It was the wife of a liberal editor; her husband was out of town, and he stayed over there, in that rich neighborhood, and later regretted it, and told me that he made a terrible mistake, that the worst people in the country are the white liberals; that they can't be trusted with anything. But I knew that he meant her, that he couldn't trust her, and it had nothing to do with trusting the white liberals."

Sylvia was overwhelmed by those revelations. An idol of hers had suddenly fallen into the gutter.

Helen continued, "He's like a child. He tells me all these things because he says I'm so different. But I don't know any more, Syl, I don't know what'll happen after we return from this convention."

She stopped walking and, looking at Sylvia with dull, sad eyes, whispered, "I never felt so alone, so miserable, when it first happened."

"You want to come home with me, to see Ma and Dad?" Sylvia asked, in an attempt to heal all her sister's wounds with the comforting suggestion of returning home for one night.

"Gosh, Sylvia, that would be wonderful! But no, no, we shouldn't! I mean I shouldn't. You ought to go, but I don't think you should tell them that I was here for this convention. Just tell them that you heard I was all right. It wouldn't be good for them to see me like this. They wouldn't understand and they'd blame Art for everything. No, no! But you must go, Sylvia. You must see them, you must see them more often," Helen said with longing for her aging parents.

Their conversation somehow drifted towards their bedroom, and the items they had left on the dresser, and on the closet shelves. They called on those items to bring them a little closer to the days of their comfort and security. They spoke of their basement, and about the old discarded bureau in which the two sisters used to hide their cherished possessions.

"It's not there any more," Sylvia said slowly, cautiously bringing the sad news. "The basement got flooded this spring in one of those terrible downpours, and all my things, and some of yours, got washed away with the drawers of the bureau. I lost my graduation picture."

"Oh, gosh, Sylvia!" Helen said, and the prolonged silence that ensued recorded their sadness.

Sylvia also confessed to her older sister that she had broken the promise to send twenty dollars a month to her parents.

"After the big March sixth demonstration, I had no money left and no way of getting it to send them help. I was locked up for two weeks, and had to pay a fine. I used some of the savings for that. When I came out of jail I telephoned them, but the operator said the telephone was disconnected. And I haven't seen them but twice since I left home. But I think I'm going there tonight; I'll sleep in our bedroom tonight, and I'll visit with them. Tomorrow I can hitchhike to Gary in a couple of hours, and get there in time to report about the convention. Maybe you should come with me to see them, just this one time?"

"No, no!" Helen answered quickly. "I can't leave Art alone. He wants me to come along with him when he enters his home again." She informed her sister that Art did not go home for the funeral when the great tragedy in the Walton family occurred. He was returning now for the first time, to face his widowed mother and the "Duchess", and he wanted Helen by his side.

V

Sylvia's gentle ring on the doorbell went unanswered. She waited and studied the familiar low fence around the house, recalling the summer her father had carried the narrow planks all the way from the distant lumber yard to build the most artistic fence on the entire block. Neighbors would stop to watch Mendel Kanofsky shape the tops of the boards with his crude tools, and later they'd watch him paint the fence and add a coat of rainproof varnish.

Sylvia examined the white gate leading to the back porch and knew, from the low sounds coming from the rear, that her parents were sitting there now, enjoying the soft breezes that had blown in from the lake. Not wanting to startle them, she waited a while longer . . . she now remembered standing next to Betty Dunhill at that same gate one day long ago, talking about their parents, when Betty asked, "What color eyes does your mother have?"

"Blue. Why do you ask?"

"Because very few people notice the color of the eyes; you're making a mistake, too, your mother's eyes aren't blue."

And Sylvia remembered getting angry for having told her that she didn't know her own mother, when her father happened to be coming out of the house through that little gate. "Pa, what color eyes does Ma have?" Sylvia asked him kiddingly.

He looked at the two young girls, and smiled. "Just a minute. I'll go back and see, she's sitting on the porch."

They were both on that porch now, talking softly. "Last year was a good year for us, Frimma, a good year for everybody," Mendel said.

"What do you mean 'good for everybody'? Everybody's children brought home their pay envelopes to their mother, like our Louie, and Helen, and our 'Baby'? Sometimes you talk nonsense, Mendel—you and I had a good year—I don't know about everybody else."

Frimma had very little contact with the other neighbors, and now she believed that only the Kanofskys, only her family, were faced with imminent disaster.

She was a woman of considerable "old country education", literate and articulate. She wrote the minutes of her Woman's Society, and read them back with such dramatic flair that she made the routine decisions sound like stanzas of lovely poetry, written by Poetess Frimma Kanofsky. Once a year the entire synagogue honored her for that contribution with a dinner and a personal gift.

However, there were moments in the Kanofsky family life when Frimma felt left out, imagining that all attention was directed to their father, to Mendel; although it was quite obvious that her shrewdness and her delicate beauty of distinction had naturally put Frimma Kanofsky in the limelight most of the time.

Sylvia often thought of Mendel's nimble fingers, and of his dream to produce, on a paying basis, the miniature figurines which he had carved as a hobby. He had actually succeeded in assembling those tiny, wooden images inside bottles with narrow necks, creating a genuine reproduction of a European Tea Room, and a Village School. Sylvia recalled telling him then, "But, Pa, you know yourself, that if you made some money from your hobby you'd give it away to people who are poorer than we are," and Mendel smiled with satisfaction, recognizing those words as a great compliment from his youngest child.

He was, indeed, known as "Mendel der Malech," Mendel the Angel, in the entire neighborhood, where people with serious problems would seek him out for help or for advice. Then, when alone with his wife, he would tell her what was going on "in the world."

Frimma, however, found it necessary—especially when they had visitors, company—to elaborate Mendel's observations and comments, to put them in her own words, as if to lend weight to them, by making his ideas sound like her own. Mendel would smile approvingly or nod his head, to indicate that his wife was right, perhaps even believing that those ideas had originated with her.

Even now, while sitting on the back porch alone, without any need to convince anyone that her Mendel had told her something of considerable importance, she repeated his words, and added, "Last year you had a lot of work, Mendel. They even wanted you to come in on Saturdays to work; ah, remember?"

"A bunch of 'goyim,' even the Jews my own age—all chasing the dollar. Sabbath means nothing, nothing to them—last year or now!"

Last year was the most prosperous year since the turn of the century, "and the most prosperous year for many other families," Mendel reminded her again. But now it seemed to the two Kanofskys that fate had deliberately conspired to destroy them.

"Why does it have to be like this? I can understand losing a job; I can understand losing your home when you can't make the payments. Things can happen. But losing two daughters!" Frimma said, her eyes looking into the distance.

"What kind of talk is this about losing two daughters?" Mendel replied sharply. "You sound like our girls are dead!"

"Well? I ask you, Mendel, did Helen have to run off with a goy? Aren't there enough nice Jewish fellows in Chicago?" Frimma repeated the question Mendel had asked her in a previous discussion.

After putting it in her own words, she added, "And why did Sylvia have to go to Gary? What is there in Gary? Is it a bigger city than Chicago? Are there more people in Gary than here? Why Gary?" she repeated. "Ever hear of a seventeen-year-old girl, a child, leaving home and going off to a strange city? All right, if she said, 'Ma, I want to see what New York is like,' or 'I want to see what San Francisco is like. I'm going to San Francisco.' But why Gary? And I believe her, Mendel, she didn't go to Gary on account of some boy. I believe her when she told us she was going there because she was asked to go there, asked to help the young people of Gary."

The Kanofskys always trusted their daughters, and their boy, Louie, too. They knew that neither Helen nor Sylvia would ever mix the dishes, silverware, or towels, when cleaning up after meals, even though neither of them believed any longer in the traditional Kosher rituals—of strictly separating all items used in the consumption of dairy from meat products.

It was not so long ago, in a moment of deep loneliness for the children, but wishing to justify them, that Mendel asked his wife, "How many girls do you know who would leave a good Kosher home, to help others organize unions and clubs, so the people could have a better life? Think, Frimma, think!" They often shared their pride in their children.

Helen they hardly even mentioned, and the name of the man she went away with was a sinful name.

"Elope! A new word! And it has to happen to us. It's not enough she runs off with a 'goy,' she has to elope yet!"

"Please, Frimma, keep quiet! Leave me alone," Mendel said softly. He was annoyed now to hear his own words reechoed. He never talked harshly to his wife, but on rare occasions, when he told her to keep quiet, Frimma would stop talking immediately, as if insulted. This time, however, she felt the need to add, "and Sylvia has to go off to Gary," making it sound like their daughter had enlisted in the Foreign Legion.

At times they'd compare their son with the girls, and marvel how different he was, although raised in the same home: how quiet and disinterested in politics or in heated discussions. Louie had been reading Shakespeare ever since he learned how to read; he had been playing chess ever since his boyfriend, Max, gave him a chess set on his thirteenth birthay. He never argued with his sisters, but would tell them frequently that they were not Jews any more, that they were more interested in the life of the colored people than the Jewish people. He never said it with rancor; and they all knew, of course, that Louie would always be grateful to them for introducing him to his Sophiele. Everybody called her with the diminutive endearing term. When Louie decided to get married to his Sophiele, it made good sense, and they all agreed that it was quite all right for his young wife to continue working in the millinery shop until they saved up enough to pay for their furniture.

The only objection the elder Kanofskys had was that their son had moved too far away, and it took almost two hours each way, on the street cars, and because of that they seldom visited each other.

"Louie could have taken a place a little nearer to us, no, Mendel? You know how long it's been since they were here?" Frimma asked, hoping to keep the conversation with her husband going.

"How long?"

"Seven or eight months, I think. When all that noise about the stock market came out, remember? I think it was October, or early November, the last time we saw Sophiele and Lou."

None, not even the "wise Frimma" could have foreseen the effects upon their lives since the storm broke, in October of last year. Events of the recent past had moved so fast that the Kanofskys failed to grasp what had brought on the disastrous family situation. Louie got married and moved out; two weeks later Helen elopes, then Sylvia leaves them—but that was in the year of prosperity, and had nothing to do with the great crash—the Kanofskys reasoned. Yet, perhaps their situation was related somehow to it, they thought; Mendel is without work since March, and no one is hiring any more in the cigar shops—he has been to all of them—and the Kanofskys were closer to total disaster than ever before.

They had trouble before, lots of trouble. It was never easy for Mendel to raise three children on his small earnings—but he never panicked. During his younger years he came up with a variety of schemes, novel plans, on how to break out of their precarious economic situations, but Frimma would tell him to stop making a fool of himself, and she usually stopped him in time.

Mendel, however, was not only a kind and considerate man, but also stubborn, and some of his general ideas prevailed, even against the wishes of his wife. He reminded her that it was a good thing he didn't listen to her when he "loaned" the fifteen dollars to the new grocer who had opened up a small store on the corner; later that grocer returned the fifteen dollars, and also sent over a large quantity of supplies, and the Kanofskys lived on that for almost a full week—by coincidence the week Mendel had no pay because of illness.

Now Frimma began to sense that her Mendel was scheming something, was planning a way out of their impending ruin, and that soon he'd start talking to her about it. She noticed that several times he had looked at her with narrowed eyes, which she recognized as "Mendel is up to something."

"I'll have to build my own factory, there's no other way out," he said in his usual gentle voice, and Frimma knew that it was useless to say anything, because she couldn't get through to him when he looked at her like that.

"Come here I'll show you," he continued, and led her out to their back porch. Pointing to the wall on the left, over which he had already placed a white chalk mark, he began to unfold his plans. "I'll put a door right here." Mendel raised his hand over his head, to assure her that he had measured correctly, that it would be high enough even for a tall person to walk through. Frimma understood from his gestures that he wanted her to say nothing, not yet. From his pocket he took out a small piece of paper with several pencil drawings, and added, "Here I'll cut a small window facing the yard."

"What do you mean you'll cut a small window? Where? Into the air?"

Mendel was no fool, by any means. He recognized instantly that this was her way of telling him to go ahead and explain more, that maybe this time he had something she'd agree with. He smiled softly, as he always did in gratitude for her cooperation.

"I'm putting up several boards over here, by the steps, and that'll give me a place for a window."

Now Frimma began to see visions of their back porch "factory" for Mendel's cigar-making because he had already measured the size of the boards he would need, and told her that it would cost $11.60, and that "Moishe is coming over to help me this Sunday; he knows how to cut glass." There was no use trying to stop him, Frimma thought.

"I have three molds in the basement," Mendel reminded her, changing the subject from his architectural plans to the purposes of his "factory." "Ereb Reiner promised me two more molds. He isn't using them since he lost his business this spring. I'll be able to make fifty cigars at a time with five molds."

"And what will you do with the fifty cigars?" she asked resignedly.

"What do you mean? I'll sell them, to the two delicatessen stores on Division Street and one on North Avenue." Mendel checked himself abruptly, trying to remember something very important. He caressed his neatly trimmed goatee, as was his habit whenever he needed help in remembering something.

131

Frimma knew that he was thinking hard, and she tried to help him by not moving a muscle.

"Yes, yes, I know now. Mr. Tuckerman. He'll get me two, and maybe even three, customers."

Frimma was just about to interrupt, but Mendel anticipated her comment. "So I'll give Mr. Tuckerman a few cigars for his troubles, so what?" Their old boarder never did favors gratis.

"Where will you get your tobaccos, and your boxes, and your labels?" Frimma asked in a cooperative tone.

"Where, where? In the jewelry store," he replied, and they both laughed. Mendel seldom told jokes, or retaliated with negative humor, but he recalled now asking Frimma where she found such good pumpernickel bread, and in ridicule she told him, "where, where? In the jewelry store." They loved their grown-up games!

"And who'll do the stripping, and the labelling while you pack the molds?" she asked.

"You will."

She knew how to strip the heavy center vein from the leaf, without damaging it, having done it many times for Mendel when he was ill, and when they could not afford to miss a full pay. She knew the difference between leaves used for inside and outside the cigar, and she could smell tobaccos and tell their quality. Frimma knew all along that Mendel was expecting her to help him.

"So we'll have a Kanofsky factory on our back porch, ah?" she told him, and smiled assuringly. Mendel had found a way out.

"We'll tell our children that the Kanofsky cigar factory is one hundred percent union," he said, and walked inside the house to answer the loud ringing of the bell. In the narrow vestibule, when he recognized Sylvia through the outer door-window, his joy was so overwhelming that he turned around and shouted, "Frimma, Frimma, come here, quick, quick!"

Frimma rushed to his side, and seeing the familiar face in the shadow of the street light, almost shrieked unnaturally, "Why don't you let your daughter in? What are you waiting for, Mendel?"

Early the following morning, Sylvia found breakfast waiting

for her; Mendel had already eaten, and Frimma pretended to be too occupied at the stove to engage in conversation.

The atmosphere was so different from last night's joyful reunion, Sylvia thought. Both her parents were deliberately looking away from her, avoiding her eyes. After sitting down in her old, usual place, Mendel asked her:

"How soon do you have to leave, Miss Connors?"

Sylvia looked into her father's sad eyes, and understood that he expected an explanation from her for discarding the Kanofsky name.

"I never deny that I'm Jewish, never! I'm proud to be a Jew," was her quick reply.

"If you're so proud to be a Jew then why did you have to change your name to a Christian name?" Mendel asked with disappointment in his low voice.

"When we received your money order and saw that name, we were going to return it to you," Frimma added.

"But Ma, you of all people should understand that we're not liked; sometimes we get thrown into jail. Radicals are treated like outcasts, like criminals, in this country. Sometimes they also punish the relatives, and families of people like me. This way we try to protect the other Kanofskys from being harassed." She deliberately addressed herself to her mother, as she had often done in the past, when forgiveness was sought by her. From her father she always felt approval of her conduct. His daughter would never do anything that he'd be ashamed of. "There must be a good reason for a Jewish girl to do a thing like this," he said to himself, and his disarming smile appeared on his wrinkled face. Sylvia offered no other explanations; instead she shifted the conversation.

"Ma, don't you think it would be a good idea if the 'shames' of your synagogue also changed his name?" There was mischief in her voice, and her head tilted, in anticipation of her mother's cooperation.

"Why? Is he in Gary, too?" Frimma responded to her daughter's teasing humor, fully aware that their deacon's name was frequently ridiculed. She continued: "We've known Yankel Smatchky for over twenty years; is that right, Mendel? About twenty years? He always answers to his name, and after all, isn't that what a name is for?"

"But a name like Yankel Smatchky!" Sylvia continued, her eyes begging for her mother's help.

"Next time I see him, I'll tell him that my youngest daughter thinks he ought to change his name to Kenneth Smatchky," Frimma said.

Sylvia jumped up from the table, embraced her mother and kissed her with a loud smack, while Mendel looked on with pride in his two women, whom he loved so dearly that it hurt. Only God knows, he thought, when he'd see her again, and what will happen to her after she leaves them today.

Sylvia was the happiest girl she had been in months: visiting with her parents, making them laugh, eating a hot breakfast with them. She kept up her clowning, telling them about her visit with her friend, Rina, in the Catholic hospital, where the patients praised the dedicated, good Christian doctors and nurses.

"It's true," Sylvia told her parents solemnly. "When Rina's doctor came in to see her, I noticed how gentle he was; he also assured her that she'd recover despite her serious illness. I was really impressed with this Catholic hospital. After the doctor left, Rina told me with deep respect for the man who had saved her life, 'That's my surgeon, Dr. Israel Jacobson.' "

Frimma laughed approvingly, adding, "What else do you expect from a Jewish doctor?"

Her mother was in fine form now. "But don't think that all Jewish doctors are that good," Frimma said casually, and Sylvia knew that she was getting ready for more of their own kind of humor. "Some of the Jewish doctors, when they don't know what's wrong with you, tell you it's age, like that elderly woman who was complaining about her right leg aching her all the time. The doctor told her, 'Don't complain so much, my dear, after all, you have to consider your age.' The woman didn't like his answer and asked him: 'How about my left leg, doctor, isn't it the same age? How come it doesn't bother me at all?' "

Of course, Sylvia never told her parents the real reason why she had decided to change her name to Connors, on the very first day she went "into the field."

There were about a dozen other young radical organizers scattered all over the vast area of Illinois-Indiana, hiking between towns, stopping off in distant places to talk to a lone contact. Some went into the mining regions of Southern Illinois or a small steel community of Indiana to set up islands of radical organizations with their contacts and "leads." These full-time young people never discussed their hardships or personal sacrifices, and Sylvia, too, understood that she was expected to hike to Gary and to other places, when the need arose.

The day she received her final instructions and a list of names and addresses to be contacted by her, she felt her stomach drop each time she thought of getting on the highway, and thumbing a ride with a stranger, to a town that was strange, to meet people who were strangers. She took the piece of paper and casually put it in her pocketbook.

"You ought to hide this list on your body, Sylvia, instead of carrying it like this. In case you get picked up on the way to Gary, we don't want the police to find the names of these young steelworkers. They are very valuable contacts, and we don't want them to lose their jobs because of our carelessness."

Outwardly Sylvia was a cheerful hitch-hiker the following morning when she proceeded "into the field". The old farmer who picked her up was delighted with the young girl's pleasant conversation, and with her easy talk about the Windy City, and the many interesting places of Chicago. Thanking him several times for bringing her so close to the steel city of Gary, the farmer asked her congenially:

"What's your name, young lady?"

"My name's Sylvia. Sylvia Kanofsky," she answered.

"Jewish?"

"That's right! Jewish!" Sylvia answered, still smiling pleasantly.

The old farmer's face turned red with anger, as if he had just let out a notorious criminal whom he should have beaten up instead of given a ride. As he pulled away in his pickup truck, Sylvia heard him cuss in an ugly voice, loud enough for her to hear, "Those goddamn Jews! Never thought I'd be giving a ride to one of them!"

She was stunned. She stood there glued to the spot where he had let her out, and for some time after the dust behind him had settled wondered if it was all real. Staring into the distance after the disappearing old farmer, and reevaluating the anti-

Semitic outburst, Sylvia began to walk into the city of Gary. In her mind she listed the names of several other organizers whom she had met, Jewish, but with non-Jewish names.

The name Kanofsky had suddenly become an obstacle to her: the anti-Semites of the Gary steel community would point to her name to denounce all Jews; there would be false arguments about the American radicals and about the movement being a foreign-influenced movement, she reasoned. As if defying all tradition and pushing aside everything that might narrow her horizons on her first assignment and limit her opportunities for work, Sylvia began to try out the sounds of Christian names that resembled her own.

At last she repeated several times, "Sylvia Connors, Sylvia Connors," and felt relieved, unburdened of an artificial obstacle.

Sylvia didn't tell her parents about any of the other encounters with anti-Semitism. How could she talk to her own kin about that dying woman, the striker at the Queen Ann factory, who had been beaten by a scab, and almost bled to death . . .

"We need blood for my mother, right away, Sylvia; we can still save her life if we get some people to come here right away to give her blood; you must help, Sylvia, please; see if you can round up a couple of young people, and I'll get some that I know—tell them to come here, to emergency, right away . . ." Paul Hammond took off in his old Ford to look for blood donors, and dropped Sylvia near the Queen Ann picket line. She persuaded two young strikers to return with her to emergency. Paul was also back, with three young friends, and was waiting to be called in to check their blood for direct transfusions into his mother's veins.

"Of the seven of us, somebody's blood ought to be right for your mother," Sylvia consoled the pale, distraught young son.

"Sylvia, please, I'll explain later, we have no time now; but please, don't go in there, let's try the six of us first, please Sylvia!"

"But why? I'm just as healthy as any of you fellows; I don't mind . . ." she became indignant at such exclusion.

"No, no, it's not that, believe me, Sylvia. You'll understand later when I explain to you; please don't go in there. In case my mother is conscious, when the transfusion takes place, she shouldn't see you."

"Look, Paul, I don't give a hoot about what your reasons are to keep me out of there. Your mother needs blood—if mine matches, she can have it!" She was annoyed to be told not to participate in the first such emergency she had run into since she became the organizer of that community. She didn't like to be told what to do under such circumstances, and for some inexplicable reason, she suspected that Paul Hammond was trying to protect her, to spare her the consequences of a direct blood transfusion. A nurse appeared while she and Paul were whispering between themselves.

"Sylvia Connors, please come in. The others may go."

Disappointment was written on the faces of all the would-be donors; they agreed immediately to rush back to the picket line and seek out other volunteers.

"Mom will die if she recognizes you when you lie next to her, giving her your blood. She hates Jews, Sylvia, and I didn't know how to . . ."

Sylvia pushed him away. "Then I'll have to tell the nurse to make sure that your mother is blind-folded, so she won't see me," Sylvia told him, and in an authoritative voice ordered the others out. "Don't waste your time here! Get some more people up here. Come on, get moving all of you, you too, Paul!"

VI

Mirko found the cold, immobile body, in front of her mirror, on the bedroom floor—too late for help, too late for tears. His mother was dead!

He was to blame, it was his fault, he, he, only he, Mirko Yanich! "I knew she was all alone—Kate a governess, Nick married," he said to himself over and over, as he became obsessed with feelings of guilt.

Speechless and stunned, he stared with glazed eyes, with gnawing thoughts that he, only he, was responsible for his mother's untimely death. ". . . alone with her the whole night, while she lay dead in her bedroom," Mirko repeated the incredible. "Why didn't I knock on her door sooner? Why did I wait till now?"

Willie came during the day and tried to talk to him; he came again the next day, and brought him food.

At last Mirko shook himself loose for a moment from the paralyzing shock, and talked absentmindedly, to no one in particular. "It's like being tied down with a heavy rope, being held back against your will, torn inside, wanting to do something, but unable, unable to help her any longer, too late, too late, because Ma was dead!" He snapped his finger lightly, emphasizing the finality her death had marked.

"But all day long I get filled up inside, and I keep asking myself, why didn't I watch her? Why didn't I bring her some food? Why didn't I steal, like others are doing, and get some food for Ma?" Mirko started again, looking now at Willie's sad face, both men filled with grief. "I know she couldn't have lived, I mean she couldn't have lasted long on that food she's been eating for a long time; I know, I know. It isn't that I took her food away from her, Willie; it wasn't that at all! No! I ate a meal once in a while with Madeline, and with you. I was hungry, but I wasn't starving! But Ma? Why didn't I watch her?" He looked with empty eyes at his friend for an answer.

"What's the matter with Madeline?" he suddenly asked Willie, who had said nothing—who was listening and waiting, waiting for Mirko to empty himself of his painful feelings. "What's the matter with Madeline? Why does she always wait till I ask her where she's eating her supper; doesn't she know herself that when a man gets hungry he wants a meal? No, she doesn't, she's never been hungry!" and again he snapped his fingers, relieved to have found someone to share his guilt with in some way.

"She seems to like it when I ask her to take me home with her, or take me to the Village Restaurant! I'm through with her! Through for good!"

Willie welcomed this outburst of anger against Madeline. He welcomed his return to other subjects. Willie had tried several times to talk to him about Zal and Chris, about the new Unemployed Council that he and Mirko had set up, but he couldn't get through to him. Now it seemed to Willie that he could direct their conversation away from the tragedy that had set in with the death of Ma Yanich.

Willie said, "Maybe you started thinking like that about Madeline after you met Chris. Could be. You didn't talk that way about Madeline till Chris Wesly showed up."

"Well, what's wrong with that? Chris is a lot different from Madeline—that helps me see Madeline in a different light, too."

"I'm not saying there's anything wrong, and get me straight.

138

I'm not saying anything against Chris or Madeline, either. But until she came around, you thought Madeline was tops. Remember what you've been telling me about her only a few weeks ago?"

"Madeline's all right, in many ways. But all this time she's been making me feel like she had me on a string like I was a puppet or something, while Chris is just the opposite, makes you feel you're somebody, makes you feel important."

Chris and others had stayed over for several days after the convention adjourned. It wasn't safe for all the delegates to pour out on the highways and risk getting picked up again. Many stalled in Chicago, like Chris, while Zal Harris proceeded to Omaha immediately.

"She thinks about other people's feelings," Mirko continued. "She likes Zal a lot, of course she does, but like a brother, a co-worker. Zal had other ideas, and Chris had to find a way of telling him that she could never become serious with him; she wanted to tell it to him without hurting him. See what I'm talking about? She put on a show, she pretended she wasn't excited when she got into the hall, but she was bubbling inside like a volcano, she was so excited. Instead of misleading Zal, she played a little game, and pretended to be interested in me—a total stranger. She had figured that it would be the best way to get Zal off her back. She was waiting for something like this to happen—and here I was, standing right next to Zal, and I tell you, she starts flirting with me like it was love at first sight; and while Zal gets shaken up, all right, and becomes jealous, and all that—he gets the point for the first time in the two years he had known Chris."

"How do you know so much?" Willie asked.

"She told me later, after Zal got on the highway, and after I accused her of being a cold-blooded cucumber, acting like she didn't see Zal in the hall and all that. Then she told me that Zal, and others in Omaha, had ideas that she was his girlfriend because they work together so much in the movement. But when she got separated from him, while hiking to the convention, and she had lots of time to think this whole thing out, she said that would be a good time to put a stop to all that nonsense between her and Zal. And you know what she said? Get this: she said the first man she'd see together with Zal, she'd either hug or kiss him, and pretend that she knew him for a

139

long time, that he was a lost boyfriend of hers; and if she had any trouble with that, she'd say it was a mistake, that she mistook him for someone else. Then here I am, I'm the one who comes out of the meeting on the balcony with Zal in front of me, and she's so busy looking me over, trying to decide how she'd act out her little game, that she really began to think of me as a nice guy to get to know, and from then on I told you . . . anyway."

"Anyway what?"

"Anyway she's just the opposite of Madeline; when she knows you're in trouble, that something is wrong, she waits to talk to you in such a way as not to hurt you more. She came up here yesterday, before she left for home, and asked me, 'Did Kate know that mother was starving to death?' 'No, nobody knew,' I told her. 'Maybe Ma Yanich died of heart failure, in her sleep? It happens to a lot of people, who die like that, in their sleep,' and you know, it was the way Chris was talking to me that made me come out of this—this pain inside, that it was all my fault that Ma died."

CHAPTER V

Three Dead Men on Guard

I

The chilly drizzle settling on the snow is turning the Windy City into a slushy, mourning grey. Umbrellas, fighting the rain and wind, collapse into hopeless shambles, and ropes strung around the edge of Loop sidewalks give way to the pull of clinging pedestrians.

In unheated buildings the penetrating cold of the second winter of the Great Catastrophe is driving families into one room, huddling the young and old into one bed to keep each other warm, while hundreds of destitute single men and women flock to the lower level of the streets, to the loading platforms of the heated skyscrapers, for a night's shelter. Corridors of Loop buildings and railroad depots are swarming with the homeless men, stretched out on the floors and in out-of-the-way corners. Grimly, at all hours, thousands push their daily search for scraps of food—men and women fighting over barrels of garbage put out by the back doors of restaurants.

The reading rooms of the libraries are filled with gaunt, hollow-eyed people, who stare at the front pages of the newspapers, at President Hoover's picture, and mechanically read: "I am convinced that we have passed the worst and with continued unity of effort we shall rapidly recover." Federal relief, the President tells these millions of desperate people, would be nothing more than a "dole" and would harm the character of Americans by undermining their "rugged individualism."

His words are reechoed by another president—William Green of the American Federation of Labor—who shouts that "the dole system embodies a vicious principle . . . (it) develops paternalism that is demoralizing," and together with the other high-salaried officialdom, he harangues the delegates at its 1930 convention to vote down resolutions calling for unemployment insurance.

Confusion and desperation deepen as the increasing throngs of unemployed read everywhere they turn huge advertisements of the National Association of Manufacturers—"MENACE OF UNEMPLOYMENT INSURANCE! AVOID THE PLAGUE!"

At last! At last a solution to the suffering is offered! At last the President and his cabinet members call upon the people to share with the "unfortunate and underprivileged." The country responds to its Chief. "I Will Share" becomes almost the new pledge of allegiance. "I Will Share" skits are given gratis in the theaters; "I Will Share" parties are listed in the calendar columns of the society pages; 20,000 movie houses ask the people to see an extra midnight show and thereby help those on relief and the other unfortunates. "I Will Share" turns America into the greatest apple-eating nation in the world, as the International Apple Shippers Association promotes the sale of its surplus product with its own slogan: "Buy an Apple a Day and Send the Depression Away!" Soon, it appears, every street corner has its stand—an upturned wooden crate on top of which brightly polished apples are pyramided—and tens of thousands of unemployed go into business for themselves as apple merchants.

The airways boom joyfully the good news that at last the country understands that man is his brother's keeper, and again the President speaks to the nation, telling his listeners that this is the great trial, "it is a trial of the heart and conscience, of individual men and women." Solemnly he repeats his encouraging words that "no governmental action, no economic plan or project can replace that God-imposed responsibility of the individual man and woman to their neighbors. That is a vital part of the very soul of the people."

And America pours out its heart and launches in every city and township the greatest charity-giving campaign ever witnessed. Donations to community chests for the health and welfare organizations come in from all quarters; the radio and press hail the Chief as a man who is stalwart and principled, and they announce that spectacular drives for fund-raising events have been initiated throughout the land by the President's Organization for Unemployment Relief.

II

In millions of homes the lights remain dimmed, gas and electricity are disconnected, telephones are silent; thousands of tenants, unable to pay rent, are evicted, the make-shift Hoovervilles are unable to absorb the families sitting on the sidewalks with their belongings. Outrage of the hungry mounts; they respond to the leaders of the Unemployed Councils and send delegations to the city, state, and federal governments for help.

In the small township of Tonawanda, over a thousand demonstrators come to the City Hall with their families, with infants in the arms of their mothers to demand milk for their starving children. They crowd inside the chambers of the small council, and as they fill the rows of empty seats, they see a chain of ugly men standing against the walls, surrounding them on all sides, as if geared for violence against the assembled. A spokesman of the Unemployed Council approaches the railing separating the members from the crowded demonstrators, and says calmly:

"There's ample milk for all the children of the needy families in our community, but it is being poured into the gutters; there's plenty of fruit and vegetables in the state, but it is being destroyed in the fields. We appeal to you to stop that destruction of vitality needed foods; we appeal to you to help us get that food to our starving children."

Several mothers push themselves close to the railing, for the City Fathers to see the sallow faces of their hungry children, and a small woman with a husky voice asks the City Council to memorialize Congress to enact an Unemployment Insurance Bill, and save this country from even greater suffering and destruction.

Unmoved by the pleas of their constituents, sitting in their tall leather chairs, without any sign of hearing or understanding the pleas of the people, they rise slowly, without replying to any of the speakers' demands, and casually saunter out, one after the other, through the rear door of the chambers, deserting the people.

Enraged over the callousness to their pleas for help, they shout in unison "Cowards, Cowards" and begin to leave the City Hall chambers; they move towards the exits, filing outside, where hundreds of other hungry people await the report from their leaders.

Suddenly bedlam breaks out in all parts of the chambers as the ugly men, standing at attention by the walls, pull their hidden billies and brass knuckles, and bear down upon the helpless crowd of men, women and children who're unable to get outdoors. Some break through the man-made chain of sadists, and reach the streets in time to avoid a beating, but others are trapped inside. The diminutive leader with the husky voice jumps over the wooden railing, on the platform where the councilmen had been sitting moments before, and shouts, "Push towards the doors! Get outside! Don't be provoked!" Pointing towards the exits, she repeats the same words in an attempt to calm the trapped people—until she suddenly feels her body squeezed tightly, her abdomen and back a single painful mess. An ugly man with a swinging club having seized her, was pressing his club against her lower part of the body, forcing her over the railing, both of them falling to the ground, the man on top of her, the wooden object pressing her middle, cutting her breathing. . . .

"He's killing her! He's killing her!" a woman with an infant in her arms shouts, and continues her incoherent, hysterical warnings, as another ugly man pulls a gun at the woman. "Shut up or I'll shoot!" he barks. From nowhere, amidst the confusion and melee, another leader appears between the gun and the hysterical woman, and hoarsely whispers through tightly drawn lips, "Shoot, you bastard! Go ahead and shoot!" as he stretches his arms out sideways, shielding the body of the screaming mother and child. The gunman puts his weapon down, and drags the man outside where he pushes and kicks him into the waiting paddy wagon.

Three demonstrators are hospitalized with head and body injuries, in the small township of Tonawanda, and later sentenced to a year in the County Penitentiary.

III

Everywhere, all over the country, in Tonawanda, Omaha, or San Francisco, people are demonstrating at city halls, at county and state seats; people are demanding help from their government. They heed the leaders who have arisen from their midst, they follow them with the banner "Don't Starve, Fight!"; they heed their black ministers in the ghettos, and stay close to them.

The Reverend Ralph Green leads his parishioners to Chicago's City Hall. "We're given a few onions and a few potatoes, but we can't live on that. My people have no place to cook the potatoes because their gas is cut off; some have nothing, they are on the sidewalks, evicted," he tells the guard at the door. But he's turned back, he's not admitted into the building. He leaves the petition for help, signed by hundreds of neighbors, and takes his followers back to the ghetto—to an Unemployed Council.

"Willie Rivers!" he exclaims in surprise and shakes hands with him. "We haven't seen you in a long time, long time, son." Their eyes meet, both understand the meaning of the "we". Neither one refers to the past.

"You're about to start your meeting, I see," the Reverend Green says, and asks permission for a short prayer.

They all stand, some pray. The Reverend Green reports to the assembled unemployed men and women that they had just come from the Loop, that no one pays any attention to them. "The people in City Hall wouldn't see us or talk to us. But they must see us, they must hear the truth, we must tell them what goes on here! Two of my families are sitting on the street, evicted from their homes for nonpayment of the rent; there's an infant among them; we can't let them sit there and freeze to death!"

Willie Rivers, looking at the back of the head of the man now talking hears the familiar voice of desperation; he hears Mr. Green tell about the suffering of his people and his plea that something be done by them, all together, or they'll all perish.

Willie responds, "We'll have to go to the City Hall in larger numbers; we'll have to go there together with the others, with the whites from the West Side and Northwest Side, who're as bad off as us here."

It is the first time that Willie had called upon a black assembly of destitute people to march together with whites to stave off disaster. Somehow he thinks of Mirko at that moment—not recalling anything special, but feeling his presence—and drawing now on ideas they had discussed and argued over, and sometimes agreed upon.

There's the smell of death in their midst now, and Willie

continues, "Meantime we must do something about that infant and the two families near the Reverend's church."

He looks at the black faces before him. A woman's hand is raised hestitantly; Willie points to her to speak. She offers to share her home with the mother and infant. "But we ain't got nothing to eat in my house." Someone else speaks up—he'll get the milk for that infant by evening and he'll bring it to the woman's house.

The Reverend waits for more help, but none is forthcoming. They have nothing to share, they have nothing to give to each other—except the coffee that's brewing on the kitchen stove of this cold flat where the Unemployed Council is in continuous session. Somehow they keep a pot of coffee going all day: in the morning when they first make it, it's fresh, it's good. But now, in the mid-afternoon, the grains are flat and tasteless, but the hot water is there all the time. Some gather around the kitchen stove to warm their hands, Willie and the reverend resume their earlier conversation.

"How's Mrs. Green, and the others?" Willie asks.

"We're all fine, Willie. You look mighty good to me," Mr. Green replies. Neither man has mentioned yet Hattie's name.

A woman has opened the outside door and shouts loudly, "Telephone call for you, Mr. Rivers." Willie excuses himself, and rushes outside the building to answer the telephone at the corner tavern.

"Hattie never says anything about Willie; maybe it's best that way. We should keep it that way," Mrs. Green tells her husband, as she's being informed about seeing Willie Rivers that afternoon.

Hattie had dated other boys since Willie's disappearance from their life. She went to dances with some, and after graduating from the white high school, she found employment at the Sopkin Dress Company, and became even more reserved, more reticent, than in her younger years.

"Willie didn't ask you about Hattie—he didn't want to see her—that's what it means, that's why he never called on us," Mrs. Green summarizes. "We ought to keep it that way."

"It's best to tell her the truth, Rebecca. I'll tell her I saw Willie Rivers today, and we said little to each other—that's the truth." He closed their discussion on how to handle this new situation that had arisen. It was their custom to first discuss between the two of them matters involving their children. And that is how Hattie learned that evening, while eating her supper, that Willie Rivers was only a few blocks away from them, and when she went to her room, which she used to share with her sister Ella Mae, she began to think again about that dance with Willie Rivers . . .

We danced together, right here, in this house, he held me close and then suddenly I felt that a shiver had gone through his entire body—something had happened, and he stopped dancing. What was it? What had happened to him? She had just turned fifteen, she recalls, and together with Ella Mae, and several other young girls, decided to go dancing at the Neighborhood Dance Hall, but her parents wouldn't allow them to go alone, and their brother refused to chaperone them. Hattie pleaded with her mother, but Mrs. Green told her, "Your dad says that you'll have plenty of time to go dancing later, when you start dating."

"But I'm dating, Mother," Hattie insisted. "Willie would take me and Ella Mae, but he's too bashful or something, and he doesn't know how to dance. It isn't fair to wait till I find somebody else to date."

All her pleas to be allowed to go dancing were in vain—until her father suggested that they dance there, in their own home. "Get your friends together, and make a party here. They're all welcome in our home," he said.

"But, Father, there are so many of us, it'll be so crowded here."

Their home was large, airy, clean. Six sprawling rooms on the top floor of the building.

"Use your imagination, girl! You're big enough to go dancing, you're big enough to come up with some answers. Look at this living room! Take a good look at the bedrooms! Start thinking what you could do to make room for a dance for the kids—no one will bother you here, and it won't cost them any admission."

Never had there been so much excitement in the Green home. Never were the two sisters so happy before! They called on their friends, girls and boys, they asked Willie to help them get the bigger boys from his gym. They came together and planned their dance in that very same room where she was now sitting; they received permission to move the big pieces of furniture against the walls, into the unused corners—and that Friday they turned the flat into a dance room, and thirty-two kids came.

The Reverend Green was a happy man when he saw the results of his own idea. The Victrola was playing and the children were dancing continuously, until ten, ten-thirty . . . then they came—the police came and pushed the door wide open and with billies in their hands, as if raised to strike—the young boys and girls, dressed in their best, dancing and holding hands, and a policeman shouting, "Hey, you fellows, boys, all the boys, leave, leave now!"

The Reverend and Mrs. Green appeared quickly, in front of the policemen. "I'm Reverend Ralph Green. I live here with my family and nobody tells anybody in my home to leave. These are my children, and they'll stay here as long as they wish. If you have any complaint against any of my children, make that complaint to me," he said politely, firmly, waving his hand to the children. "Go on with your dancing, go on!" Mrs Green added.

"There's a complaint from a neighbor that there's lots of noise coming from here," the policeman informed Hattie's father.

"Hattie, turn down the music a little, it's too noisy for some neighbor," Mr. Green told his daughter . . . and that is how Hattie still remembers clearly that evening. They continued dancing until past eleven and for many more Friday evenings they danced in that room, when something happened, and Willie told her that he wouldn't come there any more.

Hattie kept returning to that scene, and to the eight girls who stayed overnight with her, and helped her mother make the oatmeal cookies and the cocoa—and when Hattie and the girls went to sleep that night, she kept going over and over in her mind the words Willie had told her, when they were dancing together: "I'm quitting school. I'm going to Virginia where I can get into a good school, on account of my basketball playing."

Hattie didn't ask him for more explanation, but she knew that he was leaving her because things were getting too serious between them: she felt it when they were dancing together, close. She knew that many of the girls in the neighborhood were pregnant and were dropping out of school, and Willie told her he wanted her to continue studying, and maybe later, when they were both all grown up, they might meet again, but he wouldn't hold her to waiting for him. She saw Willie Rivers only once more—the evening he came by the house to tell her that he was leaving for Virginia, and that he'd be away for a long time, maybe two or three years, and that she should find another boy to date—and that is how Willie Rivers walked out of her life. She hadn't seen him or heard about him until tonight's supper, when her father spoke about Willie and the Unemployed Council.

"What if he comes back here and asks me about Sis? What'll I tell him about Ella Mae?" she kept saying to herself. "He always saw us together, all the time, and he didn't like that, but I couldn't tell Ella Mae to leave us alone; I promised Ma to take Ella Mae with me. I know he'll ask about her, and I'll tell him the truth, I'll tell him Ella Mae died about a year after you left, Willie. She was only fourteen when she died, Willie. No, no! I won't tell him how, what for?" She kept thinking that Ella Mae wasn't the only one, the other kids in school also took the test for TB, the patch test, and they were all warned like Ella Mae and I was, that if the arm breaks out or begins to swell to report immediately, or see a doctor. Ella Mae's arm broke out, but why is it that nobody believed us that Ella Mae had TB —she looked so healthy—that's why," she mused softly.

Hattie tried to reconstruct the scene in school, when she took Ella Mae to see the nurse, and she remembered telling her, "Please, do something, my sister is going to be sick." But the nurse said nothing, she remembered so vividly now. She just shrugged her shoulders and looked helpless, because so many kids came to her with their arms swollen, asking her to do something. Yes, she'll have to tell Willie about Ella Mae, "but I won't tell him about the nightmares, those awful dreams . . ." She won't tell him how she kept blaming herself all along for Ella Mae's death. Even now, she kept thinking that it might have been her fault, that she should have taken Ella Mae with her to the white school—then maybe Ella Mae would be alive today, then maybe she wouldn't get those crazy ideas that she was seeing Ella Mae and hearing Ella Mae's voice—even now. Again Hattie was getting that strange chilly sensation, fearing to stretch her hand out, fearing she might touch her sister if she did—because that's where her sister was lying when she had the TB sickness, on that cot in the corner. Oh, Ella Mae, Ella Mae, why didn't I take you with me to the white school . . .

IV

The winter stretches unendingly, madly, with its raging fury whipping man and living matter in the sub-zero frost; angrily spewing its blizzards into the Windy City, covering the streets and rooftops with layers of deep snow, driving freezing humanity off the streets, back into the unheated homes, into the churches and libraries, into the store-fronts and flats of the Unemployed Councils.

Day upon day they huddle indoors, some talking, attempting to explain to the others what had happened to their prosperous country, and to millions of people like themselves all over the land. Some are listening to Willie, and Mirko, and Isaac answer their ceaseless question Why? Why? Why? Many listen but hear nothing. The old year behind them had left them hungry, cold, and numbed.

Willie is wearing his "new" coat, heavy with lamb's wool inter-lining, the small matching velvet collar fitting snuggly, neatly, and the high padded shoulders—suggesting another period, perhaps another century. He talks quietly to the few men around the table, and bends his head sideways, telling the woman next to him in a whisper, "We'll try, Mrs. Thornton, we'll try it once more tonight, as soon as it gets dark. We'll be over." The gas had been opened up for her by members of the Unemployed Council, but something went wrong. She has no heat of any kind; the electricity, too, had been cut off long ago; she must get gas reopened by Willie and his men—she must! They all know it, and Willie promises to return after dark; he promises to come before they start on other homes, on other emergency cases where the gas has to be reopened.

Other groups are meeting in other corners; many who had come to the unemployed headquarters early in the morning are still there, sitting around, staying off the cold, windy streets. Some are reading the newspaper that is being passed around and shared in sections; a few have their eyes closed, but they are not asleep—they'll be ready to listen again as soon as the gavel comes down calling for attention.

150

At the table Willie asks, "How do you like it?" He caresses the narrow, velvet collar.

"Is it warm?" one of the men asks him.

"Is it warm?" he replies, looking at Mirko. "His old man brought it with him from Croatia."

"From Yugoslavia," Mirko corrects him.

"Fits like it was made for me, ah?" Willie says, pulling the sleeves towards the wrists.

It was the first day Willie was trying out Pa Yanich's overcoat that had been put away years ago, after his burial. Some ancient family tradition in that distant mountainous village prevented the sons of the family from wearing the deceased's clothes. But Mirko remembered this overcoat, which was still sturdy and very warm. Now Willie had repeated the story for the third time, telling everybody how he happened to have come upon this bonanza.

"I been thinking, Mirko," he says, walking away from the others. "Remember me telling you about a school kid I used to carry books for, and see her home almost every day?"

"You never told me anything about carrying a girl's books to school; you haven't been in school almost as long as I," Mirko chided him.

"Sometimes you don't want to hear right, you don't like admitting that you can't hear right. I noticed that. You telling me now that you never heard me talk about my girl when I went to school. I did tell you! You and I have been talking about her—but that ain't what I aim to tell you now—it's her father, the Reverend Ralph Green. I was getting ready to tell you about him."

"Oh, why didn't you start with that? Sure I remember you talking about him," Mirko said sincerely. He had completely forgotten about the others, but he could recall many things that Willie had said about that minister, and about his wife.

"Yesterday Reverend Green comes up here with a large group, maybe thirty, maybe more, and I been thinking."

"I get it now, I get it! You been thinking about that girl, his daughter. Go on, what about his daughter?"

Willie laughed for the first time in days. Mirko did that to him. So many times it had happened: he'd just give him a hint, and this guy with the blond hair would pick it up, right away, and finish his thought for him. Sometimes Willie didn't like

151

that at all, because it seemed like Mirko could read his mind, read his thoughts he didn't want made known to anybody.

"I've known Hattie since we both started school together, only she continued in that white school, and I went down to Virginia for a short spell, and I've never seen her since. But yesterday, when Mr. Green told me that I looked pretty good to him, I could tell he was warming up to asking me over his house. I wouldn't go there without being asked first. But I don't even know if Hattie is alive, if she's at home, or gotten married. I just don't know anything about Hattie Green any more, but . . ."

"But you've been thinking about her," Mirko finished.

"Yep!"

"Why don't you go up and knock on the door—but take off this crazy cap of yours—and ask if Hattie's home. That's easy. Say, where did you get that damned thing you're wearing on your head? It's no good! It doesn't go with Dad's coat," Mirko said seriously. He was telling the truth. Willie also knew that it didn't look right with that velvet collar coat, but it was very warm, and he wasn't going to tell Mirko that he had found that crazy-looking thing in the deep inside pocket of his father's old coat. He must have brought it over here half a century ago, Willie calculated, and now it made him look like a monk or some other ancient.

Willie Rivers had been thinking for some time about knocking on the door of the Greens, but he wasn't going to do it— not for a while. He only wanted to talk to someone about it, about seeing Hattie again some time, now that she's all grown up, and must have had her nineteenth birthday already. He wondered whether she was still thin in the waist, like she used to be. Willie dropped the subject as soon as Mirko showed he understood what he was thinking about. He never talked again about Hattie, even when the Reverend Green showed up at the Unemployed Council several weeks later to ask Willie for some help, help for his parishioners. They talked long about how they'd have to find food for a couple of families or they'd die, die just like that!

But Willie thought a great deal when he was alone—he thought often about that girl of his school days. The Green home had been something special to him all his life, all during those years he'd been going with Hattie. It was like the only

152

good home he had ever known. He always looked upon it as his own home, because he was always welcome there, and always was asked to stay and eat with them, if he happened to bring Hattie home late after some school function. It was so different from his own home with Aunt Matilda, who was bringing back from the South Side Cafeteria all kinds of leftovers she had saved for him. At the Green home everything smelled like it was cooked fresh, and was brought in steaming hot to the table by Mrs. Green or by Ella Mae, who liked to bake and cook, and help her mother bring in the hot dishes from the kitchen.

But Willie wasn't ready to go visiting Hattie Green. He wasn't ready those cold winter months to go knocking on their door, because they'd all think he came to them to eat something hot; they might think that he was using Hattie as an excuse to get a good meal, a hot meal. The Reverend wasn't telling him the truth yesterday when he told him he looked mighty good to him. Willie didn't look good at all—he had gone without a hot or home-cooked meal a long time, maybe since they stopped throwing down those innards from the stockyards, maybe since . . . . oh, he couldn't remember, and he didn't want to think about that, he told himself. But he was sure he couldn't go calling on Hattie again until he'd be invited, directly, openly, by Mr. Green and Mrs. Green. But that, Mr. Green never did, never mentioned Hattie in those few trips he had made to the Unemployed Council.

Now it was the spring months that were pushing their way into the lives of the people who had been following him, and Mirko, and Isaac, and still Willie hadn't called on Hattie.

He won't go there—ever! Best to leave it that way, leave the past alone. It might be bad seeing her the way she's now, a woman of nineteen! He wants to remember her the way she was before he left for Virginia—that's how he wants to leave Hattie in his mind.

Then March and April burst forth with shocking news which took Willie's mind off himself and off Hattie Green, and push it back to Alabama, to Scottsboro, where nine black youths were taken off a train, charged with rape—and where a mob was screaming, "We're going to kill you niggers! Going to kill you!"

And once again Willie Rivers sees in his mind that other lynching, in all its gruesome detail, that he had witnessed years ago when a small boy. But it is happening again, yes, it is happening again—only this time they have nine blacks! and that crowd of farmers had massed around the jail house, with guns—the newspapers say, mothers with small tots in their arms, bicycles and wagons parked nearby, a brass band ready to celebrate the lynching of nine black boys in Scottsboro, Alabama, now, now, in April of 1931!

Willie Rivers shutters, breaks out in a sweat as he reads the latest reports . . . all boys indicted; Judge E. A. Hawkins rules that eight must die in the electric chair in the Kilby Prison on July 10th—only the thirteen-year-old one, only Roy Wright, will be spared burning in the chair on account of his youth.

"Oh, God, it must not happen!" Willie says. He had not prayed in years, but now he repeats to himself, "Oh, God, don't let it happen!"

He remembers once again his mother in back of him, her strong hands heavy on his shoulders, protecting him, shielding him, during that other lynching. But now it's nine boys! Who'll protect nine black boys? Whose hands will shield them? Some are only kids, thirteen, fifteen years old!

Suddenly he sits up, straightens his shoulders and reads aloud —he shouts—everybody must hear him now; hear me out now, "Listen here, all of you, listen!" Willie shouts, stretching his lips. He looks into the anxious eyes of the unemployed who've crowded into the hall, all seats taken, some standing in the back; they came to get the latest news about that big case, the Scottsboro news, and Willie shouts so all would hear him. "The New York office of the International Labor Defense has sent Judge Hawkins a telegram . . ." He reads, he shouts:

WE DEMAND STAY OF EXECUTION AND OPPORTUNITY TO INVESTIGATE AND PREPARE FOR NEW TRIAL OR APPEAL. WE DEMAND RIGHT FOR OUR ATTORNEY TO INTERVIEW DEFENDANTS AND TO OBTAIN FORMAL APPROVAL OF DEFENSE COUNSEL. AND, ABOVE ALL, WE DEMAND ABSOLUTE SAFETY FOR THE DEFENDANTS AGAINST LYNCHING.

At first there is a hush, then seconds later a burst of applause and people on their feet, talking, shouting, praying. Willie holds up his hand.

"The paper says that the I.L.D. has sent its chief counsel, Mr. Joseph R. Brodsky, to Alabama to see Judge E. A. Hawkins."

Mirko grabs the paper out of Willie's hands and reads the

telegram again, and reads the news about this New York lawyer going to Alabama; Isaac follows him with his eyes, and a broad smile spreads on his genial face.

Roy Wright, thirteen-year-old boy, he won't die in the electric chair, on account of his youth—the judge says.

Willie wonders why did his older brother, Andy Wright, take him on that train ride, away from their Chattanooga home? Why? Willie wants to know all about this young boy, this Roy Wright, the youngest of the Nine Scottsboro Boys. Why did they go looking for work in Alabama? Didn't they know that there's no work any place, no work for black boys, North or South?

Willie reads on and now he knows the answer: There are four of them from Chattanooga—they've talked to this lawyer from New York, this white man sent by the I.L.D.; Roy and Andy Wright have told him that they left their home with two other friends, with Haywood Patterson and Eugene Williams, and all four, the two Wright brothers and their two friends, keep telling the same thing, that the four of them are friends, they wanted to make it easier for their parents who have no food for them all. The four Chattanooga friends left home to look for work and for food, to spare their parents. They don't know the other five black boys; they met them when all black boys were rounded up on that train and taken to jail, where they've all been accused of raping two white girls on that train—Victoria Price, and Ruby Bates[5] of Huntsville, Alabama.

They've told Attorney Joseph R. Brodsky that they're innocent: they had never seen the two white girls; they had a fight on that train with a few white boys, and gave them a good whupping—that is what had happened on that train. Willie reads on, and thinks aloud: they were looking for work like you and me, they left their Chattanooga home, like others have been doing all over the country; they're innocent—they're like me— Willie repeats again. It could have been me on that train, it could have been any other black boys looking for work and food.

They listen to Willie Rivers talk about those Nine Scottsboro Boys—eight already sentenced to die in the electric chair on July 10—but they all feel that Willie Rivers is talking about himself, it's like sending him up to that chair. If they send those eight boys to burn, then they should all be burning, all the unemployed; it could have happened to all of them!

They hear Willie out well, they understand him when he says that it could have been him on that train, looking for work, and for food.

Within three months the Scottsboro Boys will burn in the electric chair, all black Americans will burn, all poor whites looking for work and food, will burn—Willie is consumed with that idea. He collects every scrap of information, all news items, all bulletins of the I.L.D. about the Scottsboro Boys, and leads the fight for their freedom—for his own freedom—he reminds his followers.

Everywhere Willie makes his appearance now, he carries with him the copy of a cable sent by the chairman of the Transport Workers Union of Berlin, Germany, demanding the immediate release of the innocent Scottsboro Boys, and Willie promises that "This is the beginning of a great movement that is bound to develop all over the world against this mass legal lynching of black boys, once the people get to know the facts, once the people understand that what is involved is the freedom of millions, and not only of nine black boys."

The three months until Execution Day are filled with protest actions all over the country and abroad: Harlem arranges its first Scottsboro protest parade; Theodore Dreiser calls for a new trial; over a quarter of a million blacks and whites celebrate May Day, 1931, demanding release of the innocent boys; Attorney Joseph R. Brodsky makes a motion for a new trial and is denied.

JULY 10: Execution Day of the Scottsboro Boys. EXECUTION POSTPONED PENDING APPEALS TO HIGHER COURTS. World-wide protest mounts; at home labor unions, church groups, Negro and white organizations demand freedom of all nine black youths, and when Reverend Ralph Green appears again at the Unemployed Council, he asks all to rise in prayer for the Nine Scottsboro Boys, and then whispers to Willie the purpose of his visit.

The country was not the same any longer, not since the nine black youths had been rescued from the executioners; Chicago's South Side was not the same, and neither was Willie Rivers. Willie Rivers was now possessed of a new pride and a new courage, and kept thinking so often about Roy Wright, about that thirteen-year-old boy, the youngest of the Nine Scottsboro

Boys; and somehow Willie would be coining original phrases, mottos; "They are innocent as Roy Wright!" he'd say when speaking to a new audience, to some white gatherings in Rogers Park, or other middle-class communities of the Windy City.

"Who's Roy Wright?" he'd ask rhetorically, and that question would start Willie Rivers off on a long oratorical journey about "my folk, my people, is an honorable people." He'd trace the honorable history of the blacks in rebelling against slavery and saving white America the agony of becoming even more brutalized that it already was, on the eve of the Civil War. Willie Rivers would tell how black America had built this country with its unpaid labor, stolen from them for over three hundred years, and by the time Willie Rivers reached the story of the Nine Scottsboro Boys, he was able to tell his white listeners about his pride he had in being black, and being part of a courageous people that was pushing for its own recognition, and its own full nationhood in the future.

Willie was deeply influenced by the current studies widespread in the movement, which had uncovered the grandeur of the many black leaders. He read with great pride the biographies of the black scholars, poets, musicians and athletes, and he would often end his appeals by saying, "Who knows which of the Scottsboro Boys would have been listed among some of our future leaders of our country, given the opportunity to an education, to food and clothing; and who knows if that isn't where they were traveling when they took that train out of Chattanooga, Tennessee, going to Alabama—traveling away from their hunger and suffering—looking for a job and an education and looking for food which they wanted to share with their parents." And then he'd talk in great detail about Roy Wright, how he was like any other thirteen-year-old black boy.

But Willie Rivers didn't talk in whispers about anything any longer, and to the surprise of the Reverend Green, he put his gavel down with a loud bang, and announced, "The Reverend Green has just whispered to me that Mrs. Diana Gross, a seventy-year-old widow, has been evicted. The woman is ill—old and ill, and she must be put back into her flat. Mr. Green wants to know if some of us will help him get her back into her flat—quietly, without too much noise."

They all understood what he meant. They would try to get

the widow back into her old flat before the police or sheriffs would get there.

Quietly the Reverend walked towards the door of the Unemployed Council, followed by Willie Rivers, and quietly over a hundred other unemployed men and women walked out behind them, and without any talk among themselves, they reached the aging widow, sitting in front of her home with all her belongings; they form a chain of hands and begin moving things back into the widow's flat; faster now, faster, faster, but be careful don't break any of her dishes; be careful you fellows carrying her mirror; what you stopping for? keep it moving, man! keep it moving! Faster, let's get her back in before they come, before they . . .

There goes the screeching of sirens, heard coming from a distance. Faster now, men. Get the heavy things in first; don't pass them things up any longer, take them in yourself, take them in and come back for more! The line of men and women trudges in with the widow's belongings and returns back to the sidewalk for more; the crowd has grown to several hundred, neighbors from the other streets have come to help, the sirens are heard in their midst, they have arrived . . . the clubs are swinging, the widow's remaining things are being broken on the sidewalk with loud crashes—but no one heeds the police's orders to disperse; more screeching sirens in the distance, more clubbing and shouting and screams of people pained. Now shots are heard somewhere in the block, and again—more shots. Hattie Green is hanging out of her top floor window and sees below the milling hundreds of neighbors; she recognizes her father who's waving to her, he's shouting to her but she can't understand what he wants; he motions excitedly to come down; he's waving one hand to her to hurry down and with the other hand he's dragging somebody. Hattie runs now quickly into the melee, and pushes her way towards her father, she helps him pull away a wounded man—and she begins to recognize the familiar, bleeding face—yes, it's Willie, Willie Rivers' eyes are closed, he's unconscious.

"Take him by the legs, I got him up here, just go on, girl, go on, stop staring, move on, quick!" the Reverend shouts to his daughter. "Hurry, don't stop now, keep pushing!" They push their way and carry Willie Rivers into their door entrance, and now they slow down, carefully they lift him, step by step, floor by floor—they're up on the top floor—carefully, slowly they lay him down on the cot, and Mrs. Green pulls away the pillow so the wounded man's head would lie flat; she hurries to the kitchen and returns quickly with a basin of water and clean towels and begins washing away the blood, and presses the dry towel to the open wound over the cheek, and motions her daughter and husband away from the cot where she's working on the bleeding man. "Take off his shoes, Hattie! Ralph, remove his clothes! Get me another clean towel, Hattie, and stop gawking like a fool. . . ." Mrs. Green is in full charge, she has taken care of troubled people before, she knows what to do. Slowly she drops the bloody towel on the floor and replaces a clean one, pressing gently over Willie's face, keeping his nostrils free for air, she orders her daughter to the medicine cabinet. "Bring the wide bandage," she says. Carefully she bandages the cheek and eye, and the top of the head. "We got to get him to a doctor, soon—he'll need stitches under his eye," she informs them.

"Not now, maybe later when things simmer down below; they might be looking for him now," the Reverend says.

"Who'd be looking for him?" Hattie asks with alarm.

"The police. They'll be looking for him, they'll want him," he says. "We must find Isaac, or that white fellow who's always with him; one of them will know what to do, how to get him to a doctor."

"No, we'll get the doctor to come here; he shouldn't be moved," Hattie says and moves closer to the cot, as if to warn them that she won't let anybody move him out of their home.

Willie has fallen into a restless sleep as Hattie takes up her vigil by the cot. The Reverend and his wife have left . . . gone to get help, to look for Isaac or Mirko. They've been gone for hours, Hattie muses to herself, as she watches Willie fall into a deeper, quieter sleep.

She tries to recapture in memory some scene when Willie had embarrassed her with his bashfulness; he was so helpless then, like now, helpless; and she bends down to listen to his breathing—he's been so still that it frightens her. She recalls now her father telling her that Willie was like a natural-born young gentleman, opening the door for her, and later, later. . . . Father would ask me questions about him, and I'd tell him that Willie never learned how to dance, but he was such a good athlete, yet

I couldn't understand why he never learned how to dance. She wonders now, too, about that, but he was so clumsy when he tried to dance with her. "Maybe that's the reason Dad liked him so much, he wanted Willie to become a minister some day, like himself, and then he'd take him into his church to help him build it up into a bigger church." She talks to herself, "maybe he expected Willie to keep those kids off the street, like Dad was trying to do all by himself," and somehow Hattie Green keeps holding in her thoughts those two men together, her father and Willie Rivers.

Hattie always coupled people, or thought that people naturally paired up, like her father and Willie—how alike they were—and how destined to meet again. Everything seemed to her to have been arranged deliberately, by an outside power, like her believing all the time that some day she and Willie would meet again.

She was a religious girl, and like her father, Hattie believed that good done, at any time, at any place, would ultimately be compensated. "One good deed will always bring another good deed," she now whispered her father's phrase, making it her own. Hasn't her father dragged Willie away from the flying bullets and the swinging clubs, risking his own life, and bringing Willie back to her—to her!

The street below has cleared, there's no one in sight anywhere, not a soul seen in the block, as Hattie looks out the window again. Everything seems to have gone dead—dead? She wonders now about those shots she had heard, as she returns to the cot. What about those bullets? Whom did they hit? Where's everybody gone to? Why is it so quiet? She touches Willie's bandage, and silently thanks God that he's alive, that it was only a light head wound. He's asleep—good, good! She thinks again about that last time she had seen Willie and she doesn't hear the back door open, and doesn't hear her parents walk in, and stop by the cot.

"They killed three of our brothers," her father says mournfully. "Three men dead!"

"Whom did they kill?" Hattie asks in a hushed voice.

"Abe Gray," her father begins to list, as Hattie lets out a cry of grief, and puts both her hands over her mouth. She stares in disbelief—Abe Gray had been to their home only last week, he had gone to their church, he belonged . . . . Why did they kill Abe Gray?

Her father continues, "John O'Neil, Frank Armstrong— dead! All three men dead!"

Quietly her parents walk away, and leave Hattie once more with her own thoughts, on her own vigil. She turns her head towards the cot as if to reassure herself that he was there, alive, and notices that Willie had moved slightly, and slowly was now dragging his hand towards his head, touching the bandage. Slowly he opens his free eye and looks at the girl who had removed his hand from his head, and was holding it between her own warm hands.

He questions, "Hattie?"

"Yes, Wilbur, it's me," she says and for the first time that day she smiles, and her white, large teeth, and round, big eyes, and deep black skin radiate. When she called him "Wilbur" she noticed that he, too, smiled with a familiar boyish bashfulness. "Wilbur" was something special between them two only, like a code of theirs, when they were in school together—when Hattie had teased him once and said, "I'm not so sure any more that you don't have white blood in you; they should have christened you Wilbur, instead of Willie," and from then on, whenever she called him "Wilbur," Hattie now recalled, that he would slap her joshingly on her behind and run, run, run fast, far away while she'd continue shouting to him, "All right, Wilbur, all right, Wilbur, I'll remember this!"

But now neither of them could run away, and Willie didn't want to run any place because he knew now that he had come back to the Green home—to Hattie.

V

Hattie's vigil had stretched into the late night, guarding the wounded man through half-closed eyes, responding to Willie's every twist and bodily movement, alert to the sounds on the streets, to the sounds of the doors in the building, waiting for Isaac to bring a doctor to the feverish Willie.

They come after midnight.

The doctor talks reassuringly after examining Willie, telling them not to worry. "He'll be all right in a few days—has a fine constitution."

161

The doctor is a tired, weary man. He has been in neighborhood homes all evening, taking care of others like Willie. He asks now who had bandaged Willie.

"I did the best I know how, Doctor," Mrs. Green says apologetically, and pressing her hands against her mouth, just like Hattie had done earlier when Abe Gray's name was listed among the three dead men.

"Would you mind helping me while I stitch him up, and—" turning to the others, adds, "if you please, it won't take us very long."

Sensing the confidence the doctor had shown towards her as his assistant, Mrs. Green gently shooes the others out of the room and the two go to work immediately on Willie.

As they file out of the sick room and enter the large, well-lit kitchen, Hattie sees for the first time that besides her father and Isaac, there is also a white woman with them.

"We got booted out so fast I didn't have a chance to tell you my name," the white woman says with a kind, natural smile, and extends her hand to Hattie.

"I thought you knew each other," Isaac interrupts. "This is Lillian Goodman, of the International Labor Defense. She has been making the rounds with the doctor, until I caught up with her, and brought the two of them up here. Excuse me, Lillian, this is Miss Green, the Reverend's daughter."

"I know you'll take good care of our patient; we all need him," Lillian adds, still holding Hattie's hand in hers, while studying, with understanding, the tired face before her.

Hattie said nothing, but for the first time in her entire life, she had a strong urge to kiss a white person. She wanted to thank this woman, and tell her that she would be welcome to come again to them, soon. Maybe she could come again tomorrow, and bring with her that doctor who's now working on Willie's face.

But Hattie says nothing. She keeps pressing Lillian's hand in both of hers. She hears her father tell her to put up some water for tea.

"Would you like to join us for a cup of tea, Miss Goodman?" he asks.

"I'd love it, but it's up to the doctor. He promised to drop me off on his way home. Willie is our last patient."

Hattie is still confused over all the many things happening

during those last few minutes: having been told to leave her vigil at Willie's bed, her mother in there working with that white man on Willie's face; and now being told by her father to make something to drink for this woman! Perhaps she had become disoriented from sheer tiredness, from so many hours of staring at Willie, unable to do anything for him? Perhaps Hattie Green didn't understand what this Lillian was doing there, bringing a doctor with her at such a late hour, and telling her "we all need him. . . ." Why does she need Willie Rivers?

Hattie had feared all along that someone would show up and claim Willie—someone might even come in suddenly and introduce herself as Mrs. Willie Rivers. She knew no more now about Willie than the previous afternoon, when she and her father had carried him up to their home. During her long vigil, while her parents were out of the house looking for help, Hattie was unable to get anything out of Willie himself, and she even began to wonder if he'd remember her, if he'd recognize her. He had changed so much in those five years, she thought; maybe she, too, had changed so Willie wouldn't know her any more. Yet, he did recognize her, he did smile when she called him "Wilbur." And now this pleasant white woman shows up, and talks about Willie as if he belonged to her. Hattie could tell that this white woman cared, and would even risk her life . . . well, she did risk her life coming up at this hour to bring a doctor for Willie.

"Hattie, get some cups out," her father orders her, and breaks the trance. She obeys his command. Automatically she sets things out on the table without saying anything or looking at that white woman, of whom she had suddenly become suspicious. That woman was talking with her father and with Isaac about the arrests of several other people after the shooting, and Hattie wondered how come she knew so much—she wasn't from their neighborhood, she didn't know the three dead men, she had never met Abe Gray.

"It'll be best to keep Willie here a while, until he mends a bit," Lillian says with concern about his safety.

"Mrs. Green and I have talked about it, and both of us think that way, too. Things will blow over, and after the funeral of the three men, it'll be quiet here for a while, and they'll probably leave him alone," Mr. Green says, pointing with his head towards the room where Willie was lying.

As predicted by the Reverend, things were, indeed, quiet in the neighborhood after the shooting of the three black men. A peculiar stillness had spread over the entire ghetto, and had penetrated the homes of the poor. It was a stillness of silent mourners who were preparing to bury their dead, preparing for a funeral befitting three men who had given their lives so that the aged widow, and thousands of others, would not have to sit on the sidewalks any longer.

It was a stillness that had also penetrated the Green home, and made it seem natural for Hattie to sit in silence for many hours, near the window facing the street, constantly on the watch, seeing Willie sit up and eat hot soups, seeing Willie fall into peaceful, restful naps. And on the third day he asked her not to look. "I'll go myself this time," and a few minutes later, on returning to his cot, exhausted, he sees Hattie rocking on the chair, calmly, contentedly closing her eyes—asleep.

But only moments later, it seemed to Hattie, perhaps only a few minutes—or could it have been an hour, or a day later— she couldn't tell, she had been asleep, something happens to the tired Hattie which she knew she'd never forget in her entire life: it was real, it was true; this was not her imagination playing tricks, no! Willie was bending over, caressing her cheek with his tender palm, and kissing her closed eyes, and she hears him whisper:

"Stand up a minute, willya, Hattie."

Half asleep, surprised at such a request, but thinking that perhaps he wanted to sit down in her rocker, she obeys, and as she turns around to move away, Willie slaps her gently on the behind, and adds: "I can't run, Hattie, my legs don't feel like running," and she answers him, "It's all right, Wilbur, I won't hold you to it this time."

He returns to his cot in the corner and keeps staring with his one eye at the girl on whom he had tried out his last name—in his dreams—and once was shaken out of a nightmare when he had screamed, "Mrs. Rivers, Mrs. Rivers," and his aunt kept asking him as she shook him awake "which Mrs. Rivers was he dreaming about," and Willie couldn't answer her honestly, he wasn't going to tell her that he'd never see Hattie again; that he had said goodbye to her for good, forever.

But now Willie feels dizzy from his efforts, and he rests his head on the high pillow, stretches his upper lip a trifle, and closing his mouth tightly, as if to swallow a sigh—or was it a sound of a cry, a cry of joy—as he dozes off again, and lets his body and soul relax, and heal in this home, where Hattie is watching him and watching the street below.

In the street below, where the three men were killed, the mourning for those three blacks had been turned into the strangest procession ever witnessed anywhere in the country. There is no crying, no wailing, no disturbing noises anywhere. The silence is broken only by the tread of marching feet of tens of thousands. Tens of thousands keep coming from every corner of the Windy City, traveling from the North Side, from the "Slave Market" areas around Halsted Street, from the Jewish-Polish neighborhoods, from the Italian and Irish ghettos; tens of thousands are merging with the blacks behind the three biers carrying the three murdered black men—all are walking in silence, without song, without prayer, as thousands of others standing on the sidewalks, with glazed eyes, weld a rare, and an unspoken tie that binds people, that transcends mourning and sorrow, and somehow becomes transformed into . . . into a happening!

A hundred thousand people of all color and all religion communicate with each other in total silence—yet they say to each other: there will be no more evictions; they will not allow any more evictions in their city streets.

And through this strange mourning for the three murdered black men, a deafening, silent warning is sent across the avenues and boulevards of Chicago that there must be no more evictions in the black or Polish ghettos, in the Irish or Jewish ghettos; no more will families be allowed from then on, from the funeral on, to sit on the streets—these tens of thousands of silent mourners pledge to the three dead men in front of them.

And from this strange procession of mourners, new unuttered words appear which bind the blacks and whites, unuttered words—as if coming from the caskets, from the three dead men—as if suddenly Chicago shouts those words aloud, and they are heard everywhere, in the city, in the suburbs, all over the nation: "Moratorium on Evictions! Moratorium on Evictions!"

The three murdered black men lead the procession—long after they had been put to rest in their graves, they continue leading—and the mayor of Chicago declares a moratorium on evictions! Other cities follow, and the black martyred men seem to stand guard, from then on—before thousands of homes throughout the nation, and with their buried bodies seem to hold back evictions, hold back any further suffering of their fellowmen which the evil of evictions had brought to the South Side and to other places in the country. "There must be no more evictions anywhere in this land!" the three dead men continue to shout from their graves—and the country hears them!

Willie continues to recover from his wounds while other battles on the outside rage on, unevenly, unpredictably. The country is in turmoil: millions now fighting against hunger through a network of Unemployed Councils in forty-six states; every city and town in the country resisting bodily, en masse. Beginnings of a profound change are felt everywhere, even as evictions continue in various places. But the change is there, as if a tide had been turned: moratoriums on evictions continue spottily, relief allotments for the starving millions increase; organized power of the unemployed, often acting in unison with the employed, is felt everywhere. There is virtually no scabbing during these years of great suffering, as unemployed appear frequently on picket lines under their Unemployed Council banners in support of striking workers. The cry for unemployment insurance and for public works projects is raised all over the country.

Hattie—suddenly thrust into the center of it all—is unable to grasp the broad sweep, or the direction of the movement. She is too close to the turmoil, too deeply moved by the upheaval that has taken place in her own personal life, to be able to answer some of the questions that Willie was asking.

"I've been wondering, Hattie, why you never showed up at the Unemployed Council. Your father came several times, but you never showed up. Didn't he tell you he had seen me?"

"Yes, he told us the first time he been there."

"Didn't you want to see me again?" Willie pushed his questioning.

"I don't know. Five years is a long time."

She didn't know how to explain many things. To her it appeared as if two worlds were colliding. There was her own, quiet, uninvolved world of the simple life—doing household chores, helping her mother, and occasionally her father in some church functions. Since losing her employment as an operator

166

at the Sopkin Dress Company several months back, a certain inertia had set in with the knowledge that there was no other work available for her elsewhere. There was no major driving force to propel her out of her routine in the home. The sweeping developments on the outside had not touched her yet—when suddenly she was thrown into that other world, the world of Willie Rivers, of Mr. Isaac and Mirko Yanich, who were daily visitors in their home.

Hattie heard discussions now between the three of them, then more detailed, intimate talks between Willie and Mirko, and she began to feel more and more excluded from that other world. They never asked her to leave the room, but they froze her out by ignoring her presence. She was, indeed, a total stranger in her own home.

As Willie continued to recover and move about of his own volition, and talk more seriously about returning to the outside, to the other world, the fear of losing him again became real. However, Hattie stayed close to reality, and in silence had examined the scraps of information she had gathered. Willie had known many other girls since they went to school together, she reasoned. He had grown up during those years into a sophisticated political leader, who was respected not only on the South Side of Chicago, but all over the city. She had found out during the long vigil that Willie had been in high demand as a speaker, as well as an organizer, on the other side of the city, in the white communities, and that he often became the spokesman for all, blacks and whites—when petitioning the local or state government bodies for relief or for food.

She would then ask herself: "Who are his girlfriends? Why don't they show up here? Is there someone waiting for him to return?" "No!" she argued against herself. "Such a woman would have shown up by now. Then why doesn't he have a girlfriend? Why isn't he married? Why is it that I can't even broach such questions now, now that the time is rapidly approaching for him to leave our home?"

The other questions that Willie asked casually, which she could not answer—the political questions, or those dealing with the multitude of intricate developments in their community life, or questions pertaining to the progress in the famous case of the Nine Scottsboro Boys—those were the empty spaces between her and Willie. Those were the areas that she had to fill

167

with knowledge and understanding, if the two worlds—her own and Willie's—were to become one some day.

She began to await Isaac's and Mirko's visits with even greater anxiety than Willie himself, and she became an attentive listener during their involved discussions. On rare occasions, when she sensed that her presence was welcome, she would ask a question for clarity in her hushed, soft voice.

"What do you mean that all the contradictions of our society are coming to a head in this crisis?"

"Well, you take this Draft Bill for unemployment insurance; you've seen it. Have you studied it? No? You should, then you'll see that everybody, including the men belonging to the American Federation of Labor, the A.F.L., all would benefit if Congress passed such legislation. Right?" Isaac asked, addressing himself to Willie. Again she felt left out, but she knew it was her own fault—she should have read that bill.

"But the leaders of the A.F.L. say that it would be bad for the United States to get saddled with a government Unemployment Insurance Bill; that it would be the same as getting a dole. All right! Now, let's take a closer look at this. The vice-president of the A.F.L., Mr. Matthew Woll, is a wealthy attorney, but he's also president of the Union Labor Life Insurance Company, and like the executives of other insurance companies, Mr. Woll is opposed to insurance for the unemployed because it would cut into the profits of their companies. There's a contradiction here, right? The membership, and the eleven million unemployed, and part-time workers need unemployment insurance. But vice-president Woll and president Green don't need it. These leaders then don't represent any more the needs of their own members, but they're still up there on top, making decisions for them."

"So what happens to such a contradiction?" Hattie asked.

"Well, it's coming to a head. You can't live with it and it won't die by itself. The people inside the A.F.L. are on the move, too. A rank-and-file painter by the name of Louis Weinstock started a big movement among the A.F.L. members for this Unemployment Insurance Bill, and it's catching on like wildfire.[6] Three thousand locals have already voted in favor of an Unemployment Insurance Bill—but the leaders are against it."

"So?" Hattie pursued.

"So, there'll have to be a showdown on this. I'm ready to

168

predict that the rank-and-file will win this point, if not at the next convention, then at the following, or the following. They'll vote down the leadership on this. That's how one of the contradictions will get settled," Isaac said with scholarly assurance.

But he wasn't through yet; he sensed that Hattie was following his reasoning and he wanted very much to have her stay with him on that subject until he had his full say. Ever since he started visiting Willie at the Green home, he had observed that Hattie was a logical thinker, calculating but isolated, and unaware of the great doings outside her home.

"Have you seen yet this afternoon's paper?" he asked.

"Yes, I've read most of it to Willie," Hattie replied.

"Then you've read what this young feller, this painter, said when he testified before the Senate Labor Committee; then you've seen for yourself how he takes this fight for unemployment insurance all over the country. He's making appearances wherever people will hear him out."

Isaac was referring to the testimony of Louis Weinstock before the Senate Labor Committee where he argued that this country must set up an unemployment insurance system for all unemployed people. He told the senators that there were over ten million totally jobless, and millions of others working part time, and that a man needs at least eighteen dollars a week to survive.

"That means you're asking for almost ten billion dollars a year, young man! Do you know that this is a lot of money?" one of the senators said.

"But this is war, sir! This is a war which the country must win! It's a war against hunger, misery and total starvation, and what I'm asking you to do is to raise money as if a war was going on right now."

Isaac had more to say now; he had also an attentive, captive audience of two.

"I got some more to say about this Mr. Matthew Woll, this vice-president of the A.F.L., who made a speech and said that the ten percent wage cuts that the railroad workers are accepting willingly, to save the companies from going bankrupt—this he calls 'the greatest achievement in the history of our country.' Hogwash! I say hogwash! The greatest achievement in the history of our country, in my own lifetime, will come when the Unemployment Insurance Bill is passed, and when at last this country will join the civilized world and establish some form of social security for its citizens. Even if it takes our helping to kick President Hoover out of the White House in next year's elections, it'll have to be done!"

"Is that one of those contradictions you're still talking about?" Hattie asked, looking at Willie for approval of her participation in the discussion.

"That it is, girl," Isaac answered, and felt encouraged to continue a while longer. "Organized labor isn't protecting even its own members in this crisis; the leadership is letting the employers cut them up, whup them good, while the T.U.U.L. moves ahead and fights back the wage-cutting campaigns."

Hattie pondered that last point, and she didn't feel like asking what the T.U.U.L. was all about, hesitating to admit her ignorance about so many subjects. She wasn't even sure that she understood how that was a contradiction, but she decided against asking other questions.

Isaac was talking about the labor leaders, about William Green and Matthew Woll, as if they were more responsible than the employers for the bad labor situation in the country, and she was wondering about that, too. She never had any experiences in a labor union, but for the year-and-a-half that she had worked at the Sopkin dress shop, she found out that the employers had used all kinds of methods to keep a legitimate union out of there. And here Isaac was talking like that about a union president and vice-president—and it bothered her a lot. But she kept quiet.

"You're talking about contradictions, girl," Isaac was warming up again.

"I wasn't talking about contradictions, Mr. Isaac. You were! I'm just listening," and she looked at Willie whose grin had spread slowly all over his face.

"You know why I'm so sure that this country is going to get an Unemployment Insurance Bill passed finally? You know why I think this must eventually happen in this country?" Isaac asked, resuming his soapbox style, and raising his voice as if he were addressing a large crowd. "Because a big contradiction is being overcome, being smashed up into tiny bits of fine grains of sand and blown away during this big storm."

"H-m-m-m" Willie cleared his throat. He put his finger against his lips for Isaac to lower his voice.

"What was I saying there?" he continued quietly, embarrassed before this daughter of the Reverend Green, to have been so loud.

"Please go on, Mr. Isaac. Maybe Willie knows all these things, but I'm hearing them for the first time. You've been saying that you're sure that this country is going to have an Unemployment Insurance Bill passed because . . ."

"Because another big thing is coming to a head in this country. It makes no difference when one's hungry, or one is evicted, whether he's black or white. Makes no difference! For centuries people have been thinking that there's a big difference; now they're finding out that whites can't get any place by themselves; they're finding out they got to work together with the Negroes. I've never seen anything like this in my life—Willie will tell you the same thing, Hattie. Whites and blacks acting together like brothers. Many whites now speaking up for the Nine Scottsboro Boys like they were their own children."

He would have continued in that same tone but Hattie noticed that Willie's mouth was open, his breathing loud, like it always was when napping. She touched Isaac lightly on the arm, and pointed towards the cot. Isaac stopped talking immediately, shaking his head in self-admonition. Quietly he got up and on tiptoe began moving out of the room, but Willie opened his eye and asked:

"Why did you stop talking? I liked what you said."

"You sure did. It helped put you to sleep," Isaac said, and they all laughed.

Willie told them both to sit down, as he had something to say to them. "I didn't get around to telling you that the labor delegation leaving for the celebration of the Russian Revolution, this fall, wanted to make sure it had several Negroes in it, and I was asked if they could nominate me as one of the delegates." He said it slowly, pretending that it was an ordinary matter he was discussing with them—and not one of the biggest things that had happened in his young life. "Before all this came up," he pointed to his bandaged head, and laughed artificially.

"You never said anything about being asked to go to Russia. Why did you keep quiet about this?" Isaac wanted to know. "You should have told us that you had a chance to go over there as a delegate."

Isaac often wondered how those delegations were put to-

171

gether. Sometimes he thought to himself that the selection of all those delegations traveling to Europe in the midst of such a deep economic crisis was up to some power far beyond his own reach—in the hands of the gods—decided upon by people who were his superiors, who were involved in big international and national activities. And now he began to look upon Willie, for the first time, as upon a very important man, as one who was also being considered for such an important trip, a man who would probably become known nationally some day in the future.

Willie had mentioned several times to Isaac how he would like to see what the Soviet Union was like. "If I ever get to see that country, I want to spend some time over there finding out how the colored peoples in the U.S.S.R. are treated; I want to see with my own eyes if it's true that it's the only place in the whole world where the colored people are treated like equals."

Both Hattie and Isaac understood by the way Willie had revealed this information to them that he had given up one of his most cherished dreams.

Isaac asked, "Why did you wait till now to say all this?"

"I couldn't tell you before," Willie answered. "If you had known about that offer, you wouldn't have let me come out to demonstrations and to other doings."

"You think stopping the widow's eviction and getting your head bashed in and being laid up here for weeks . . . . I don't get you, Willie," Isaac reproached him. "You should have laid low and made sure that you'd get on that delegation and make the trip."

Travel was slow. It meant taking a steamship across the Atlantic, which took over a week; and then days and days on some other boat going from London to Leningrad, and then a train ride to Moscow. Preparations for sending the delegations to the anniversary celebrations were usually started months in advance. It was on the eve of that widow's eviction when Willie learned about being nominated for that trip.

"See, that's the reason I didn't tell you. You would have had me stay out of everything until I got safely on the boat. No, sir! There will be another time. Maybe they'll include me in the May Day celebration, next spring. I don't know, and I tell you, right now I don't care."

172

But he cared a lot. He thought a lot about having missed the opportunity to travel with a labor delegation to European capitals and to the Soviet Union. Even though his body still ached, and he was healing too slowly for his impatient temperament, his head remained clear and alert all along.

After his visitor left him, he asked Hattie to read to him the papers, and some articles from the magazines that Isaac and Mirko collected for him. When alone, he reread slowly some items and evaluated carefully the changing trends in the country. Being removed from immediate physical involvement in the daily routine of leadership, his horizons broadened; he began to see things in their relationship, in perspective. He made summaries in his own mind, and tried them out on Hattie.

"Look at this, Hattie," he said one afternoon, and handed her a New York City newspaper in which a reporter described a scene at the City Hall which outraged him.

. . . women struck in the face with blackjacks, boys beaten by gangs of seven and eight policemen, and an old man backed into a doorway and knocked down time after time, only to be dragged to his feet and struck with fist and club . . .

"Same thing all over the country," Hattie commented.

"That's the truth. But look what the editorial of the same paper says. It admits that some form of relief will have to be given to the unemployed, and soon; that the large-scale arrests and beatings aren't solving the problem, even if they do feed them in the jails."

But often, when left alone during those convalescing days, Willie dwelt on thoughts that went beyond the obvious. He began to discern a pattern throughout the country: the spontaneous battles that were raging all over for food and milk and other necessities were turning into a disciplined, well-sustained movement that was gaining momentum and was beginning to demand in serious tones that the federal government assume responsibilities to the people.

"Hey, Hattie, where are you?" he called aloud, urgently. "Come here a minute!"

She hurried to his bedside, expecting to see him in some serious trouble. Instead, however, he was sitting up, with the pillows firmly behind his back, and his wide eye open with excitement, bringing back memories to her of years ago, when Willie had beaten up some rowdy who had used insulting language to Hattie, and was compelled to apologize to her.

"Last year, at the July Convention, we talked about unemployment insurance, and said that the government of this country has a responsibility to the people, but you remember, there wasn't much response."

"No, honey, I don't remember nothing, 'cause I wasn't interested in what that convention talked about; I was working on Sopkin dresses, and was mighty happy that I still had work," Hattie replied teasingly.

She was wearing a cool summer dress, neatly fitted around her thin waistline, and her hair was piled high on top of her head, pinned down in secure curls. She had just replaced fresh lipstick, and Willie's eye was on her shapely mouth, thinking to himself how pretty she had become during the years since he had last seen her.

"No, you didn't know last year that we were setting up these Unemployed Councils to help the people fight their way out of that chaos and confusion. But look what's going on now: the councils are leading all these big fights in the country, and are squeezing some things out of those city and state governments. They've begun to grant relief in some places where they'd refuse to even talk to the poor; and the people are now listening to us when we tell them that we ought to march on Washington and force the President and Congress to pass an Unemployment Insurance Bill."

He was actually thinking aloud, working out a thought that he felt was extremely important. Yet he could see that Hattie was not interested, and after blowing a kiss to him, said, "Tell me the rest when I come back."

He kept pondering in silence: the people knew better than I, that they had to get something to eat first, right away. They had to get their furniture and things back into their homes, right away. But unemployment insurance would take some time to get—they knew that they couldn't obtain it right away. That's why they agreed that it was a good idea, but we had to wait over a year before we could get them behind this Washington March for an Unemployment Insurance Bill.

He closed his eyes and put his head back on the pillows. Now his thoughts were on the details of the biggest event of the year —on the plans that were announced for the National Hunger March to Washington, D.C.

CHAPTER VI

Professors All

I

The storm rages on, uprooting people and tradition, equalizing millions into a common heap of suffering humanity, pushing the nation into a new way of life—a life of hunger marches, Scottsboro parades, peace demonstrations, eviction battles, strikes and picket lines—rounding out its second year of devastation and compelling millions to question everything: themselves, their leaders, and their country. Young and old are studying the sources and the reasons for this great disaster; they are investigating the bases of the economy; in the halls, on the street corners, and at Unemployed Councils, in school auditoriums and churches, they are debating the cloudy international upheavals and are beginning to interpret the danger signals being flashed from abroad to the shores of the United States. New words and new phrases are entering the language, and *Mein Kampf,* "Invasion of Manchuria," "Planned Economy" become commonplace in speech.

People are comparing the system of socialism in the Soviet Union with the system in the Scandinavian countries and Great Britain. Tolerance is shown to all ideas, and in the midst of this broad national search for the truth, provocateurs, as well as ordinary two-bit stoolpigeons, make their appearance—confusing and befuddling the naive and the uninitiated.

The country has become a land of orators and preachers, of theoreticians and writers—professors all.

Mirko, too, is caught in this swirl of the new life. He tells Willie that he, too, will take a closer look at this country, and find out how it's run, how the crisis affects the nation and the world. He needs to know more, much more than he understands now, if he's to continue leading others, who are asking the same questions.

The deserted Yanich home, now also Willie's temporary home, has become a veritable miniature university, a place of study and reading and investigation. Ma Yanich's bedroom, never touched by anyone since her passing, had become Willie's refuge. They pushed the bed against the wall, removed the rocking chair, placed Willie's folding table near the window where he is sitting now and studying the early announcements of plans for a national hunger march upon Washington. He hears Mirko knock on the door, "Can I come in?"

"It's open."

Mirko bursts into the room, loaded with newspapers, current magazines, and samples of leaflets and calls to action, from all over the city and state. In the bright daylight Willie's scar under his eye bulges in a straight line clear to his ear, to remain there as a permanent monument to a battle that had taken three black lives.

Mirko's voice, excited and anxious, fills the small room. "I got several things to tell you, but you'll have to listen to me first, before you start reading these papers from Alabama," he tells Willie. "Brought you also a copy of the Baltimore *Afro-American* with a good piece—but let it rest—it won't run away." He remains standing by the door, hands full, unable to co-ordinate his movements.

"Oney once before I seen you look crazy like you do now," Willie tells him. "Take a look at yourself in that mirror."

"Don't start giving me any lectures today; I'm gonna get plenty of lectures soon, maybe for ten full weeks, and when willya learn to say 'only' instead of 'oney'?"

"You mean you agreed to go to the New York school?" Willie asks, ignoring Mirko's correction.

"He threatened to discipline me if I didn't go, that bastard!" Mirko said and at last unloaded, and plunked himself on the edge of the bed. For the first time he noticed that Willie's hair had receded at the temples, making his face appear bigger, and older.

"I got some more news for you. I'm gonna see Al next week, in New York City!"

"How do you know he'll be there next week? And how the hell are you gonna get there that fast? You taking a train?" Willie asked. He hadn't met anyone yet who had traveled by train, or even by bus. The country was in perpetual motion,

177

hundreds of thousands shifting from place to place, hitch-hiking everywhere, in all seasons, all hours of the day.

"I'm gonna see Al in New York City if I have to sit there and wait for him to come back from Germany. He said he won't stay there an extra minute, if he can help it; that he might be on his way home by the time I got this letter."

"You said nothing about a letter from Germany," Willie said surprised. All of Al Ross' letters had been seen by Willie, ever since he became acquainted with Mirko.

"I know, I know. I'll let you read it in a minute; got it too late yesterday, and then I forgot to show it to you in the evening. But don't rush me. I got other things to talk about first."

"All right, talk! You're gonna talk about leaving for that New York school, ah?" Willie said, reading Mirko's mind.

"I had a fight with C.A. I told him I couldn't leave Chicago now, not now; too busy to pull out in the middle of all kinds of things I'm involved in. But I also told him that I was no intellectual in the first place. I told him that maybe a guy like Willie Rivers should have been picked instead of me because I think you're an intellectual."

"Stop calling me names just because I can't give you a good whupping," Willie interrupted. "You had more education than I, so don't go calling me an intellectual."

"Well, I told him that I won't be able to concentrate on lectures and books while we got all those men in packing trying to give the company union a kick in the pants. I told him I was right in the middle of it all, doing what I can from the outside so the man on the inside don't get exposed and fired."

"What'd he say to that?"

"He says to me this is the very reason why I gotta go to this school in New York. He says to me that the whole country is studying and reading and getting an education like never before. Everybody's got time to do a lot of reading and thinking. Then he says to me, 'Mirko, the movement needs people like you for leadership, and you have to know more than you do now if you're to grow with this big movement and lead the people. The leaders must know what they're talking about,' C.A. says to me. 'And without getting firmed up in your theories, you'll be working in the dark, in a blind alley,' he says."

"I bet that shut you up."

" 'I can refuse to go to that school, can't I?' I says to him. And you know why I said that? Telling me to go away now was like telling me that I wasn't doing my work right, like I was a kid, and that they had to send me back to school for ten weeks. I didn't like it, and I said so."

" 'Yes, you can refuse to go, Mirko,' C.A. answers, 'but then we'll have to discuss this matter again in the District Committee, where we selected the list of students from our areas for the National Training School. We'll have to tell them that you think you're too valuable at the stock yards to fall out for ten weeks; that the movement will collapse if you disappear for ten weeks,' and his sarcastic talk hurt. I didn't like it and I told him so. 'But if the Committee decides that despite your objections you should go to the school for ten weeks, you'll accept that decision, and you'll go? Am I right?' he asks me.

" 'That's putting me on the spot,' I tell him. I felt like he had me trapped.

" 'What do you mean putting you on the spot? If the majority decides the minority has to subordinate itself, and has to go along with the decision. That's democratic procedure, isn't it?' he says.

" 'This business of democratic procedure can be carried too far,' I says to him. 'I don't go along with the idea that I should leave the field now, with a new Unemployed Council getting on its feet right near the yards, with Willie Rivers,' I told him that 'with Willie Rivers not too strong yet to be left alone. I tell you this ain't the time to leave the field and go away to study from books.' That's what I told him. But wait now, Willie, I wasn't angry inside as I sounded, 'cause I had this letter from Al sitting here, in this pocket since yesterday, and I've been wanting to see Al before I get too old and grow a beard, and he can't recognize me any more."

"Then you weren't on the level with C.A. You did want to go to New York?"

"It's not just like that, goddamit! I did, and I didn't want to go. Sure I want to go to see Al, but not to get stuck there studying from books, not now!"

"How did it all wind up?"

"Well, he says that he doesn't blame me for not wanting to go, being so wrapped up in my work, 'but you'll feel different when you come back from that school, and you'll be sorry it lasted only ten weeks,' he says. Then he gave me some of that

179

usual stuff we've heard about in our movement about not having a good appreciation for theory. I thought he was teasing me with some ideas that I've never thought about and knew nothing about."

"Like what?" Willie urged him on.

"I ought to be fair to that guy. He first asked me if I'd mind taking just a couple of extra minutes, that he wanted to tell me something. I told him to go ahead, of course. I like that fellow, I'd trust him with my life—but he's such a sad-looking guy, like it's a crime to crack a joke in his presence. I think he's buried with his political work so much that he don't see anything else. I bet he don't know the difference between a basketball and a volleyball."

"But what happened? What did he want to tell you?"

"After apologizing-like to me, he gave me a lecture, telling me that the workers in this country haven't cut loose yet from the mental apron strings of the capitalist class. Get that now! I told him to slow down and tell me just what he meant by that, and the only time I ever seen C.A. laugh was when I said to him, 'What do you think would happen if I told the men in the slaughter houses that what was wrong with them was that they haven't cut loose from the mental apron strings of capitalism?' And boy, when C.A. Hathaway starts laughing real good, you can hear him all over the place. Then he stopped all of a sudden, and still apologizing to me for taking my time, says, 'The American workers don't feel that they belong to a class, or that their interests are the opposite to the interests of the capitalist class; they are not class-conscious,' he says, and get this—I tell you you can love that guy for the way he says something nice about the American working class after criticizing it first. 'The American workers have a strong class *instinct,* and a good fighting spirit as workers, but they don't draw a sharp ideological line between themselves and the capitalists,' and here come his punch line. He tells me that 'this ideological backwardness is the greatest drag on the trade unions of this country.' When I told him that I don't savvy, he started giving me some figures like the one about John L. Lewis, the president of the miners' union. 'He's among the best labor leaders, but he makes $12,000 a year while he asks the miners to take a wage cut.' Then he tells me that the high officials of the A.F.L. unions, and the railroad brotherhoods, receive salaries equal to those of a cabinet member, or a vice-president of the U.S.A., something like $15,000 a year, and the allowance they have for expenses sometimes runs up to fifty percent more. 'Don't you see,' he says to me, 'there's something lopsided all around when a labor movement permits its leaders to become wealthy men—you invite corruption when you do that.' He was just settling down to giving me a good talk about this, when . . .''

Willie laughed aloud, interrupting Mirko.

"All right, give," Mirko said, and waited.

"I'll betcha I know what you told C.A.—but on the level with me. If I guess right you tell me. On the level?" and Mirko clenched his fist, indicating that he was swearing to the truth. Long ago these two friends had drifted into the habit of confirming the truth by lifting their clenched fists inconspicuously.

"You told him that the Soviet Union has proved already that the workers can get along without the capitalists, but the capitalists can't get along without the workers, ah?" Willie asked, his fist on his lap, to be opened after Mirko's reply.

Mirko smiled goodnaturedly, softly, and said, "No, I didn't tell him that. But I stopped him and told him that when I go to New York to that school, I'll find out more about all this class-consciousness, and that he ought to stop lecturing me as I have lots of things to take care of before leaving."

"Then you told him you'd go?"

"I did," Mirko replied. "There's five of us going from here, and C.A. asked me to be in charge, and drive this beatup tin-can standing in front of the house. I don't know if it'll make it all the way to New York, but it's better to get started with it, than to scatter ourselves now on the highways."

"How soon do you have to leave?"

"Right away, in a day or two. No later than the end of this week," Mirko said.

"C.A. hinted that the director of the New York School, Dr. A. Markoff, might arrange the work in such a way that the entire student body would be able to go to Washington for that hunger march that they're already talking about. But that's a long way off. Still, I might wind up going to Washington, D.C. before I return home from school. You'll have to hold the fort, pal, for yourself and for me, too."

Mirko was a happy man. On his way from the Loop, where he had spent almost the entire morning with C.A., Mirko had worked out plans for disentanglement from his various responsibilities to the packinghouse workers, and to the unemployed. He was happy also to see Willie settled in the Yanich home, in some fairly reasonable comfort, and close to where he'd be giving leadership soon.

"This letter here, from Al, you got to read it now; I'll be needing it. I want to write an answer to him; gotta tell him where he can find me in case I miss him at his union headquarters."

Mirko opened the letter from Germany, and placed it on Willie's table, and started walking out. "See you later. Got too many things on my mind now."

Willie began to read the letter from Al Ross, from Germany.

Martial law has been declared. The economic crisis has reached out here, and the country isn't what I've seen in the past. All leaflets must be O.K.'d by the police. No more outside assemblies are permitted. Over 60 workers' newspapers have been suppressed.

Demonstrations are illegal . . . . Strikes are breaking out and mass demonstrations are taking place despite the terrorism . . . The main struggle is on the waterfront. The International Seamen's Club has been raided three times, and the General Secretary of the International of Seamen and Harborworkers, a member of the Burgershaft (State Legislator) has been arrested together with the members of the strike committee.

Police in special cars with searchlights in front are continuously circling the waterfront district. Police assigned for this work, besides receiving special pay, are primed for action. Just like soldiers going over the top they are given a stiff shot of rum. When they arrive in time for a demonstration they immediately wade in slugging all in sight, spectators and demonstrators alike, men, women and children. They show no mercy. They show no hesitation in shooting. In order to prevent any attack from above all windows are immediately ordered shut; the order is backed with warning shots in the air.

I'm coming back home immediately. Will write more to you what I've seen here. These Hitlerites are terrorizing the waterfront . . .

He signed off abruptly. Willie was wondering if he had gotten into some kind of trouble. But he decided not to mention his concern to Mirko. Mirko had too many other things on his mind; should be left alone, he decided.

Willie now began to sort the other reading material Mirko had brought him, and read half-aloud from the *Afro-American, Baltimore*:

No Menacing Reds: The Reds are going our way. Like ourselves, they represent a feared and hated cause. They are the first white group since Emancipation to advocate race, social equality and intermarriage for those who wish it. In fact, there is more real Christianity among white Communists than in the white YMCA, the white Christian Endeavor Societies, or the white so-called Christian churches.

If the Communists ran Baltimore, for example, Negroes could get jobs on the police force, or drive city garbage carts, at least. Shields Alley would be paved. Negroes would sit on the school board, the jail board, and when qualified, on the Board of Awards. They could get a bed in Hopkins Hospital or attend the Maryland University Law School which they are taxed to support. They could even attend the nearest church, whether it happened to be predominantly black or white.

The Reds are no menace to Negroes. In fact, it is very comforting to find groups of such people as Communists in this color-mad western world.

As if wishing to drown his own thinking in the reading material piled before him, Willie reached for the Alabama newspaper, and turned to the paragraph Mirko had already penciled out for him.

The frequent appeals of the communists to American Negroes is causing the black man to think more seriously of his new-found friends and to consider more at length their doctrines for the progress of the workers. No cause of white men has made so bold an attempt to defend the Negro and to work religiously for his protection as the communists. . . . The communists have shown a total disregard for color prejudice, and lack of appreciation for station and title. They have accepted the black man on an equal plane with all other workers throughout their work and seem willing to toil for his elevation as they do for all others of their group.

Willie's hunger for knowledge had often led him astray in his reading, pushing his inquisitive mind through the numerous open doors which promised to take him to sources of deeper understanding. He had learned during the weeks of convalescence to be alone with his own thoughts for long stretches of time, and to allow himself the luxury of analyzing, in detachment, some obscure comment or reference to an event.

This late afternoon, after Mirko had left him to begin preparations for his trip to New York, Willie's mind lingered on an analogy made by an eastern journalist of the Scottsboro case with that of the young Jew, Beilis, who was prosecuted in

Czarist Russia on the charge of murdering a Christian child—in an alleged customary ritual of Jews while celebrating Passover with Christian blood. Willie thought that he would like to use that analogy when speaking to white audiences, and to Jewish audiences in particular.

He thought about the South and the rest of this country, how it had accepted the idea that Negro males, even children of thirteen and fourteen, like Eugene Williams and Roy Wright, the two youngest of the Nine Scottsboro Boys, were supposed to have a "natural" tendency to commit sexual violence upon white women. "Therefore the admitted fact that Negro boys were riding a freight train and even fighting white boys on the train, on which two white women were riding in male attire, is all that was needed to bring about the death sentence," the journalist wrote in pursuit of his analogy.

For the first time Willie read and understood the word "pogrom" and decided to add it to his vocabulary. In the kitchen, where he later joined Mirko, he said, "So far we have been able to stop a pogrom. Now it's up to the country to work harder, until the Nine Boys are set free altogether."

Mirko was aware that his friend was feeding him with new ideas and a new word, but he asked to be left alone, or he'd never get himself together for that long trip and long absence from his work.

II

The small, rundown Model T Ford, puffing its way past the Indiana sand dunes into the open fields, carried a cargo of five unusual scholars. Besides Mirko Yanich at the helm, there was Peter Edgehill from the Gary big steel mill, middle-aged, stocky Beatrice Grandhal from the North Halsted Street community of Chicago, and two coal miners from Southern Illinois.

At the approach of every city and hamlet, the five students announced their arrival by singing "Hold the Fort For We Are Coming" through the open windows, and during their long hours of travel over the countryside, when silence was precious, Beatrice, who took upon herself the role of matron, would keep everybody awake and on the alert by raising her voice to an impossible pitch with "Avanti Popolo, Alla Riscossa"; and the others, not to be outdone, would go through the first two stanzas of the famous Italian workers' song, and allow their matron to complete the round with a shrill "Viva!"

Only Mirko, who was driving most of the time, was silent, his eyes glued to the sign ahead, and when at last he was able to read Gallion, Ohio, he pulled off to the side and informed his passengers that "we're out of gas, we're out of money, and we better split up right here and start hiking the rest of the way. We can't make it to New York with this jalopy—it just won't go any farther."

They were still a considerable distance from New York and each of the five passengers was evaluating in his own mind the situation, and was silently working out a solution. Only Beatrice, who spoke up first, admonished Mirko.

"You should have thought of this before we left Chicago. The school isn't going to wait for us until we get there."

"But there was no choice, Beatrice. It was either hiking all the way or taking a chance that this tincan would get us there," Mirko replied.

"Then why didn't you tell us before we left Chicago? Why are you telling us that now?" She was irritable, and loud. "Maybe we could have collected a few more dollars if we had known before that there might be this trouble with the car; or maybe some of us wouldn't have gone altogether."

The others looked angrily at their matron. This was no time to start blaming each other; this was the time to come up with some ideas on how to get to New York without missing too much of the studies.

"What's the name of this town?" Peter asked.

"The sign said Gallion," Mirko answered sadly.

"Gallion, Gallion, Gallion, Ohio!" Peter shouted at the top of his voice, and opened the door on his side. "This is Gallion, Ohio! Let's go to the Bishop! All of us to the Bad, Bad Bishop!" he shouted still louder.

"You gone nuts?" Mirko asked, and looked at him skeptically. As the leader of the group, Mirko was told a few pertinent facts about each of the passengers in his car, and he knew that Peter Edgehill, in his mid-twenties, had a history of TB. He was a tall, good-looking man, with thick black hair. His voice, however, was weak, and no matter how loud he spoke or shouted one could hear the sound of a heaving whistle in his chest, as if coming from the depth of his tubes. But now this man was full of joy, his black eyes shining with the good news he was about to reveal.

"I've always wanted to meet the Bishop personally, and I'll be goddamned if I could have planned it better." Peter clapped his hands together in self-applause, and repeated, "Let's all go to the Bishop."

Now Mirko, too, recalled the name and realized that Peter was referring to Bishop William Montgomery Brown, known throughout the country as the Bad, Bad Bishop.

"What will we tell him?" Mirko asked.

"The truth! That we're on our way to New York City to a Marxist school, and that we ran out of gas and money and food," Pete said. "Nothing but the truth when you deal with the Red Bishop. That's what he'll like—to level with him."

They rolled the car into the center of the town; on the way they were directed to the most famous citizen of Gallion, Ohio— to the Bad Bishop's home.

The Bishop answered the bell himself—he had been watching, through the large front window—and he was not surprised when Mirko told him their problem. Other people had used his home before for similar emergencies, it seemed.

The Bishop's long, white hair, combed smoothly over his ears, made the round, rosy-cheeked face with the broad smile look like the closest image to a living angel this group of students had ever met. He welcomed them all "home," shaking each one's hand, and immediately instructed his housekeeper to prepare hot baths, and a hot meal for the five. He telephoned his mechanic—who within minutes arrived and picked up the car. Three hours later the mechanic returned with the car in top shape, the gas tank filled full. When the five were ready to continue with their travels to New York, the Bishop handed Mirko a ten dollar bill, and in a soft, almost feminine, voice, said:

"I would like to make a request of you, my children. Would you sing for me the *International?*"

When the five lined up to sing, Bishop Brown closed his eyes and did not see the tears rolling down Beatrice's face, as she led the group in the singing.

III

The soft-spoken director of the national school, Dr. A. Markoff, had just begun his opening remarks to the student body when Mirko and his contingent walked in.

"Illinois?" Markoff asked with a broad smile.

"Illinois and one from Indiana," Mirko reported.

"Welcome, welcome! Please be seated; we'll check you in later."

Already checked in were several who came directly from the Pennsylvania coal community, where thousands of unemployed miners had been evicted from the company-owned houses, and were now huddled on the mountains, crowded three and four families together in one-room shacks, living on dandelions and wild weedroots.

Checked in was the blond young girl, recently released from the Monroe County Penitentiary for her participation in a warehouse raid for food. Mirko sat down between her and a man of about thirty. This man, known to his colleagues for his humor, had written on his application, when he checked in: Today I completed the Draft Law for a system of unemployment insurance for this country. Some day it'll become the Social Security Law of the land.[7] However, today will go down in history for another reason: today there appeared crooner Rudy Vallee's song "Life Is Just a Bowl of Cherries."

A number of those who had checked in had natural inclinations towards theoretical research and studies, and had already contributed to the radical publications. They felt at home when Markoff continued with his welcoming remarks: "You, the leaders from all parts of the country, will be expected to become teachers and educators of large masses of people. Upon your return to the fields from which you had been torn away—the unemployed, the strikers, the A.F.L. rank-and-file movement—you'll be expected to guide them more wisely and more intelligently; to share with them the knowledge you will have stored up in these ten weeks. In short, to teach others."

To Mirko such a welcome was enough to make him wish he could pick himself up, walk out of that classroom, out of the Bronx Cooperative Building, and disappear for good, and get lost until it was all over. He could not see himself as a teacher and educator—under any circumstances.

"I'll never be a teacher of anything, and I don't give a damn what this director is telling me. I'll be lucky to keep up with the reading assignments," he said to himself, already embarrassed over his future failures to share his newly acquired knowledge with others. He had strong feelings of personal inedaquacy, constantly blaming his lack of formal education for his slowness in grasping new theories, or for his inability to keep up with the vast amount of reading that was brought into the ranks of the masses of unemployed.

He looked around the large classroom to see if others felt as he did, and his eyes met the familiar face of Christine Wesly, who smiled back to him in recognition. Her shining, brown eyes were lit with joy in response to his salutation. For seconds after, Mirko could barely believe that the Omaha girl, sitting several rows away from him was the same Christine he had met before. He was unable to catch the many details that were responsible for her changed appearance. Yet he noticed that her bright red hair was combed in thick braids, encircling her head like a crown, and revealing tiny ears with tiny button-earrings. Later he saw that she wore no lipstick or other makeup, yet there was a high glow on her cheek.

Trying not to be conspicuous, he turned his head again in her direction, but Chris had already begun to take notes, and she was totally unaware of Mirko's observation.

Mirko shifted his attention to Dr. Markoff, whose novel methods of bringing political education to large groups of workers without previous academic preparation had made him a popular figure throughout the country. Until this opening session, however, Mirko was not acquainted with the details of the great successes of this labor educator, but now the gentle director reported to his class in his usual, unassuming manner.

"Approximately one thousand workers have attended the political courses of our labor school in New York City. In Chicago, Boston, Detroit, Cleveland, and other big cities, there are similar schools. We also have a network of evening courses, weekend courses, and this, our third national school. Political science, the scientific study of our society—is very much wanted by large groups of people. It will be up to you to help them get that knowledge. We'll begin our studies now."

Without any other preliminaries, he began the teaching

process instantly, and gave the students a taste of his method. "Many Americans do not consider this country an imperialist nation. Except for Puerto Rico, it is a fact that the U.S.A. has no colonial system of any kind. Is America an imperialist country?"

"Of course, it is!" several voices responded.

"How can one call this nation imperialist when it is so unlike the classical British, Dutch or French imperialisms?" he continued, and took special note of those students who responded. A number of hands were waving, and a short debate ensued immediately.

Peter, the Gary steelworker, was on his feet arguing. "The U.S.A. is a latecomer among the imperialist nations. By the time America appeared on the scene as a big power, the world had already been divided up, and most of the undeveloped countries had already been grabbed up by other imperialist powers. That's why the illusion is created that America is not an imperialist country."

"Very well. You're giving a good reason why America is not an imperialist country," Markoff said, smiling appreciatively of such a lively opening of the first session.

"But I didn't say it wasn't an imperialist country; I only said it came upon the world scene very late . . ." and Pete repeated his point and became angry that such a simple thing wasn't understood by a man like Dr. Markoff. In the excitement, and rapid exchange of words, between student and teacher, Peter began to cough and had to sit down, his face somewhat flushed.

Markoff assured him that he agreed with him, but "by repeating the same argument twice, or twenty times, you are not actually bringing more knowledge to the opponent. You have to come up with something more as soon as you are challenged." He smiled assuringly to Peter, and pointed his hand to Christine.

"Go ahead, if you think you have something to add to his argument."

"I think I have another point: America has used different methods than the crude methods of the other imperialists to establish its domination."

"What kind of methods?" Markoff asked.

"There's a big colonial liberation movement afoot, and it's

becoming almost impossible to transform the remaining countries into paying colonies. So America uses financial and political pressures to establish her domination—or as it's usually called, American leadership—especially since America came out so strong from the last World War."

"You could add to what you have just said that America was also using military pressures. But that's what we're going to study tonight; when you do your reading of the assigned material, we're going to find out exactly how these military, financial, and political pressures of the U.S.A. were even more effective that the earlier crude methods of the old imperialists —to establish American influence and domination." Markoff closed the first hour of free exchange of opinion.

A faint wave of panic brushed Mirko's consciousness as he listened to the debate between students and the director, and as he saw students all around him writing, with heads bent over their notebooks, keeping up with the new ideas, while his own pencil remained immobile on his pad, and his thought somehow riveted on the braided redhead in that room. He thought that Chris had pleased Markoff very much with her clear ideas, expressed so simply that even he, Mirko, had already learned something new.

Several of those who had spoken up strongly, convincingly, indicating that they had come with some previously accumulated political knowledge, were selected by Markoff as Group Leaders, and the large classroom of people was soon subdivided into several groups. There was general commotion, with all students moving freely forth and back in their choice of Group Leader, reshuffling alliances and allegiances. Mirko quickly attached himself to Chris' group, and sighed with relief when the first session of the school took its first rest period.

"Is Zal here, too?" Mirko asked casually, indicating that he hadn't had a good look around the place yet.

"No, he's holding the fort in Omaha. We couldn't both leave the field, but I'll tell you more during the lunch hour," Chris said, and it would seem that from that moment on, Mirko Yanich had run into an unexpected obstacle that he had not foreseen at all—he simply could not concentrate or take notes.

The groups stayed close together; they usually ate during their lunch hour at the same table, in an attempt to get better

190

acquainted with each other and with their Group Leaders. Mirko had already noticed that Chris' attitude to Peter Edgehill had the familiar pattern he had seen once before—when she had decided to ignore Zal Harris. He saw the same calculating reserve, centering her attentions on other students, but especially on Peter, and ignoring him completely. Once or twice she asked him about his work in Chicago, and about his sister—whose name she had forgotten. But it was her aloofness and her calculated behavior which was confusing him most. On more than one occasion she seemed to be telling him with her eyes, or with a gesture, that she had no intentions to get involved with him in any way. "Then why use Pete for that, as she had used me once in Chicago?" he asked himself.

The fortuitous selection of Chris as Group Leader by the others did not apply to him. Mirko had deliberately moved himself into a position that had put him in the same group with her, believing that Chris had encouraged him and welcomed him. Was she now playing a game with him, too, as she did with Zal? He wondered. Had he made a mistake in getting into her group for the duration of the school? He began to consider the idea of shifting over into another group before the situation had jelled. There was still time to move himself elsewhere. He looked around the room and saw several other large tables with their respective groups, eating together with the Group Leaders, as they were doing now with Chris.

He was about to get up and do something to change the arrangement, when Chris asked in a friendly, soft voice, "Mirko, would you like to use my notes of this morning's session? I write fast, but if you can read my writing, you're welcome."

"That would be swell, Chris," Mirko answered sincerely, grateful for her assistance. "Have never been any good in taking notes, and I didn't even catch the reading assignments for this afternoon."

"Neither did I," two other students said.

Chris repeated the pages assigned by Markoff and added, "This afternoon we're supposed to be reading this material by ourselves, but in the evening when we reconvene as a group, we're supposed to have lots of questions and debate among ourselves."

Writing down the page numbers in his unused notebook, a

certain calm had begun to set in Mirko's mind, replacing the earlier confusion that had beset him.

The routine pursued during the days that followed created numerous difficulties for Mirko. Chris was assisting two other students besides Pete, and found very little time for Mirko. As his difficulties mounted in keeping up with the studies, his anger at his Group Leader also mounted. The early spark that he had detected when they first recognized each other on the opening day of school seemed to have disappeared completely. The original aloofness had gradually grown into a total indifference to him. Yet he was constantly aware that Christine was not indifferent to Pete, who asked and received daily assistance from her. As the day approached for the students to hand in their first major composition, dealing with The Main Characteristics of American Imperialism, Mirko's restlessness and inner turmoil reappeared. Much of the material he was reading in preparation, he could not grasp in full, and was thoroughly helpless in putting down any of his own original thoughts on paper.

Twice he approached Chris, but twice she told him that she was occupied, assisting Peter with his assignment. She was speaking the truth, for Chris was frequently entering and leaving Peter's room and was seen sitting in a chair and reading aloud to him, while he had his eyes closed, resting. In a very peculiar, undefinable way, Mirko felt that Chris was teasing him, challenging him, telling him that she was glad he was so near her, yet telling him also to leave her alone.

His frustration and anger came to a head in a most unexpected fashion. The morning the students were to hand in their compositions, Dr. Markoff called on Mirko to read his paper to the class. Embarrassed, he admitted that he had not written it yet, but added, "I can say without hesitation that American imperialism stinks worse than the Chicago stockyards on a windy day." The class burst out laughing; Dr. Markoff, joining in the laughter, was unable to extract a better definition from the red-faced Mirko.

"I agree with you, Mirko, but if you tried to tell a Chicago stockyard worker something about American imperialism the

way you told us, he wouldn't learn anything from you. Right?"
Dr. Markoff asked, and looking directly at Mirko, added, "I'd
suggest that your Group Leader—you're in Chris' group, I believe, I'd suggest that Chris go over with you some of the material we discussed here and in the group . . ."

Mirko interrupted him in an angry voice, "I don't need any
dame to help me, I'll have my assignment ready this weekend."

He sat down without looking at anybody. The strained silence in the classroom hung over all, for several seconds. Chris
raised her hand and was recognized.

"I think I should explain here that Mirko asked me several
times to assist him, but I was working with Pete during most of
my free time, helping him. Tonight Pete will be leaving us, and
I'll have more time, as Mirko's Group Leader, to work with him
on his composition."

"Thank you, Chris," Dr. Markoff said and quickly called on
another student.

No other explanation was given. No one said why Pete was
leaving the school. Mirko began to wonder if he was the only
one in that large room who was deliberately kept in ignorance.
There was such an estrangement between him and Pete that
when the announcement of his departure was made, he was certain that it had something to do with the relationship that had
set in between Chris and Pete; and he now scolded himself for
being so blind and stupid. Upon adjournment for the evening,
he quickly returned to his room, deliberately avoiding all the
others, skipping his evening meal, and attempted to lose himself
in his studies—which now made even less sense than before.

Mirko wanted time to put the new facts together into some
meaningful pattern, and to straighten himself out emotionally
so that he could benefit from his schooling. Otherwise, he
argued in silence, he would have to admit to total failure and
request permission to return to Chicago. He was occupied with
these thoughts for some time before he heard the knock on his
door.

"I should have spoken to you sooner, Mirko, and explained
to you," Chris said upon entering. "It was too heart-breaking for
me to see this situation develop in my own group, and somehow
I must have completely overlooked my duties as the Group
Leader, and ignored your request."

"You don't have to apologize. All dames are alike," Mirko

replied without getting up, or offering Chris a chair. His original jealous suspicion was now corroborated by Chris herself, and a strong urge to pick her up and throw her out and never see her again overwhelmed him. "Pete should have said something to me; I'm responsible for him in a way. I brought him here and am expected to see him back home safely."

"He's not going back home. Pete is very ill and has to be hospitalized."

"Lungs?" Mirko asked in a subdued voice.

"Yes. It's bad. He didn't want to miss any of the class work and he asked me to read to him, and keep him informed of everything that was going on in school, while waiting to be admitted to the sanitarium. Dr. Markoff asked me to keep an eye on him, after he was moved into a room by himself, and to be careful not to mix too much with the others."

"That's why I didn't see him at our conferences," Mirko said, feeling a need to confirm aloud the accuracy of Chris' story. "I thought you were deliberately avoiding me, giving me the brush-off. I guess I owe you an apology."

"Not me, but the class," Chris replied, and walked out.

Alone again, Mirko's thoughts drifted to Pete, recalling his coughing fits during their long trip, not complaining ever, reassuring the others that he was all right. He admonished himself for not having noticed Pete's absence sooner, and for having been so completely consumed with his own selfish thoughts about Christine.

"Of course I owe the class an apology, like she said, for blowing my top, and calling her a 'dame.' I owe her, too, an apology. But how can I apologize to her and make her understand that she keeps confusing me," he mused to himself.

Mirko frequently felt inadequate in the presence of others who were able to speak glibly, convincingly. Somehow he began to believe that people tried to win the upper hand over him by confusing him. And now he was wondering if Chris, too, was doing the same thing.

His heart, however, quickly filled with warmth for her, and with renewed desires to see her soon, to talk to her freely, and to tell her that for weeks and months after they had met in Chicago, he kept thinking of her, and hoping that some day he would meet her again. "How am I going to tell her all that after the way I behaved?" he asked himself.

He knew he would be seeing her every day, many times a day; he would be eating with her, and studying with her for many weeks ahead, and he began to think of ways to approach her. Perhaps an invitation to go to the movies with him, or for a long walk in the Bronx Park? Maybe he could obtain a couple of tickets to a Broadway play—she'd like that! At last he decided that the best thing he could do for the present was to apply himself to his studies, to begin to work on his composition, and if the opportunity arose, to ask her to read it before turning it over to the director.

The material he was reading began to make sense to him for the first time. Slowly he copied new words which he looked up in the dictionary, and slowly he formulated ideas with those new words. He worked the rest of the evening, writing and rewriting, checking against the textbook—unconsciously he was preparing himself to face Chris with his finished product the following day. Deep in the recesses of his mind he was harboring the hope that she would approve his effort, that she would forgive him for his boorish behavior.

During the morning break, when Mirko showed his paper to Chris, he said goodnaturedly, "I hope they don't laugh again. I sweated on this piece almost all night."

"Don't worry. I'll bet it's good," Chris replied.

She read its contents as he stood by and watched her facial expression. Once, when she looked up into his expectant eyes, he caught a glimpse of her encouraging smile, and felt the heavy burden that had weighed him down for days slip away, relieving the tension from his taut body.

"Give it to him now," Chris said, "then he'll know that you were working on it last night instead of attending the general assembly—without an excuse."

"Oh, my god! I forgot all about that! Don't you want to fix it up a little before I hand it in?"

"What for? This is your own work, it sounds just like you, and I think it's good, too," she replied, handing him back his paper. "Go ahead, give it to him now."

The days and weeks that followed raced by rapidly for Mirko. He spoke up frequently during the debates in his group and in the general sessions, stubbornly arguing for his viewpoint, as he was doing this particular session. The entire student body was discussing the lecture they had heard the previous day on "The Status of the American Labor Movement." Mirko's notebook was wide open on his lap; he was staring at his own large scribbling, repeating to himself in silence

> only 3½ million now in unions
> mostly skilled, aristocracy of labor
> Negroes not accepted in major unions
> basic industries still unorganized

He raised his hand and said that he took serious issue with the lecturer on one point. "The most important thing facing the country is the simple matter of getting relief for the hungry. If this isn't done quickly, the people will demoralize and there will be lots of pressure on the unemployed to become scabs. In the meantime the mood of the unemployed to fight through the Unemployed Councils will drop, because they are hungry and need immediate relief." Mirko spoke with urgency in his voice, almost begging the others to grasp this point. "The Unemployed Councils should even consider using their headquarters for giving out relief themselves, so the militancy of the unemployed won't dwindle. This is the most important thing."

There seemed to be general agreement, but several students argued that Mirko was boxing himself into a tight corner if he continued to see only what is going on among the unemployed.

A Pittsburgh coal miner argued, "You seem to forget that last year when the Trade Union Unity League was set up, it pledged itself to go into the big unorganized industries and that is exactly what they did. The miners, the steel workers, the textile workers turned down the wage-cutting offer of the employers; instead they organized strikes against such a program and thousands of new members came into these militant trade unions. What we really need now is to get the organized workers and the unemployed to work together, and not against each other. That's why I agree in part with Mirko: we have to get relief to the hungry so they don't become scabs, but we have to get the A.F.L. also to come out for unemployment insurance, and for a program that will relieve the suffering of millions of Americans."

Dr. Markoff recognized the middle-aged Beatrice, the "matron" of the Chicago contingent, who was waving her hand vigorously. "I think we should insist that the unemployed members, who belong to the A.F.L., or to other unions, should be exempted from paying dues and union assessments so that they would feel that they are still union members, and would hesitate to become scabs on other union members; also it would be a good idea to request that all those big salaried bureaucrats of the A.F.L. take some cuts in their salaries and the money saved be used to give relief to their unemployed members. I agree with Mirko one hundred percent; we must not allow the unemployed to demoralize. Their fighting spirit must be kept up until this country provides some form of insurance against starvation for our people."

Mirko had never heard this woman speak up before and he often wondered why she had been chosen to go to this school. But as he looked at her he could easily visualize her addressing large audiences, speaking with ease, without any oratorical gestures, talking plainly and sincerely. It pleased him to get her backing.

Chris, too, argued in favor of Mirko's viewpoint. "I know what it means to starve of hunger. When you reach that low point, there isn't much fight left in you. That's the real danger now: that all fight will be drained off the militant unemployed movement in this country and then all kinds of demagogues will take over the leadership. Even the American bourgeoisie itself will undertake to grant all kinds of charity panaceas instead of genuine unemployment insurance."

Mirko was observing intently the tall redhead and silently thanking her for all the help she had already given him. She had taught him how to extract the most pertinent facts from the assigned reading material and how to use those facts to broaden his vision. Even now, as he was studying her face and her convincing presentation, he wished he knew more about her, and was wondering what had brought her to the radical movement in the first place. What did Zal Harris have to do with that? Somehow the idea kept persisting in his mind that some day he would have to get a direct answer from Chris, herself, about Zal, and what he really meant in her life. He kept thinking that Zal was still standing in his way, was still blocking him here somehow, in New York.

That thought frequently pursued him and this evening, instead of studying in his room, he sought out Chris and asked her to go with him for a walk in the Bronx Park. "For a little fresh air, and something I want to ask you." He refused to tell her what it was that he wanted to ask her but cautioned her that she might be disappointed; that it was something that had been bothering him since he first met her in Chicago, and never fully cleared up. Hurriedly Chris slipped on her corduroy jacket over her turtle neck sweater, and as she met Mirko at the door, she quickly protected her hands from the cold evening air by slipping one hand under his arm and putting the other into her deep jacket pocket.

"What is that big question that's been bothering you?" Chris asked amiably. She was in a good mood, happy to have had the opportunity to go outside for a while, and curious, at the same time, what Mirko was up to.

"How did you ever happen to become a Red? And what did Zal have to do with it all?" Mirko asked, surprising Chris.

She laughed loudly, and teased him, "You really don't care how I happened to have become a Red; it's Zal that you want to know about, I mean Zal and me. Am I right?"

"Not altogether. I want to know about Zal all right, but today when you talked in the class about relief for the unemployed, I also began to wonder about those millions of Americans, all those people now on the move, milions of them, and so many talking radical, like Marxism comes naturally to them. . . ."

"I don't know about the others, but as for me—it's too late to go all the way back, from the very beginning. Some other time I'll tell you about the place where I was born, on the outskirts of Omaha City, in a small farm community. Maybe it all began over there, and not when Zal knocked on my door after I got fired."

CHAPTER VII

Birth of a Rebel

Chris remembered making frequent trips to the big city with her parents. As an only child they took her with them everywhere. Later, in school, the entire class would sometimes come in for an important event—a school play, or for an inter-school oratorical contest. It was during her high school years that Chris was drawn more frequently into the booming metropolis, where she began to feel that she belonged there, instead of on the isolated, dull farm.

The city was growing rapidly, with new movie houses opening up and one of them advertising that it would soon introduce the very latest, the most astonishing new invention—the "talkie". And Chris was indeed among the first few hundred people who had heard the music sung live, and saw the beautiful acting and talking, as if the performer were there in full life.

There were other attractions that kept the tall, healthy redhead in the city: there were places for a girl to go to work, and to make her own way in life, and not have to depend on her middle-aged parents.

Soon Chris found herself working side by side with some thirty other young girls, on a large sprawled loft, where a variety of items were being processed for the Midwest Bakery. The excitement over being able to sustain herself in this large city, and earn enough to be totally independent, wore off rapidly.

Her body began to ache from sitting on a stiff high stool, nine hours a day, cracking open hundreds of raw eggs, and separating the whites from the yolks into large containers. She was not allowed to get up to carry the filled containers to the other end of the loft—the foreman did that. Only during the half-hour lunch period could she stretch her long legs, and take her eyes off the crates of eggs, and the tiny sharp knife to which she had to give her undivided attention every second of the day, or make the error of throwing a yolk into a large container of whites and then lose precious minutes fishing out that yolk. It was piece work, speedup work, back-breaking work, even for the husky, healthy Christine Wesly. There was no conversation among the workers until the lunch break; the toilet facilities were at the front of the building, and a trip away from your high stool was a conspicuous act, seen by everybody on the loft, and embarrassing if made too often. But at the end of the week, after fifty-four hours work, Chris received in her envelope about twenty dollars—sometimes a quarter more, and sometimes less. There was no way she had of controlling the count of the filled containers. The foreman kept that count. When she decided once to keep track of what she had turned in each day, she made the discovery that she had been cheated of nearly two dollars for that one week, but she had no proof, and no way of getting it back.

One mid-morning, during her first year of employment, Chris found a leaflet signed by the Trade Union Educational League, Bakers Industrial Division. What completely overwhelmed her was not so much finding this leaflet securely on the toilet seat, but to learn that someone else in her department knew all about the cheating that was going on, and all about the back-breaking work she and the others were doing, and how difficult it was for the single girls who had come in from the countryside to live on those earnings during the years of prosperity and high prices. She read the leaflet very carefully and put it back on the toilet seat exactly as she found it. That, she soon learned, was the most serious error Chris Wesly had yet made since coming to work in the city.

Minutes after returning to her stool, she was called into the office and was asked who had been working with her on that leaflet which she had left on the toilet seat. She was told that she need not deny that she was the one who had left it there because she was the last one in that toilet. Chris was asked to "cooperate" and to tell who else belonged to the T.U.E.L. Baker group; whom else did she know up front, in the main bakery building? She was promised better work in another department, with more pay; she was told that she would be more secure helping the company build its own Employees Association, than working with this group of Reds that was there to make trouble for everybody.

Her honest answers to all those questions were not believed. To prove to the company that she was innocent, she was told, she could join those people who had been issuing leaflets, and then she could tell the company who in the plant was doing all that Red work, and making trouble for everybody.

Chris had never heard about such a thing; at first she did not even understand what they were talking about; but then the management representative made it all clear to her. She was fired! Fired for refusing to cooperate.

Chris was so bewildered over the rapid developments of the last few minutes that as she walked home, she first began to reconstruct in her mind what she had read in that leaflet, and recalled several items: the eight-hour day had been won long ago, but in the Midwest Bakery, everybody worked nine hours a day, six days a week. She remembered it talking about not knowing at the end of the week how much one earned because they were at the mercy of a cheating foreman. But Chris could not remember the address that was given at the bottom of the leaflet. She was now admonishing herself for not having pocketed that leaflet; had she done that she might still be working, and then she could have found where those people from her plant, who knew what was going on, were meeting.

It was not until Sunday of that week that a strange boy and girl knocked on her door and after making sure that she was the Christine Wesly who had been fired from the bakery, they asked permission to come inside to talk with her.

The boy said very little. "I'm Zalman Harris, from packing, but my friend here, Joann, is from the bakery." Joann explained that she had witnessed what had happened, and that she knew Chris to be absolutely innocent because Joann was acquainted with everyone in the small group of militants in the bakery plant. But now, since Chris had already lost her job, would she work with this group that was trying to organize the bakery into a genuine industrial union? Would she cooperate with them in their efforts to change conditions there?

The entire thing appeared to Chris like a fairy tale: this was her first contact with unionism, and with a frameup; her first contact with people who wanted her, Chris Wesly, to help build a union. She looked at the two of them with her head slightly to the side, as was her habit when suspicious of anyone; she was studying them to make sure that they were on the level, and when Joann told her that the T.U.E.L. group was acquainted with similar situations, similar frameups of people in an attempt to make stoolpigeons out of them, and that they knew all about the foreman's cheating, and that they were preparing to take strike action, which, if successful, could change the whole picture inside that plant—then Chris began to enumerate several other things that ought to be done in the egg-cracking department, and she added that a rest period in the morning is something that all the girls would very much appreciate; also that the egg-cracking department ought to get a toilet of its own. She listed grievances which Joann was fully familiar with, and had already written about in previous leaflets which never reached Chris. Zal, in the meantime, advised her to try to get work in one of the packing houses that was hiring women.

"We have some members of the T.U.E.L. in there already, but it would be good to have a girl like you help them out. They won't suspect you, and you could do some good work in there."

To Chris the picture was still unbelievable, unreal. When Zal and Joann said their goodbyes, Chris was sure that she would never see them again. She had a strange feeling that she might be getting into something that could change things for her for the rest of her life; that these two people were probably the kind of Reds she had heard her Dad talk about, the ones who wanted to make a revolution like they did in Russia, and take away all the freedoms that the Americans were enjoying. She kept thinking about that point: she had nothing to draw on for arguments either way. She wasn't interested in politics or in unionism. She only wanted to get another job without getting mixed up with Reds or unions.

Chris decided to forget about the visit she had from those two strangers and forget what they told her. Instead she would go to work in the other large bakery plant. She could tell them that she had experience in the egg-cracking department of the Midwest Bakery, but she would accept any other work too. When she applied and was asked to wait a while, the interviewer then asked her if she had made some mistake in the spelling of her name.

"No. I guess that's why we are a little different from the other Wesleys," she said smiling, using the standing family joke. "We spell it simply, without the extra 'e' ".

"You're right. You sure are different! You're a troublemaker, Miss Wesly! We have no work for a troublemaker," he said and with anger on his face, he pointed to the door.

She walked away from this large plant and again began to reconstruct what had happened to her those past few days, and began to recall something else she had read in that first leaflet she had ever seen. She remembered a warning about a blacklist system that was going on in all the big plants. Now she understood what that meant. She didn't at first, when she read it. It was a strange phrase and a strange idea. But now she realized that she was being blacklisted: the company she had been working for had informed others that Christine Wesly was a troublemaker. That's the way it works, she thought to herself. What if the same thing happens in other places? What if they have my name in other plants? And she suddenly was struck by the monstrosity of the situation: what if she couldn't get work any place in the city, or in the state because somebody thought that she was the one who gave out that leaflet? But, Chris concluded, this was impossible; it could never happen! Maybe they cooperate with each other within the industry; maybe the owners help each other that way, she consoled herself.

But when Christine Wesly applied for work at the packing house where Zalman Harris told her women were being hired, she was shocked when the man asked her: "How do you spell your last name, miss?" She spelled it, and then decided to lie to him and say that this was her first job in the city.

He, too, returned moments later and asked, "Are you sure now? Never worked before in another plant in town?" And Chris began to feel like a woman who was being shadowed, who would be on a blacklist the rest of her days; who may even have to move out of Omaha, or of Nebraska. For a moment she even considered the idea of going back home, but quickly decided that it would be like going back to a graveyard, to take up residence as the caretaker of the graves. Bewildered and somewhat scared, she knew that she could never again go back to the farm of her parents.

But her being in the middle of a "labor situation" without ever having done anything, and being thrown out of work in the midst of this prosperity, was so shocking, so confusing, that she found herself walking away from the plant, and crying in grief.

Chris then began to study carefully the want ads for girls, and to her amazement saw the large advertisement of the Midwest Bakery: "Need thirty girls immediately. Good pay." It was some time before she fully realized that it was the egg-cracking department that was out on strike, and that important developments in the rest of the sprawling plant were expected momentarily, "which," according to a news item, "could become one of the serious labor troubles sparked by the Reds."

Her mood changed; a ray of joy had entered her furnished room, and the very thought of joining the other girls from the egg-cracking department on their picket line, in her white apron and cap, made her jump up as she began to sing loudly and boisterously. She suddenly thought of that boy who came with Joann. The name "Zal" stuck in her mind because it was so unusual. She remembered him saying something about intelligent people learning to work in a plant without getting themselves fired or blacklisted—as if criticising her for being fired. Yet, she reassured herself, the only thing she did wrong was not to have taken that leaflet. But that wasn't fair! She didn't take it because she was sure that it was meant for others to read, too. And now, for the first time, Chris began to examine the real reason why she did not fold that leaflet and put it in her pocket. The more she thought about that, the closer she came to realizing that she had left that leaflet on that toilet seat because she was afraid to take it! Yes, she was afraid to take it! But how did he, that Zal, know whether I was afraid or not? And what if I was afraid? Why shouldn't I be? How did I know what would happen to me if I walked out with a leaflet on me, a Red leaflet, telling me where I could find them, if I ever got in trouble.

That is how Chris kept recalling and telling Mirko in slow detail, as they walked on deeper into the Bronx Park, the circumstances under which she had met Zalman Harris, the boy who got her started in the labor movement.

The evening was calm and clear. The cool November air was soothing as they walked in step across the park. Everything

Chris was saying seemed soothing and comforting to Mirko. He barely made a comment, and barely looked at Chris as she recalled the days when she became associated with the militants.

Only once Mirko stopped and took her hands into his and kissed them softly, as if to keep them warm, and to shield them. He wanted to shield Chris the rest of his life, and wished he could tell her at that moment of the great surge of love he felt for her; he wished he could tell her that with her he would change the world and change himself. But he said nothing as he placed her hands on his chest and drew her close to him, and kissed her tenderly.

"Mirko, let's go back," Chris whispered into his ear.

They walked back to the building, holding hands, saying nothing more to each other until Mirko opened the door for her.

"Will you help me with my home work tonight?" he asked.

They smiled at each other and both knew that life had changed for them with that evening walk into the Bronx Park.

From then on Mirko and Chris were constantly together during the so-called free, or social time, and when Dr. Markoff designated one evening for the students to "get better acquainted with the movement in other parts of the country," Mirko and Chris paired up, as did the rest of the student body.

Several students from the Midwest accompanied their New York hosts to the famous Yokinen Trial* which was reported extensively by the press, and which had aroused interest throughout the country. Yokinen, a Finnish-American Communist, was accused of practicing social discrimination against a Harlem Negro. He was charged with white chauvinism and given a public trial at the Finnish Club in Harlem, before fifteen hundred spectators. Yokinen was found guilty by a workers' jury and by the audience, and was expelled from the party. Similar trials then followed in various parts of the United States, exposing racism, and calling upon the people to fight it as a menace which could eventually lead this nation to disaster.

The school, led by Dr. Markoff, used numerous novel methods. "Getting Acquainted Evenings," the director explained, were meant as evenings of study of American life directly from a fellow student.

* March, 1931.

205

"We better make this an evening of study, and come up with something when Markoff calls on us," Chris told Mirko. "What shall we talk about?"

"About you," Mirko answered quickly.

"Why only about me? Let's talk about us," Chris suggested.

"If Markoff calls on me tomorrow and says, 'Mirko Yanich, you're next. Tell us what you've learned.' I'll say, 'Dr. Markoff, I've learned, about a year ago, when I first met Christine Wesly, that she was a calm, principled leader in Nebraska. The boy with whom she was hiking from Omaha, arrived in time, but alone, without Chris. He was sick with worry about her. He was in love with her, and I took it for granted that Chris was his girlfriend. But something strange happened. I couldn't figure out, until much later, that Chris was not in love with that boy. Then I remember inviting her to come with me to the movies, and it was in that movie house that I found out that she likes to appear tough and calculating, but that she's really the softest and the kindest girl I had ever taken out on a date. I saw her cry in the movies, when the picture ended with the death of the little orphan. She's a very sentimental girl, and falls hard for all the tear-jerker scenes. And after that movie, I began to think of her, and dream about her, and if I wasn't an atheist, I'd say, I began to pray that some day I'd meet her again. Now I met her again and I must admit, Dr. Markoff, that I don't know what to do. I'm in love with Chris and I'd like her to come back with me as my wife.' Then Markoff would ask, 'What does Chris think about it?' and I'd have to answer that I don't know what she thinks about becoming my wife. Maybe you could ask her, Dr. Markoff, to give me her answer now, before all of us, before this body of students'."

Suddenly he dropped his double talk, and embraced Chris, covering her with kisses and caresses. They were alone in the "girls' dormitory," the large room used by the six women students. All the others were out for the evening, "getting acquainted" elsewhere. Mirko and Chris were now sitting on the wide couch, with Chris snuggled up closely to him, and enjoying his peculiar style of proposing marriage.

Picking up his own idea, yet responding calmly, she decided to let this discussion run its natural course.

"If Dr. Markoff calls on me, I'll say, 'I, too, am in love with Mirko. It started long ago, when we first met in Chicago. But

how can I agree to become his wife when he's about the worst
male supremacist I've run into since I've been connected with
the movement? He thinks like an old peasant in some Croatian
village'."

"Correction, honey, Yugoslav village. You know the name
was changed to Yugoslavia in 1929." He kissed her on the cheek
and sat back comfortably, looking at her with joyous eyes.

"Come on, Mirko, don't try to change the subject. This is
very serious. I can't understand how an American-born fellow,
with the kind of experiences that you've had in the packing
plant, and now a leader of so many thousands of unemployed
—how you can be so much like an old-country peasant, when it
comes to the woman question. You think that all you need is
my consent to become your wife, then you can go ahead and do
what you think is right for both of us. You expect that after we
get married I'd move in with you, and take your mother's place
in re-establishing the Yanich home for you; you expect that
we'd raise a family, that Kate would move out of the house for
good, because when we're married we'd want our privacy, without the other members of the family around. Well, I'm not
ready to turn myself into the kind of a woman that the German
Nazis propose for the German women."

He had never heard her talk like that before. The soft, lov-
able Chris seemed to have moved far, far away from him, so
she could lecture him about the woman question. Calling him
a male supremacist didn't shock him, or even disturb him as
much as seeing Chris' other side—the hard, stubborn woman,
with set ideas. He wasn't even sure that he understood the full
meaning of the term male supremacy as spelled out by Chris.
Is it wrong to expect his wife to live with him in his home? Is
it wrong to expect to raise a family while both are young? he
thought to himself. Is it wrong to follow the old Yanich tradition of leaving the newlyweds alone, letting them get adjusted
to each other and giving them opportunities to work out their
problems? Even in the worst times, he believed that old tradition was a good one. Is it wrong for him to expect to be alone
with Chris, in the home that was now practically empty? She
was confusing him again.

Mirko was proud of the men he had seen in his home, whom
his father used to invite over for a drink, or for a visit on weekends. They talked unionism, secretly they joined various com-

mittees that were building big unions; some, like his father, led stoppages and department protests, and later the big steel strike. He remembered those men as rebels, fighters, singing songs of freedom and unionism, while drinking the red wine and eating the barbequed lamb, telling jokes and having hearty laughs. Mother was somehow always at the stove, always refilling plates or the coffee mugs or wine glasses, always wearing her kitchen apron, busy keeping the house clean, and the clothes washed and pressed. To him those memories of his family life, until he was fifteen, were cherished memories of singing men, loud men, drinking men, and like his father, hard-working men. Those were the happy years, "our family years." Whenever he thought of marriage, Mirko thought of a home for himself and his wife and his offspring, like the Yaniches had when his dad was alive. Now this girl he was in love with was telling him that it was all wrong.

But she said she loved me . . . what does loving mean to her? Doesn't it mean the same thing to both of us? Is she deliberately mixing me up?

"Why so quiet?" Chris asked him after a long silence between them. "Have you changed your mind about telling Markoff that tonight you learned from Chris that you were a male supremacist? That you get jealous when you see me kidding with somebody else in the classroom . . ."

"But that isn't it at all! If I'm what you insist on calling a male chauvinist, then it's bad, and something should be done to change that situation," Mirko replied seriously.

Chris burst out laughing, and all her feminine softness returned, as she moved close to Mirko again, and kissed him on the mouth. "I guess that's the reason why I fell in love with you when I first met you in Chicago. You're so honest, and so anxious to learn and to change." She laid her head in Mirko's lap and stretched the rest of her lanky body.

"But you make fun about getting married and raising a family. And this time you don't use the old argument that during a depression it's wrong to bring children into this world, to suffer and to starve. Thank God there's a Lenin, and he came to my rescue. From now on I'll use him a lot more because now I know he's on my side." They both laughed as they recalled reading together from one of the textbooks of the school about family life for radicals.

"Don't you want to get married and raise a family?" Mirko asked, not having understood Chris' motives.

"Sure I want to get married and raise a family. But when? And under what circumstances? I'm a responsible leader in Omaha; there are several strikes on, right now in Omaha. I helped the strike committees, and the picket lines, I got support for the strikers, and when I return home those workers will expect to see me again on the picket lines, if they're still out; or they'll expect to see me at the Unemployed Council headquarters, from where they're conducting their strike activities. We have a big organization among the unemployed, and just before I left we squeezed several important concessions from the State Legislature, and I'm on the city-wide committee which is negotiating for a moratorium on all evictions. I have to get back to those fields of work," she said, as she sat up, beginning to show renewed concern for the work that she had left behind. She told him how she refused to come to this school in the first place, because she was so involved, but at last agreed. Now the thought of going to another city instead of her home town where she belonged made her feel like a traitor to the big movement of which she was such an integral part.

"The most important thing, as I see it, Mirko, is for me to help out with those classes we're running on the Negro question; we have a lot of influence among the Negroes, but we have to continue with our work of convincing the white people that without Negroes as our allies we'll lose everything, even the few concessions we've gotten," Chris added slowly, meditatively. Again there was extended silence between them, and Mirko knew that she was not quite through. He had learned her ways, and he could tell from her intonation that she was thinking aloud, sharing with him her worries.

"But you'd have me drop out of this picture, or disappear altogether. Or maybe make a public announcement that I, Christine Wesly, have just gotten married to Mirko Yanich, and from now on I'll be living in back of the yards in Chicago, and I'll keep house, do the laundry, wash the walls and floors, and keep a clean house for the master, for Mirko Yanich, and when the first baby comes, I'll quit all my activities."

"That all sounds crazy, Chris. Why do you talk like that? Why can't you transfer to Chicago, after we get married, and move into our home, and we'll both make a home of that half-run-down place; and if you insist that Kate live with us, that might not be such a bad thing that we have to quarrel about."

"No, Mirko. We're not quarreling about these things. Kate may not even want to live near the stock yards any longer. But I'm going to ask you point blank: if we get married, why don't you come to Omaha?"

"How can I? I was sent here to this school because of the work I'm involved in. Willie and I . . . oh, never mind Willie, when you see him again you'll understand how he and I, well . . . I've lived around the yards all my life, everybody knows me, our home is like an Unemployed Council headquarters since Mom passed away. Nick moved out right after he got married, Kate lives with that wealthy family where she's working as Governess, the house is all run down, nobody is looking after it, and it needs a woman who could make it again into a Yanich home. What's wrong with that, Chris? Why do you call that male supremacy?"

"Because I don't think I should spend my time fixing up an old, run-down house, or give up the next dozen years raising a family. There are more important things to be done. We're leading a big movement in this country, and the unemployed millions depend on us. They trust us, and everybody in the leadership of this movement counts, everybody counts. There'll be time to raise a family later."

"Later? When? When you're too old?" Mirko asked. "Or are you against radicals like us raising families altogether?"

"There are times when we have to give up our personal wants for the needs of the movement, and I think this is such a time. It's wrong for a man like you, or for me, to get tied up now with raising children, or fixing a home. But you see, Mirko, you don't even consider my personal wishes. As long as you have made your decision, and as long as you thought that as your wife I should come to Chicago and settle there, the subject is closed, and you can't see anything else. Why? Because I'm not an equal in your eyes, so you make decisions for both of us. You've already decided in your own mind that I'll be staying home most of the time, raise a brat or two, and you, the big man of this great mass movement will be free to go wherever you are needed, come home late, or not at all; you'll be doing whatever will be necessary for the movement, but I, Christine Wesly, will become the good wife, the good hausfrau, and find ways somehow of getting food on the table, like your mother had to do, which drove her to . . ."

"You've gone far enough, Chris," Mirko stopped her. His anger at bringing in the memory of his mother at such a moment was rising. "I know I was wrong in not seeing that she was starving herself so Kate and I would get the bread and soup. I know I was too busy getting food for others—but let's leave mother out of this . . ." and now sadness overwhelmed him, reawakening again the feeling of guilt, the self-accusation that it was his fault that she suffered so long, and that he was responsible for her untimely death.

"I'm sorry, Mirko. Sure it wasn't your fault. She wasn't the only one who died of malnutrition in the beginning of the crisis. Maybe you helped save hundreds of other mothers from dying of hunger, when you led those demonstrations, and got the relief cuts re-instated. But let's not go making a mistake between us, before we are married."

"You mean we should get married—but not make mistakes?" and again Mirko became excited with her acceptance, and drew Chris into his arms and held her for a long time, and as he kissed her she could feel the tears of joy that had gathered in his eyes and couldn't be held back by him.

"How can we talk of getting married when we have such sharp disagreements between us?" Chris said softly, unconvincingly.

"Name the first disagreement that we have to remove," Mirko said, both feeling their commitment to each other had become irreversible.

"I can't come to Chicago and live with you in the Yanich home; I belong in Omaha where I was born, raised and educated, and where the people trust me."

"All right. You go to Omaha, and I'll go to Chicago. We'll talk to the people in both cities, and they'll help us figure out for whom it's easier to break away and make the change. Maybe after you stay there a few weeks, and explain to everybody that you're planning to become Mrs. Mirko Yanich . . ."

"See, there you go again. Why should I call myself Mrs. Mirko Yanich? I could tell them I'm planning to get married to Mirko Yanich, and that it would be better if I trained somebody to take my place, and as soon as I get disentangled, I could arrange to go to Chicago where my future husband now lives . . ." Mirko didn't let her finish. "All right, Mrs. Wesly-Yanich, Mrs. Yanich-Wesly. Which do you like better? I'll clean up the joint; we'll get a couple of women from the Unemployed Council to pick up some linoleum for the kitchen floor; Kate has been stealing things from that rich family—she says they never earned all that wealth in the first place—they stole it from the poor whom they've been exploiting all their life. So now maybe she'll bring us a few more things we'll be needing. Maybe we'll arrange a welcoming party for my bride, and we'll make a real big wedding party, and raise some money for the benefit of the Unemployed Council so they could move out of our house, maybe . . ."

"Maybe you'll tell Markoff what we've learned on this Wednesday night," Chris interrupted him.

"I sure will! I'll tell him, and the whole class, that I'm a male chauvinist, and that my wife-to-be, Christine Wesly, won't come to live with me until I get rid of my 'peasant ideology' and that anyway Chris and I won't see each other for a little while, and we request that the graduation party be something different this time."

"How do you propose to make it different?" Chris asked.

"Maybe Dr. Markoff should invite the governor; they say that the New York Governor, this Mr. Roosevelt, has been going to all kinds of graduation parties. He seems to get around and this school is important," Mirko said with mischief in his eyes. "They say he has ambitions to run against President Hoover in the next elections, so he better come and talk to us; he'll need support from other places besides New York State." Again they laughed, and kidded each other about who'd tell Markoff of their decision to get married later. They called that evening their "Engagement Evening," and only the arrival of the girls, who occupied that "dormitory," brought the happiest evening for Mirko and Chris to a close.

For the remaining few days of school, they were constantly together. The other students had already become aware that Chris and Mirko were in love; and everybody treated them as if they were something special, something that happens suddenly, like a miracle, which no one has to explain, and no one has to give an account for; but everybody knew that the miracle had taken place, that Chris and Mirko were in love. And both lovers felt as if they were participants of a fast-moving race of some

212

kind, that they had to utilize every single minute together, that they had to know more about each other, and to solidify their feelings of belonging to each other so that after the separation, after their return to their own bailiwick, the feelings between them would remain as strong as upon their separation.

They met in the "dormitory" as often as possible; they took their breaks together, and spent the lunch hour and all rest periods together. They took no part in the remaining social events of the school, being too occupied with each other, and found excuses all the time for remaining behind when the other students left the grounds for "field work," or for a "cultural event."

When alone in the building one evening, Chris asked: "You talk about Willie like he was an important part of your life, Mirko, like you couldn't separate from him if you had to. Is it that way on his part, too? Then there are times when you say Willie is really your leader, although he's younger and came to the movement after you. I feel like you'd do almost anything Willie tells you to do."

"Not anything! Oh, no! You got it all wrong," Mirko protested.

Chris was usually ahead in reading his thoughts. "No, I know that you wouldn't listen to him if he told you not to marry me, all right? But look at it seriously: It seems to me like you've fallen under a spell of some kind. What's so mysterious about him? Why do you talk about Willie the way you do? I'm beginning to feel I ought to know him better."

"You will, you will. There's nothing mysterious, but Willie is teaching me things that I could never have learned without him."

"Like what?"

"Like, like . . . many things. But take for instance that company union in the plant, I mean how they leave those men from the 'killer floor' alone, they don't push them, they're afraid of them. I've in there, let me see, been in Swift's since '22, got kicked out last year, been in there almost eight years, and I've never seen those black men, how they work, what they look like. The company is afraid of them; if they begin to move towards unionism why the whole plant could be toppled over. Now Willie's never been inside the plant, but he knows those men. They talk to him, he goes to their homes, he talks unionism with them, sure he does that, but he talks something else with them. Listen to this: Willie told me once that some of those men become like brutes in their work; they kill all day long, they kill animals, living things, and then, like one guy said to him: 'I almost killed that bastard, that foreman, the same way I killed the cow!' Willie gets to the guts of this man, to his insides, and makes him talk like a black man will talk to another black man. They tell Willie how they hate their work, how disgusted they are with it all, but they make more money than the others in the plant, they make good money."

"How do they kill the animals?" Chris asked. "Do you know?"

"I know now; but it's funny you should ask that question. That's what I asked Willie myself."

"Did he know?"

"Of course he knew. That was the first thing he found out. That's the way he works. He came to my home to stay overnight several times, and he knows everything about each and every Yanich that ever lived."

"Does he know anything about the future Yaniches, too?" she asked.

Mirko didn't catch on at first. He could think only of his brother Nick, and the girl he married, as a future Yanich. Then it clicked, and Mirko's face lit up, and Chris saw that the squint in his left eye, which she had noticed before in Chicago, was now shimmering, as it did when he became emotional and excited.

"Yes, Willie knows a lot about you," Marko said slowly, and he paused. He didn't want to get too far away from the things Willie told him about the key black men in packing. "One of his buddies, the man Willie knows best on the 'killer floor' whom he calls Butch, told him that he uses a sledge hammer, and it takes a lot of strength, real muscle. The cow is chained by the hind legs and they hang it up, alive, an animal that breathes, and Butch tells him that sometimes he believes that the animal talks to him, and looks at him with a plea not to kill it. Then he takes this sledge hammer and hits that 'talking cow' hard, hard enough to stun it. First he has to stun the animal, then he slits its throat, and then they split the animal at the sides. The men wear those big, heavy aprons and high boots because they work in blood all day, and hear the screams and the sledge hammering and the cutting, all day, and once in a while a guy goes berserk and instead of cutting off the cow's head, the forem . . ."

"I got the point, all right. I got the point!" Chris stopped him quickly. "What else could anyone do? Somebody has to kill those animals," she added.

"Yeah, that's true, but Willie told Butch that if they get a union going there, a genuine union, they could find a better way of killing those animals. If they make it one of their demands the men wouldn't have to become brutalized like that."

"Maybe we better get off this subject, I'm feeling a little faint inside from your talk about all this killing," and Mirko noticed that she was telling the truth, as her normally ruddy, freckled skin had turned pale, and the freckles that he thought were only under her eyes now appeared on top of the nose, on the bridge. And he leaned over and kissed her nose.

"Never knew freckles tasted so good! How about making a lentil stew for me when you come to Chicago? The Yaniches ate a lot of lentils—used to take them off the kids' faces, then they'd add a few mushrooms, and a piece of garlic—ah, wait till I show you how to make lentil stew out of freckles . . ." And he talked on and on, deliberately trying to make her forget the earlier discussion, and soon her color returned to its natural pink.

She asked: "Why is Willie so involved with Isaac? Were they related?" and Mirko knew that she was back to her own self, and that he could now talk again about Willie.

"No, Willie and Isaac were total strangers. I was there when Willie first came to the park to hear Isaac talk, and soon Isaac began to treat him like he was his own son. Willie liked that, and he told me about it. 'I always knew I was a Negro; I was always self-conscious. My folks in Alabama always made me feel, and think, that I was inferior to whites; that there was something wrong with being black; and it was Isaac who was the first man to make me feel proud to be a black man.' Willie likes to tell me about this whenever he speaks about Isaac. And it was Isaac who made a radical out of him, too, and the way I have it figured out, Willie was like a man who had come out of some dark room into the light, blinking his eyes—not understanding, and not believing at first all those things Isaac was telling him. Then his eyes cleared, and he even began to teach Isaac some things. That's true, and Isaac used to kid him about it and tell him, 'Son, you had some schooling—I had none. You can read'n write fast, while I just about get by.' And then Isaac goes to this Loop anti-war demonstration, and C.A. makes a big anti-war speech against the Japanese, saying that September of 1931 would be remembered as the day when the Second World War got started."

"Why that date?" Chris asked.

"I asked the same thing, and Willie says that in September Japan broke its treaty and occupied the City of Mukden in Manchuria, and the rest of the world said nothing, and the German Nazis who were getting stronger seemed to like what Japan was doing. And while C.A. called on the large crowd to protest the selling of scrap iron to Japan by the American government, plainclothes cops attacked the rear of the crowd with banana stalks, and all hell broke loose. There's screaming as they beat up some women, and one girl wraps herself around a telephone pole, and the cops can't get to her while she's shouting 'We don't want another war, we had enough, stop the Japanese from drawing us into another war' and just about that time two mounted cops wade through the crowd, and yank this girl down, and this time cops with drawn guns pull her away to a waiting paddy wagon, while C.A. is still talking and telling the people that the Hoover administration is preparing for war against the Soviet Union."

"Were you there?"

"No. I was getting ready to leave that week-end for this school; I had no time to go on the demonstration."

"But Willie told you all this? And you remember it all?" Chris said.

"Willie told me this over and over. Because they had no permit for this anti-war demonstration. The people who sponsored demonstrations all over the country decided to go ahead with this national protest, with or without permits, and they worked out a new strategy: they had a large number of speakers spread out throughout the downtown area, and when one group got busted up, another one would form, and a speaker would appear, and get up there and shout slogans like WAR IN ASIA WILL LEAD TO WAR IN EUROPE, and DON'T BE

216

SILENT, PROTEST. And when the police were getting confused as to where to turn next to break up these groups of peace demonstrators, some plainclothesmen ganged up on an isolated man or woman and almost beat them to death."

"Is that what happened to Isaac?" Chris asked.

"No one knew exactly what happened to Isaac at first. Later they found out that a woman who saw two men beat Isaac with banana stalks began screaming and shouting: 'He's dead, you murdered this man.' The cops believed Isaac was dead and they walked away towards the waiting ambulance to report a death, but this woman dragged Isaac out of their sight and then a man helped her carry him two blocks to this man's car, and when they brought Isaac home he was still alive. But the doctor said that Isaac was blinded and that the head wounds were too serious—that he couldn't possibly last much longer."

With the murder of Isaac, there took place a profound change in the life of Willie Rivers—a visible change in his outward appearance as well as in his general behavior, and an invisible change which his friend, Mirko, felt and sensed and shared.

"Willie stayed with me for a few days, and we arranged Isaac's funeral. The two of us spoke in the chapel and at the grave. We didn't say much, just a few words each. From the chapel we went to the park, to the place that everybody knew as 'Isaac's Box,' and there we stopped with his body in the casket and said nothing; we just bowed our heads, and the people cried quietly. And then we took Isaac back to the streets, to the cemetery, and later, when Willie started coming out of it, when he returned to take Isaac's place, he got up on that box, and began speaking —but not any longer like the old Willie. He began in a whisper with 'My name's Willie Rivers' and those standing close to him were drying their eyes, and me thinking that Willie must have looked like Isaac, when Isaac was a young man." Mirko paused and continued thinking aloud. "Willie wasn't just copying Isaac in voice or manner, because Willie was now talking like a different kind of a man," and here Mirko again had difficulty describing what had happened to the young Negro orator of Chicago's South Side.

He was trying to tell Chris that Willie wasn't thinking any longer in his spontaneous, disconnected, and cocky manner. Now Willie seemed to have moved into another kind of frame of mind, his thoughts more complex, yet the people able to follow him closely, and understand him well.

Mirko described to her how once his friend stood there, on Isaac's box, looking so aged, and telling the people: "Since the end of March of this year something has happened to our country the likes of which we had never seen before. Since the day they've tried to frame those nine black boys at Scottsboro, Alabama, and lynch them. We've seen tens of thousands of black and white people come to their rescue. Why? I ask myself, and you ask yourselves now: Why do the Russians, and the Germans, and the French, and whites all over this country come out on the streets in big meetings, and sign petitions, and raise thousands of dollars to save those Nine Scottsboro Boys from the electric chair? Why?"

Mirko recalled that Willie wouldn't answer his own question. He'd give his listeners time to think it out for themselves. Then he'd add: "Why do over a quarter of a million whites and Negroes demonstrate for the boys' freedom? Why?"

Willie then continued telling his audiences that the motion for a new trial argued by Joseph R. Brodsky, the ILD attorney, was denied, but "that don't mean the boys are dead. No! They're far from being dead!" and he'd wait for the applause to simmer down, and he'd continue telling his people that the executions scheduled for eight of the boys had been postponed, pending appeals to the higher courts. "We'll save those boys' lives, and in doing it we'll put an end to frameups like this one."

Mirko, too, was amazed at Willie's ability to throw out a group of key questions, and let them dangle somewhere in mid-air, and then ten or fifteen minutes later, pick up his own trend and continue, with everybody in the audience seemingly thinking together, with him.

"Because for about a year-and-a-half our people, black and white, have been suffering like never before from an economic crisis that is disastrous. I tell you it's disastrous for everybody. And the men who run this country can't get away any longer blaming us for this disaster. During these months of suffering, as the blacks and whites organized, and stuck together, we got some relief, we are getting some food now, and we are getting milk for the children. We got unity between the people in this country, and that's the greatest thing that's happened to all of us." Willie now seemed to stop altogether, but his listeners

218

knew that it was his style of speaking, and they were not deceived.

"Hunger united us, suffering united us, and the people feel that lynching the nine black boys is aimed to dividing us, like we've been divided these hundreds of years. But that division has ended now! There'll be no more Scottsboros because the people, black and white, won't let it happen again."

Mirkov now kept talking, as if to himself, as if assessing what had really happened. "Willie was always grateful to Isaac, like he owed him his life because he made him feel like a man, a man of the world; and after Isaac was gone, I saw that Willie was taking on Isaac's burdens, like wanting to fill that gap."

Chris switched the discussion. "How did Willie meet this girl, where he was recuperating?"

"I don't feel like talking about Hattie Green—that's the name of this girl. You'll see her when you come to Chicago; she'll tell you herself all the rest of this reunion between them."

"What do you mean by 'the rest'? Is there a 'rest'?" Chris asked, with renewed interest in the whole thing, while Mirko was beginning to object.

"Don't go calling me a male supremacist, but I'm going to tell you this: you're no different from all the other women. Now you won't leave me alone until I tell you more about Hattie, but I'm not going to say another word, except that Hattie is now Willie's girl friend again—they were friends before he dropped out of school, and that's all you're going to get out of me."

Although Mirko was saying all this good-humoredly, joshingly, he didn't think that this was the best way for him to spend those remaining few precious hours with Chris—talking about Willie's old school friend, Hattie Green.

"We have more urgent things to talk about than what goes on between Willie and Hattie, and it's none of my business in the first place, and none of yours either, all right? Now go ahead and say it, say I'm a male supremacist!"

"What urgent things do we have to talk about?" Chris asked.

"Well, most of the students are going to Washington right after graduation to join their state contingents, which will be coming into the Capital on December 7th. We're joining the Illinois column in Washington, and we'll return home with them, with the midwest Hunger Marchers. Wish you could come along with us to Washington, but you still think you can't afford the time. All right. Then this is our last evening together; we won't see each other until . . ."

Neither of them knew until when. No one knew when the Hunger Marchers would make it back home, and Chris didn't know how things would work out for her in Omaha. It was a sad parting for both Mirko and Chris. The unknown was staring them in the face, and each wondered in his own silence: what would happen in Washington when the Hunger Marchers arrived to demand from the government emergency measures to meet this national disaster? Would they be bloodied up, like so many others who had protested to the state and city governments? Would Mirko come out alive from that battle, if there were a battle? What will happen to Chris while hitch-hiking in the cold of the winter, half-way across the country? If she gets there alive, will she uproot herself and come later to Chicago to take over the duties of a future Yanich, in the tradition of the Yaniches?

They both wondered, in their last tender farewell evening together.

CHAPTER VIII
Hunger on the March

I

The battle to survive the devastating storm has taken on new dimensions. Thousands are pushing their emaciated bodies against the doors of bulging warehouses, reaching for food, and for warm winter clothing; others improvise tools and instruments to reopen the gas and electricity in their dark and frozen flats; meanwhile hundreds of thousands everywhere brave the cold and sleet, and policemen's clubs, as they demand food for themselves and for their families.

The hungry and dispossessed are in motion—demonstrating, picketing, and marching on the city halls and state capitols; they are lining up caravans for the Hunger March to the national capital.

Washington has become the crossroads for the nation's hungry and the nation's militants. Hunger Marchers are arriving with their columns from St. Louis, Chicago, Buffalo, Boston, and other centers—on schedule, on December 7, 1931. On the Plaza, before the Capitol, the marchers come face to face with thousands of policemen and detectives who had been mobilized from all over the country. Troops held in readiness in nearby forts can be seen by the marching men and women; and as the Hunger Marchers move along Pennsylvania Avenue, to the White House, the parade is flanked on both sides by rows of marching policemen who outnumber them. Poindexter is leading the Illinois-Indiana contingent; Sylvia Connors is close by his side. Mirko Yanich has just joined them, arriving late from New York with two other students.

In her pocketbook Sylvia has tucked away the last letter from her sister, Helen, which she has read and re-read many times:

meet me inside the Washington Auditorium, at the foot of the stage.

I must see you, Sylvia. Am coming in with the Alabama contingent, but I won't return with them. Can you find room for me with your delegation?

The snow has just begun to fall and suddenly Sylvia becomes worried about her sister's clothes, imagining Helen in her light summer dress, freezing to death. She is wondering how she could obtain, in this strange city, a pair of galoshes and a scarf for her sister. That seems to Sylvia to be the most urgent thing to take care of now, or as soon as she finds Helen. Confusing thoughts are running through Sylvia's mind: she has somehow forgotten what Art Walton looks like, or how his voice sounds. She fears that if she runs into the Alabama people, she will fail to recognize him. Everything about him seems to have suddenly moved into oblivion, miles away from her perception, from her memory reservoir. Only the face of her sister, her Helen, as she remembers her when she first ran away from Art Walton that evening when he and Kikki had their reunion—only Helen's pale face and thin, diminutive body keep coming up in her mind, as she looks among the hundreds of Hunger Marchers, searching for her sister.

As if shaken out of a trance, she suddenly hears from a distance behind her the familiar high soprano, the voice of her sister leading in the singing of a labor song. Tears of joy gather in Sylvia's eyes; she turns her head in the direction of the voice; soon the two sisters wave to each other, and push their way to meet; now they are marching in step with the others, holding hands, and singing at the top of their voices.

Barred from the doors of Congress by thousands of police and detectives, who surround them, the marchers proceed to the White House, where uniformed and plainclothedmen await them. Poindexter is hoisted on the shoulders of several delegates, and with a loud, booming voice he spells out the demands of the Hunger Marchers.

Congress refuses to see them, the Senators refuse to see them, President Hoover refuses to see them. They continue marching, leaving behind them copies of their major demand, AN UNEMPLOYMENT INSURANCE BILL,[8] at each of the buildings.

At the Washington Auditorium the Hunger Marchers deliberate for many hours, and finally announce to the country that their fight for unemployment insurance, for social security, has just begun.

They leave by the same routes, and in the same manner. The two sisters return together; Mirko and his Chicago fellow students join the Illinois-Indiana caravan, and the long trek to all parts of the country begins.

II

Covered with army blankets and sitting close together in the back of the truck, Sylvia first notices the aged and haggard appearance of her sister and the lonely, empty look in her eyes. It seems to her that Helen had created an atmosphere of hushed silence around her, as if wishing to be left alone and not wanting to be disturbed.

The gap between them had deepened and it became painful as they hit the open road. This situation could not continue much longer, Sylvia decided. She had to find a way of pulling Helen through that void, of pulling Helen closer to her emotionally, by tapping some source that would enable her to open up and talk. Sylvia's feeble inquiries about Art were quickly rejected, and she avoided broaching that subject again. Perhaps she ought to tell her about their parents and their brother? She invented stories about "Mendel's Factory," and wove imaginary anecdotes their mother would have told them.

"How do they manage if Pa can't sell all his cigars?" Helen asked at last.

"They manage. They have learned to live on so little that whatever Louie gives them every once in a while just about keeps them alive. They get some vegetables from the peddler next door. You remember Mr. Horowitz?"

"Of course I remember the Horowitzes! Why do you ask such a foolish question?" Helen replied with some irritation. "But how can he afford to give Ma vegetables for nothing?"

"Well, it's a long story. He can't afford it but he insists that Ma take from his wagon whatever she needs. You know his horse has been in our barn all these years, and at first Pa used to get a few dollars a month for rent. That stopped long ago. Well, one night the barn door blew off, when we had that big storm I wrote to you about. There was nothing Pa could do about fixing it during that terrible night. But he was afraid that the horse would run away. So he decided to stay there, to sit up the rest of the night and watch the horse. In the morning when Mr. Horowitz came to the barn, he found Pa sitting there, blocking the door with his body, protecting the horse. Well, it was after that night that Mr. Horowitz began to give Ma all kinds of vegetables from his wagon. That helps a lot. And Ma kids about it, too, telling us that she always wanted to be a vegetarian anyway. Louie and Sophiele come around about once a month and leave them a few dollars. I haven't been able to send them any money from Gary. But after this trip to Washington, I think I'll be reassigned back to Chicago, and I'll stay home."

"You don't like your assignment in Gary?" Helen asked. She wanted to hear more about Sylvia's plans to return to Chicago, and had hoped all along that it would happen that way so that she, too, could move back home with her.

"It isn't that I don't like it. We have a strong Unemployed Council going there; the big mill has laid off a lot of people who are now doing practically full-time work for the movement. And soon we expect Pete—oh, you never met him, Peter Edgehill, from the mill. He's still working and has a good nucleus organized inside the plant. He's popular among the men, and when he comes back from the national school I'll be able to come back home. I want to help out in packing."

"You mean you'll go to work in some packinghouse? But aren't they laying off there, too?"

"No, it isn't that, I couldn't get work inside anyway, they are not hiring anybody now. But I could help in other ways. We have a good caucus working inside, and they issue bulletins and leaflets about their grievances, and they expose the company union in there as a phony union, and all that stuff."

"Where do you come in?"

"Well, they need help in getting those bulletins out, technical help, too."

"You think you'll move back home?" Helen now asked hopefully.

"I'd like that; maybe I can help Pa get rid of a few more boxes of his cigars, on the other side of Humboldt Park. They don't like to accept help from Louie or Sophiele. She's working only part time, and Louie took quite a cut in his pay. Ma and Pa wouldn't object if you or I helped them, that would be different."

224

"Me helping them?" Helen asked. "You think I could come back home, and Ma would . . ."

Sylvia did not let her finish. "Oh, Helen, it would be the best thing that ever happened to all of us. Ma and Pa wouldn't ask you a single, solitary thing about where you've been, or what you've done, unless you want to tell them yourself. You know that's the way they are. Helen, we'd bring them so much joy if you and I came back home, oh, Helen, Ma loves you so much, she worries about you so much; but she never complained against you when you eloped with Art. She never said a word against you to me. Helen, this is the first time I must ask you, and you shouldn't stop me: you said Art couldn't come to Washington, but you never explained why. You said he was all right when I asked you if he was sick, but that's all you said."

"Now that I'm going home with you, I don't care any more." Her voice faltered momentarily, and her drawn face was hid by the darkness of the night as they climbed the crest of the mountain. She needed time to absorb the meaning of Sylvia's plea to move back with her into their parent's home; she needed time to adjust to the thought that soon she would be surrounded again by the warmth and love of her family. Gently she leaned her head back and closed her eyes. For several long moments she remained suspended in the joyous pleasure of a forthcoming reunion. She imagined herself walking through the little white gate, and, standing by the door window, she saw the smile in her mother's blue eyes that seemed to suddenly cause her own eyes to fill.

Softly she cried in the dark of the night, and the warm tears running down her pale cheeks relieved that weight inside her, that pain that needed healing with the warmth of her sister's hand, which reached for hers. They kissed and felt each other's damp faces, and waited for the darkness to disappear, for that pain to be left behind on the mountain, and for Helen's cleansed voice to speak again.

"If I thought I could have come home, I would have left Alabama before. I didn't know where to go after Art shipped out."

"Shipped out? Why did he do that? Why didn't you let me know? How long have you been there by yourself, alone?" Sylvia asked in rapid succession. She saw Helen's face more clearly

225

now as they approached a city at the foot of the mountain, and heard her calm answer.

"He left five weeks ago. When we first began to prepare for the Hunger March, he already hinted then that he wouldn't be going along with us; he had other plans. I thought he had other plans for work somewhere else in the south which he couldn't talk about, not even with me, you know what I mean?"

"No, I don't. You mean Art kept some things from you? Didn't he tell you everything that was going on?"

How naive! Helen thought to herself: the same Sylvia I had left behind—unspoiled, trusting everything and believing everybody.

"Art was all right, Syl. He made me feel like I was the only one in the entire world that he could have fallen in love with. And I believed him, and I still do. He wasn't lying to me. That's the way I appeared to him at first. He'd spend hours teaching me new words, and I seemed to be in a race all the time: a race for new words, a race to learn their meaning and their use. He was always pushing me to grasp the deeper meaning behind those words. Art opened up to me a new world of books and ideas. I must have carried around that dictionary with me everywhere, all the time, even when I went to bed I'd keep it within reach." Helen was like a gusher until they reached their stopover. She talked on and on, for long durations.

"But he's a superficial person. When I scratched off the top, and began to look for the real Art, I found a hollow man."

"You called him a fake once, remember? Is that what you mean?"

"No, Sylvia, Art isn't a fake. I was wrong. Art, Art—that's the way he really is: jolly, cheerful, laughs easily, but inside him is like a hollow barrel, it's empty inside. I had a lot of time to figure things out. He used to leave me alone a lot, soon after we came to Alabama. And I thought he was busy with work in the movement. That's true, too, he was busy. But he used this also as an excuse to do other things. I told you about his spending some nights with that editor's wife, and then he came home and cried, I mean cried, begging forgiveness. And I never told him what it was like for me to sit in that rooming house, where we lived, sit there two and three days in a row, and once it happened that he didn't show up for a whole week. Syl, I got to know everything in that room so well that I thought I could recognize

226

a strange cockroach entering the place. I would have gone off my mind if I didn't think that he was busy doing some important work for the movement. And I knew how dangerous it was for a white man working in the South."

She checked herself as she said this, because Helen had known during those two years of life with Art, that it was equally dangerous for a northern white woman to work in the very heart of KKK territory, as it had been for Art. Yet, she never thought of it that way until just now, as she recalled in her mind the loneliness and wretchedness, always having pushed out of her conscious thinking the actual dangers to herself. She saw only Art's safety threatened . . . .

. . . Art and she walking in broad daylight, for the first time, in a black community—she recalled so vividly now—and there before them appeared a group of eight white uniformed cops, coming towards them, at them, as if on a pre-arranged schedule for an expected confrontation. Art bent down, kissed her, put his arm around her waist and proceeded to talk to her in the same sweet, love-making manner as he had done in Chicago, when he first began to court her. They looked into each other's eyes, Art smiling, Helen—having grasped the reason for Art's behavior—responding coquettishly as they continued walking, seemingly unaware that a formation of white cops was now directly in front of them . . . now passing them. They continued in that fashion for two more blocks, in pretended lover's stride, feeling deep in their hearts, in the racing beats, the full impact of the intimidating purpose of the cops' visit into the black community. They arrived in a small park and sat down on a bench, still in mock lovers' makebelieve, when they saw on several benches the pink KKK leaflet, threatening all northern whites —all Yankees, telling them to mind their own business and go back where they came from.

The ride on this truck through the mountains and wide fields had a strange effect upon Helen: her sense of time seemed to have become confused. She saw in her mind scenes of early days with Art, but they were as real and fresh as if it were happening now . . . Holding hands with Art, and he holding her back from screaming when the elderly black woman stepped down into the street to allow her and Art to pass. She felt so humiliated, so ashamed that a black woman had to do such a thing—and Art, seeing her bewildered look, caught her hand and pulled her quickly away from that spot. "You have to be more careful, Helen, or we won't last here another day."

"But did you see that? I wouldn't have believed this was real if she hadn't stepped aside to let you and me pass! Why this is the worst thing that has happened to me since we got here!" But Art smiled reassuringly. "That's why we are here, to break down this savagery. But we have to have patience and do first things first." She understood; she knew what Art was saying. But last week, only last week, when Art wasn't by her side any more, when Art was thousands of miles away from her, perhaps in some distant land on the other side of the ocean, she saw before her eyes the very thing he had predicted would come to pass in the south.

It was in Richmond, Virginia, that late afternoon, when she and the other southern Hunger Marchers arrived from Alabama, Mississippi and Georgia, on their way to Washington.* They came to the center of the city, and there on the steps of the City Hall stood a chubby redheaded man of about thirty years of age, whom they called Bill; he was making a speech but he was also arguing with a representative of the Salvation Army and the Community Chest—he was shouting for all around him to hear him clearly: "Gentlemen, I appreciate your proposal very much; you can take care of the southern delegates marching to Washington, but on one condition—without segregation and discrimination. If you can find a way of putting them up in the same place then I'll accept your proposal." This redheaded Bill stopped long enough to catch his breath and then continued: "This is a united delegation, going to Washington as one group, not two groups; and we won't stand for separating the blacks from the whites, we can't accept any offers for lodgings and a meal on a segregated basis because the people won't stand for that nonsense any longer, and we, who are in charge here, won't either." There was loud applause from the hundreds of unemployed people around him.

"Sir, but Sir, this is the South! You can't change the South in one night. What you want, and what we want also, is to take care of these tired and hungry people until tomorrow morning. You want to see them off on their way to Washington, don't

* This incident took place a year later, Dec. 6, 1932.

228

you? But they won't be able to proceed without a rest and without some food in their stomachs."

"No, we want more than a rest and a meal: we want to see the whole damned system of Jim Crowism toppled, kicked over for good; we will not be a part of this business for 'whites only' for 'colored only'; we won't accept your lodgings and your blankets and your hot meals on your terms," and this fiery speaker waved his arms, shook a fist into the face of the Salvation Army spokesman, "the Hunger Marchers are staying together like this, like this," pointing to his closed fist, "and we'll return together like this," and loud applause rang out throughout the center of the city, and the next thing Helen's mind drifted to was her sitting right there, inside the Salvation Army building, blacks and whites together, sitting together at the same tables, eating their meal together, sleeping on the floor and on the benches and on the makeshift beds without separating one from the other—all equals—equals in everything.

"It was like a miracle before my own eyes," Helen said to her sister by her side.

"What'd you say, Helen? . . . a miracle? . . . I dozed off."

"Skip it, I must have talked in my sleep," Helen said with a smile.

And then her mind swung again, like a pendulum, sometimes to the distant past, to those precious moments with Art, and sometimes back to her present, to the reality of the moment. Now both she and her sister were fully awake.

"Remember the piece I sent you about the meeting that Art and I had arranged?"

"Sure I remember," Sylvia answered. "A lot of people have read that story, and a lot of people are beginning to understand better what goes on in the South."

Sylvia's admiration for both Art's and Helen's physical courage had risen high after reading that piece Helen referred to.

A SECRET MEETING IN THE PINES*

There was a yellow moon over the pines. We drove through twenty miles of ragged farms and woodland, always on the watch for the deputies. At last we came to a lonely tenant shack in the depths of the big plantation. And here some thirty men and women were

* By Mike Gold.

waiting. Negro farm workers whom the town organizer with us had assembled to form a new branch of the International Labor Defense.

A kerosene lamp and a lantern flickered. By its light I could see the dark, silent, solemn faces of the farm workers. Most were dressed in overalls, powerful, friendly giants with soft eyes. Some of the women were in their Sunday dresses. Outside the bare little shack, some of the workers were scattered along the road and in the woods. They were our guards.

These people, sunk in the backwoods of a southern state, listened to the organizer as to an emissary from another world. It was all new to them. But in this community, three Negroes were in jail on a framed-up murder charge. A young Negro farm girl had been half-beaten to death in the fields by the boss only a week ago. There was a daily crime by the masters against these workers.

I have never spoken at a meeting that touched me so. All the truths that we repeat so often, until sometimes they become routine, took on a new fresh meaning. When you said the word, "hunger," a deep sigh came from this group, and mournful Amens. When you spoke of freedom for black and white, the Amens came louder. Two women began to cry. As I spoke I felt like crying, too. Oh, how all the centuries of slavery our class has suffered pressed in upon me. How real it was in this backwoods shack, by the light of a kerosene lamp, with the moon over the pines outside the door, and the sheriffs around.

The organizer, a giant farmer about forty-five, marked in the community by the law as a known Red, but carrying on his job fearlessly, introduced another white comrade, a local farmer, and myself. Here is one of the phrases he used:

"You have known only white bosses. You have come to hate them, and rightly so. But these are a different sort of whites. You can trust these whites. You can come into their houses, and share everything. If you need a bed, you can share their bed. If you need food, take what is on their table, they are your comrades. This is what our movement means, the unity of black and white for the freedom of both.

"Yes, you don't know such white people, but your daddies must have told you about them. They are the same people who came down from the north in '61 to help free you from chattel slavery. They mean what they say, and in them there is the indisputable spirit of Jesus Christ."

A working man organizing an I.L.D. branch in the name of Jesus Christ!

"It was the same wherever we went—some black person had to introduce us to the others, or they wouldn't accept us. Whites just aren't trusted, I mean they weren't trusted 'till people like us came around. You can talk all you want about unity of

230

Negroes and whites, but it meant nothing until some black person like this Reverend Whitman would speak up for us. He was full of resentment about the kind of life his people had to live, and he poured out his resentment in song and prayer. He couldn't make a living from his small church; it was his wife's working as a domestic in a liberal publisher's home that kept the reverend alive. Reverend Whitman introduced us once to his small congregation, telling them that we were the kind of whites who could be trusted, and from then on we held our meetings there, and things began to ease up for us. Then the one branch of the Socialist Party in that city, which had been sitting on its fanny, doing nothing, while hunger was spreading—well some of them began to come around, and before I left most of their members were working with the unemployed and helping us get started on this Hunger March."

One of the phrases caught Sylvia's attention: it was Helen's reference to that liberal publisher's home, and the publisher's wife, which Sylvia suspected had something to do with Art's absences from home.

"Was that the same publisher you told me about last year?"

"The same, the same. That's how it first got started with Art, I mean his staying away. This publisher was friendly to our cause, and he invited us, all whites, to his house. He wanted to know us better, and he wanted to see if he could help us in some way. He and the mayor were feuding over something—I forget now what about—but this liberal editor wanted to strike back at the mayor in some way, and we took advantage of it. We asked him to publish our program in his newspaper, and he did. We demanded winter relief, free clothes for the unemployed, free rent and food."

"But his wife began to notice Art? And Art enjoyed her attentions?"

"Why do you bring that up now?" Helen answered sharply. She wanted to forget that particular episode which had brought her so much grief.

Then Sylvia heard her sister use the word "promiscuity."

"Art thought that when husband and wife had to be separated for long periods of time, it wasn't promiscuity if one of them, or both of them, took up with someone else, temporarily. He kept telling me that it was only a temporary arrangement, to satisfy their physical needs, and that there was nothing wrong in that, and that it was better than for them to go to a prostitution house."

"Oh, no, Helen!" Sylvia exclaimed. "You're not serious? Art couldn't have been serious when he told you that!" She was so shocked that she wished he had been there with them, on that open truck, so she could have given him arguments that came to her mind.

"Didn't you fight with him on things like that?" Sylvia asked in the hope that her own sister hadn't been converted to immorality.

"You don't fight with Art. The Waltons never fight among themselves, Art told me. They never shout at each other, or let off steam by cursing at each other, or by breaking dishes, like Pa did once when he got mad with Ma, remember? The middle class and the upper class, and the intellectuals, discuss politely, they 'intellectualize', he said—that was quite a word for me to catch, but I've used it a few times already. I had to do a lot of reading, and had to learn how to use his own words, because with Art it's a matter of who comes out on top with words, words. I could never get to a point where he'd argue with me with feelings, with anger. When he became disgusted with me, and didn't care to get into a verbal contest, he said: 'Helen, I won't be back tonight,' and walked out. Then I knew, I knew for the first time, that Art wasn't staying out for the night on account of the movement. I knew that Art was going somewhere to have fun, to forget everything, because there would be no fun for him that evening with me, in our rooming house."

Sylvia felt so betrayed—her god having fallen so low—that somehow the need to come to his rescue, at this moment, became more important to her than her sister's suffering.

"But you know, Helen, that a lot of us don't think it right for a revolutionary, I mean for one who gives his entire life to the movement, for such people to get married and raise families. If you're going to give your entire life to the movement then you must be free to do it. I always thought that way myself."

"You're trying to find an excuse for Art. It isn't that living with me was an obstacle. No. We worked together for quite a while, we planned our meetings, which were often in secret, just one step ahead of the KKK, and one step ahead of the lynchers. But Art isn't capable of deep emotions, he's not capable of working class loyalties, of family loyalties," Helen replied.

"Now don't go accusing Art of being anti-working class just because he fell out of love with you, Helen. That isn't fair, either. You've grown up so much in these couple of years that now I can say you ought to be more objective when you review Art's personality, and you ought to see him objectively when family and children are considered."

"Some day you'll fall in love with someone in the movement, and you'll talk differently. If he's a real revolutionary, he'll love you even better than the people outside the movement, because he'll know that you, too, are a dedicated person, and that makes people like us different. We are different. Everything has to have more meaning; our lives are more intense, more sincere, and more humanistic, as Art tried to explain to me. He often told me that we are the most humanistic people because we are leading this big movement in the country from which the whole nation will benefit, even if we, as individuals, will be victimized, and will suffer."

Helen stopped talking suddenly, and Sylvia could feel the chill that had gone through Helen's body. She shivered lightly, and pulled the blanket over her mouth, as if trying to keep the cold air out. Sylvia waited, saying nothing. Helen resumed talking.

"But Art is honest; it was wrong for me to call him a fake. He's honest. He believes certain things very strongly, and he tries to get to the truth, like a thirsty man tries to get to water. But he's empty inside. I don't think he was ever really happy, with me, or with Kikki."

"What do you mean, 'or with Kikki?' " Sylvia asked in astonishment.

"He told me everything—that's why I say he's honest. He told me that when Fred—by the way, do you ever see Fred?"

"Yes, yes, I do. I'll tell you later about him. But what about Kikki? I don't get you."

"Well, it happened when Fred was away for a few days, in Pittsburgh, to some conference of metal workers or machinists, I don't remember which; there was a meeting of some kind for people who were planning to go into basic industry, to help build industrial unions. Well, he was away, and during that week-end, Art and Kikki . . . well, anyway, that's why I didn't like the way they acted when Art saw Kikki again at our Club. I could tell then that they weren't just friends. But it was all over between them, and Fred will never know about this because Kikki will never tell him."

"Why did he tell you all this, after denying that there was anything between him and Kikki? He didn't have to, did he? It was all over, and you were thousands of miles away from Chicago."

"That's just it: he's like a little boy sometimes. He seemed to want to win me over by telling me everything, like he was afraid to keep anything to himself; like he needed to be on the level with me about Kikki, too, and he said that he felt like a liberated man after telling me about her. You never saw anybody like him, Sylvia. Never! I think that was the only time I really felt I loved him: that was the time I would have done anything for Art, because of the way he treated me from then on, the way he told it to me, like he was a saint. Oh, I don't mean it in a bad way. It's just that he had to make a full confession to me, because if he didn't then I wouldn't be the saint any more in his eyes, if you know what I mean! But he was really a torn person, he was what I'd call infatuated with the working class, but he never understood working people's life; and he was infatuated with me, but never in love with me, because he doesn't know how to love. He never grew up emotionally; he's a big man, all grown up in body, but inside there's an empty, little soul, looking for a place to settle down, and Art can't find a place where to put his little soul down, because Art can't find himself."

Sylvia was completely overwhelmed at her sister's ability to verbalize such thoughts. Since her association with Art, Sylvia noticed, her sister had stopped referring to herself as an uneducated shop girl; and the last time they met in Chicago, Sylvia remembered her sister welcoming "stretching the brain," as she called a deep discussion. Now Helen spoke with ease: words came freely to her, the language she used was so different, so much like Art's, that Sylvia wanted her to go on talking.

"Art should have stayed with his crowd, with the Kikkis, and his music friends, and his university friends. With them he's a different man, I know that now. How I know that! The way he tried to make himself into something else, by making me, too, look in his eyes like someone else, someone I just wasn't. I'm the girl he was supposed to have been looking for all his life but before he shipped out we talked about this, and we both agreed that I am not that girl at all. He admitted that he had to get away from everything; that he had to find ways of taking care of himself without anybody's help. That's true. He suffered a lot; the two of us have gone hungry many times, but he never complained, and wouldn't complain now either, no matter how difficult life might be for him. He doesn't complain about anything. He thinks it's a weakness for a revolutionist to complain. I don't agree with him. I think it's petty-bourgeois to hide one's pains and suffering."

"You think something went wrong with him after his father committed suicide?" Sylvia asked.

She knew Art only from a distance, as an impressive speaker and lecturer, as the good looking teacher who fell in love with her sister and then "eloped" with her to work in the most dangerous revolutionary activity in the country. But Sylvia had never been in close contact with people from the other classes; now she had an opportunity to study Art and his family through her sister's eyes. She wondered, however, if Helen was capable of analyzing them objectively, especially now, when she was still so close in her thoughts to Art. Perhaps Helen's vision was as limited as her own, Sylvia thought. Both girls knew people who were poor, and their judgment was based on the relationships of the poor. She had seen how the illness of a member of the Kanofsky family became the concern of all; how the loss of a job for someone, especially since the Great Depression, had suddenly become a tragedy for all the relatives. Do people from the other classes also have such deep feelings of concern, such attachments, she wondered.

"Do you think Art was very much attached to his Dad, and since his death became . . ."

"No, no! You got something wrong there, Sylvia. Art wasn't attached to anybody. He doesn't know how. Maybe the closest one to him is the 'Dutchess', his sister. That's because she's so much like him—but Art has the movement, while the 'Dutchess' has nothing. Art had both his feet in the Walton setup, in the Walton life, as he was growing up, and studying, and later teaching. He never had to think about food, clothes, money—it was always there. He had everything he needed. When he decided to go to the South, and work there for the movement, he left one foot in the Walton family, and took the other foot to the Black Belt."

"I don't get you."

"I know it's hard, it's hard to understand this. He doesn't understand it himself, but I think that Art had everything he needed when he went south; you know we drove there in a good Model A Ford; he had good clothes and shoes and underwear. But that isn't it! He still had the Waltons at home, especially the 'Dutchess'. He never had to worry, like we did, when Pa cut his finger and couldn't go to work, and Ma had to take in the tobacco leaves to strip for him, if you know what I mean, what I'm driving at. We were poor all our life, and when Pa made a week's pay, he would invite someone from the synagogue to come home with him for a meal on Friday night, or Saturday, like it was a sin to enjoy a good meal while someone else was going hungry. But Art must have always felt that he could go back up north, to his secure Walton home, and always be welcomed. Maybe they would kid him a little about taking up with the radicals, and with a Jewish girl, but they were there, always there; and the big house, and the good income, the full closets of expensive clothes, and Thela Walton, with her expensive jewelry, you know what I'm saying, Syl?"

Sylvia followed her logic, her study of the man Art Walton, who at one time was high on her list of living gods. Again she was amazed at the interpretations Helen had made about his behavior. She was amazed at the ease with which she now spoke about Art, without any bitterness.

"The mind can register some things, but that doesn't mean that the heart also grasps them. Remember when I told Ma and Pa what had happened when the goons beat us up in front of my shop, as we were giving out a union leaflet? We didn't know whether it was the boss who sent them, or the union bureaucrats, or both; and Pa caught that point right away, and said it made no difference: a beating is a beating. But at the same time he asked me—remember you were paper-hanging the wall in the bedroom, and you got off the ladder and came in when Pa asked: 'Of all the thousands of people in Chicago you had to be the one to lose your job, Helen?' He didn't want to sound like he was bawling me out, or telling me that there would be no income at all; Pa was also out of work, remember? But I told him that I wasn't the only one who was trying to get a good union in my shop; that quite a number of us were fighting for better conditions. Remember how he asked me what it was we were fighting for, and when I told him we wanted the hours cut down to eight a day, and to get overtime pay for everything over eight hours, and that those of us who had been on the job a year or more should get a paid vacation, he thought it was a good idea. But then I remember that when I told him that we also wanted the company to pay for loss of time in case of some accident, he said that was the best thing we could do. But that isn't really what I'm driving at, Syl. When I told Pa that I'm young now and can take this beating, but that when I get older I will want to be able to work in the shop under better conditions than we have now, because we have to look ahead, he understood it real quick. He had no illusions about me getting rich some day, or something happening to him that would make him rich, see? And Pa liked the idea that what I was doing now would help me when I got to be his age. You know what I mean, Syl? But Art never got that point, never! When he was telling his friends about the beatings we took from the goons or the police—I remember we were sitting in Kikki's apartment that Sunday evening, and he was showing off with me—and you know what I thought his friends were doing? I thought they were looking at my finger nails, and I put my hands in back of me, like I was ashamed of them. Later I thought they were all watching my manners, how I was eating the refreshments that Kikki was serving. I know, I know that I was very self-conscious, but don't you see, I didn't feel that I belonged with those people. But Art did belong with them. He was one of them; Kikki and Fred belonged, but not me. I couldn't tell Art's friends that I wasn't ashamed about being kicked out by the Amalgamated Clothing Union."

"But you said youself that the conditions in the open shops were one hundred percent worse than in the Amalgamated shops; so maybe . . ."

"Maybe nothing!" Helen suddenly came to life, the same Helen whom Sylvia had always admired, and now loved even more; now that Helen was back in her old fighting mood.

"When they kicked me out of the union that made me even more militant. The nerve, the audacity! Taking the bread and butter away from me! I was mad all right. But when the few of us got into that unorganized, open shop, I tell you, in a few months we had the place cleaned up; I mean, we made the boss get a sweeper through that shop twice a day to pick up all that stuff from under our feet, and we made him put window shades on those hot windows. Don't you see, the boss was afraid of getting a union into his shop, so he made a lot of concessions to our rank and file committee. I learned a lot of things about unionism in the Amalgamated shop, that's true, even though they kicked me out—oh, what the hell!" She stopped good naturedly, tired of it all.

After a while Helen returned to the scene in Kikki's home, and once again used words that Sylvia had never heard in Helen's speech. "Art idolized me for all those struggles I was involved in. But what about the others who fought with me, the other girls from the T.U.U.L.? Some of them were my girl friends, like Minnie. Well, he had no use for the others, he didn't even want to meet them socially. Now I understand: he was infatuated with the working class, I mean with the image, or picture of the working class, but for his steady diet he ran to his middle class friends. And don't get me wrong, Sylvia, I don't think there's anything wrong with him going to his friends, to those professional people, and there's nothing wrong with him inviting someone in, to talk to them about dialectical-materialism—they liked it all, they ate it up. But you know, when I look back a couple of years, I can see now that Art and his crowd must have believed that we were in a revolutionary situation in this country, and they wanted to be on the right side of the revolution—now don't laugh! A lot of people I've met in our movement think that way, even now. They see the Reds leading all those big movements of the unemployed, and organizing militant caucuses in the basic industries, and leading so many important strikes, and now we're getting very close to the Negro people of this country, with the Scottsboro case helping us expose this whole system of frame-ups and racism—you know what I mean? It looks like a revolutionary situation because so much is going on, but we really don't have a revolutionary situation in the country. We have a big upheaval, like a rebellion against so much suffering in the midst of so much wealth, but we are far from a revolutionary situation."

"What about Art? Do you think that he, too, joined up for that reason?"

"Well, Art's going to the Black Belt, soon after he joined the movement, was something like people of comfort going slumming in the poor neighborhoods. And he knew it later, later when he got there. He felt it that way. That's why I say Art is an honest fellow, but he can never get close to those tenant farmers and understand their life. He found out in the South what courage really meant. But that, too, he saw in an abstract way, because he still had the Waltons up north in the comfortable home in Chicago; sure he respected that courage, but it wasn't part of him, if you know what I mean. I, too, began to see the difference between being beat up on a picket line and those black people being lynched or killed when they tried to change the situation."

"Was it part of you?" Sylvia asked.

Helen looked her kid sister in the face with eyes full of love. She always admired Sylvia for her ability to generalize and come up with theoretical implications. But now Sylvia was down to earth, and asking her something that she had asked herself during those lonely hours when Art had left her alone.

"I don't know, Sylvia, if I was part of what I saw in the South. I never before knew that there was so much suffering, so much backwardness. There's so much terror going on there against the people, every day, every night; and for a while we became part of it, and part of the black people of the South, and I never knew that there were so many people in my own country who had so much courage. It opened up my eyes to a lot of things. I remember how I felt when a black woman once took my hand at a meeting, and introduced me to the others: 'This is Sister Helen, she came here to help us. We can trust her.' Never in my life did I feel so proud, and good inside: they accepted me as their equal, you know what I mean? That's the time I felt a part of it all. I was one with the black people in that room."

"But you don't think Art was ever one with them, as you put it?"

"That, too, I asked myself many times. I don't think he fitted in for that kind of work. That's why he'd go off and look for some woman, for someone who was a little closer to his way of thinking, I mean closer to his own background. And when he was criticized for his behavior, in our closed meetings, and told that his political work would suffer if his personal life didn't get straightened out, he agreed."

"You mean others knew that he was carrying on with somebody else?" Sylvia asked in astonishment.

"Others always know. When one does important political work like we were doing there, everything was important: your personal behavior, your attitude to your wife, or to other men's wives. People thought I was Art's wife, and they treated me that way, and when Art failed to draw me into the work—and then left me behind so much—the others began to question him about that, too. You can't lead a double life and get away with it for too long—not in a movement like ours. But the more disappointed I became, the harder he tried to impress me with how much he loved me, and how he couldn't get along without me, and what I had done for him since we'd met. I believe that, too, Sylvia." Helen stopped for a moment, and Sylvia knew she was getting ready to tell her something even more important and she wanted her full attention.

"You know what he said when we talked about this the last time? 'You're emotionally involved with the working class, and you became emotionally involved with the black people here.' You see what I mean that he intellectualized this whole thing. Sure I was emotionally involved when I found out that nobody down there, not among those people I met with, had a home like we have on Potomac Avenue. We say it's a poor man's home that we live in, but to the black people I've met it would be like living in a palace. I talked with young men and women about your age, and I tell you, Sylvia, I felt like crying when I found out that they had no education, or a couple years of education that meant nothing, absolutely nothing. I started teaching them, and had three classes going: two for the young ones and one for the older. Can you imagine me teaching others! Art could have been a better teacher, you might say, but that isn't the way it came out. They didn't feel comfortable with him, he told me. He knew it."

"But with you they did?"

"Sure they did. Only somehow I always felt like crying inside each time they sat down by that kerosene lamp to learn from me how to put letters together and make words out of those letters, and then, later, having the same people writing a leaflet with me."

240

Sylvia kept thinking that she had something to tell Helen, but she couldn't remember just what it was; it was very annoying. During the ensuing silence, she suddenly recalled—

"Yes, that's what Fred once said; now I remember, you reminded me. He said he feels comfortable with the men in the shop. He got married, of course, and moved into Kikki's place. But he's been working all this time in a machine shop where he says he's learning something new every day, and he's becoming a skilled man. Maybe Art should have gone with him into that shop instead of to the Black Belt? You said Art told you how Fred begged him to do that."

"He did, he did. Art is so honest with himself. . . ."

"You keep saying that over and over. If you think he's so honest, and you understand him so much, why didn't you stay with him, and help him? Like you say yourself, help him find himself. To me it looks like you've outgrown him in many ways. Honestly, Helen, there was a time when you and I couldn't talk like this. But look what happened to you. I don't recognize you—I don't mean the way you look, sure you look terrible, just terrible! But that isn't so serious. After we stay home for a few months you'll become your old self again. But I mean you're so different now, Helen, you should have tried to help Art more."

"No, you don't understand, Syl. It wasn't a matter of helping him find himself. After his Dad committed suicide, Art became another kind of man than the one I first met. Can't you see what I've been trying to tell you? His foundation collapsed, it fell in, because his other foot that he had in the Walton family couldn't remain there any longer. The Waltons were busted, wiped out. His father, too, couldn't face up to it, when the crash came, and Mr. Walton and so many of the others like him began jumping out of their high apartment windows. And now Art had nothing to return to ever, ever. They took away the Walton home, he found out, and all the belongings, and jewelry, and everything that Mrs. Walton and the 'Dutchess' ever had in valuables was gone. You see, everything collapsed for all the Waltons, and Art is a true Walton, and he couldn't get adjusted to living the way the Kanofskys have lived most of our life. It isn't the lack of food I'm talking about. Art tried to become someone other than Art Walton after the Big Crash, but he couldn't make it."

There were fragments of ideas in Helen's mind that were suspended—they had no place to go. She could not do anything with them to fit them into a total picture. But they were there, bothering her. In the long silence between the two sisters Helen lingered on those fragments . . . he wasn't trusted by the Chicago stockyards men, but neither was he really trusted by the southern black people . . . he was sharp intellectually, keen, even when people disagreed with him; he had no qualms about how the people felt . . . but now he was cut off somehow from both the whites, who kept criticizing him, and the Negroes, who couldn't understand him, and wouldn't accept him.

Helen seemed to have reached a conclusion, and, without telling her sister what had brought her to that point, blurted out: "Don't you see what happened? He was forced to turn himself inward: he has begun to question a lot of the things that he had accepted before; but he doesn't any longer have the confidence he had when he was in Chicago, teaching those kids in the South Side School, so he ships out to sea where he'll be looking for new meanings to all these things that he couldn't handle. He doesn't really know what he's looking for, Sylvia, but he has to get out of all these pressures—he couldn't take them any longer."

"Where did he go?" Sylvia asked. She was beginning to share her sister's disenchantment with one of her idols.

"He got on a ship which isn't coming back for many months, maybe five or six months. He said he was going to start from the very bottom, shoveling coal into the furnace, or whatever you call that thing down there below. Then, he said, he'll ship out again, but he'll come to Chicago to see me."

"You want to see him when he comes back?"

"Not really! Sure, I'll see him if he calls, but I don't believe he will even come back to Chicago."

"You mean you're really not in love with Art any more? This is what you've been saying all along—are you on the level with me, or with yourself?"

"You don't understand, Syl. I don't think I'll ever love anybody else. I don't think I want to. But I have to forget Art, get him out of my mind. I keep feeling that I, too, got emptied out inside, and now I have to fill up again. I keep thinking of Ma and Pa, all this time as we get closer to home. It's strange, Sylvia, that I should keep thinking of them so much—they're so different from us, so backward, but you know, I really think the future world will be made up of people who'll be very much like them, like Ma and Pa, unselfish. That's the main thing, unselfish."

This new idea that her sister threw at her suddenly confused Sylvia. She tried not to dwell on it in her own mind, and she quickly dismissed it with the explanation that Helen was lonely, just plain lonely, and the Kanofsky home now looked to Helen like a heaven. Later she'd see her parents more objectively, and maybe she'll see Art, too, more objectively, Sylvia thought.

"What do you want to do when we get to Chicago? Have you thought about that at all?" Sylvia asked.

"Sure I've thought about it. Lots of times. I'd like to get back to a shop, if I could find one that's hiring. I'd like to find work with black women, where they have many black women . . ." But Helen had in mind to talk about something else that interested her more.

"What about you, Sylvia? Have you given up school altogether? Or do you think you might go back for a few semesters?"

Sylvia laughed aloud: it all sounded so strange to her. "Where did you get an idea like that? I'm almost twenty years old," and again she laughed. "If you hadn't returned with me to Chicago, I was going to move in with Betty. She took a small flat on North Halsted Street, and asked me if I'd share it with her."

"Betty? Who are you talking about now? Betty who?"

"Molly's cousin; you remember Betty Dunhill from the farm. She's back in Chicago; their farm is gone, her father is gone—I don't mean dead, he's just gone."

"Is she still beautiful?"

"Not the way she looked when we graduated, but she's a very pretty girl, husky like, got into the bacon department at Swift's. Mirko helped her get in." After some hesitation she added: "I think she fell for Mirko. But I forgot, you never met him. Well, he helped her get that job and now she thinks he's the cat's meow. But let's stop talking, please. I'm so sleepy."

"Well, you're doing all the talking; I was almost asleep when you came up with that Betty piece," Helen said, which reminded Sylvia of old times, when the two sisters used to argue over such things. She leaned over, kissed Helen, and pulled the blanket to her chin.

243

Helen, fully awake and exhilarated, was thinking about her reunion with her parents. "I'll tell them that maybe soon we'll be getting social security in this country, and then Pa will be able to retire and collect something—if that bill gets introduced and passed. That's why we went to Washington on this Hunger March, I'll tell them," she rehearsed to herself. "Pa seems to understand better than Ma about what we're doing, but that's natural; even if he doesn't go to union meetings, he likes to talk about Samuel Gompers, and remind you that Gompers was a cigar maker, too, like himself." And Helen was visualizing how Ma would be listening quietly, and then she'd repeat some of the things that their father would say, and put it in her own words, her own way. "Ma was always jealous in that way, but she shouldn't have been. I think we love her in one way, and Pa in another way, just like I'll always love Art. . . . I don't care where he ships to, and what he does in those ports. Art will always, always, always . . ." Helen dozed off and snuggled up closer to her sister, and she imagined, or was she dreaming? that she was on their back porch, in Pa's "factory" and Pa was telling her: "It's not cold here, not since we put this little stove in here; that was Ma's idea. We put an extension through the pantry window to the back porch, and now we have this little heater; come, I'll show you, and now I can work even when it gets very cold, cold, cold. . . ."

Everybody suddenly seemed to have become restless and wide awake—they hit a pocket of cold air, and their covers weren't sufficient to protect them.

"We're stopping for coffee on the other side of the road," the driver shouted through the little window in back of him. They were told that an Unemployed Council was waiting for them to feed them, and now the Hunger Marchers became talkative and cheerful. In all major cities they were met by large delegations of unemployed and part-time workers to whom they made reports. Daylight was breaking through; they stood up on the truck, and rode in singing.

III

Before leaving for Washington, to join the Hunger Marchers, Mirko sent a hastily scribbled note to his sister telling her that most of the students were heading for the capital, and that he would return home with the Illinois-Indiana contingent. He also wrote: "Don't be surprised if soon there will be another Yanich in the family."

Kate was not surprised. In a previous letter Mirko had spoken more seriously about Chris, hinting that he had fallen in love with her, and that some day he hoped Kate would acquire a sister.

The idea that Chris might soon be joining the Yanich clan threw the young governess into a complete tailspin. She had met the lanky redhead only once, but Kate remembered very clearly Chris' composure and calm, and the sense of reality she had brought into their household when they returned from the cemetery, after burying Ma Yanich. Chris stayed close to her the rest of the afternoon, and before leaving for Omaha she hugged the broken-hearted Kate, and reassured her, and made her feel grown-up, and made her promise to act like a Yanich woman was expected to act—with courage and fortitude. She often thought about that, and ever since receiving Mirko's note she had been in a state of suspended excitement.

Mirko, returning to his sprawling cold-water flat, expected to find his sister, but instead saw a note pasted on the door: "Call me at Madeline's."

"What the hell is she doing at Madeline's? Has she lost her job?" he asked himself. On entering the house he immediately noticed the starched lace curtains in the living room, draped gracefully over the windows which had been naked for months.

"I bet I know where they came from," he said half aloud. "Kate's been stealing again. But why is she at Madeline's?"

He continued to stare at the other changes in his home, and upon entering the bedroom that belonged to his mother he found a penciled sign, pasted on the mirror of the dresser: "WELCOME HOME!" The room was spotless, freshly cleaned, and fully made up. The dresser was covered with a colorful narrow runner of rich quality, and a matching doily was pinned to the head of his mother's rocking chair. On a small table near the bed, on which there used to be a night lamp, there now stood a tall, wide vase, filled with artificial flowers, and evidently sprayed with an expensive perfume, emitting an aroma of a rich flower garden to all parts of the house.

"I'll be goddamned!" Mirko said, as he put his hands in his pockets and leaned his thin body against the wall. He studied

245

again each detail, each tiny change that Kate had made in the musty, sickly room and wondered whether Kate had taken the expensive vase and all the other items from her employer. He recognized only the white linen spread, covering the double bed, the traditional family heirloom that had been handed down for several generations to the newlyweds.

The kitchen, too, had been scrubbed and cleaned, and it displayed new short curtains over the sink windows, with bows on both sides. Another sign in Kate's handwriting, "WEL-COME", was spread on the large, round table, and Mirko began to put the story together, and began to realize that this was all done in anticipation of the arrival of a new Yanich.

"But what is she doing at Madeline's?" he kept saying to himself, and when he telephoned her later, the story was completed for him by Kate.

". . . then the gardener caught me carrying a small painting that I found in their basement among dozens of other valuable paintings. He reported me and I got fired. But I already had all the other things in the house, so I didn't care much. Did you like the bedroom drapes?" Kate asked casually, as if she had gone out and selected exactly what she thought her brother would have chosen himself.

"Then you're not working any more as a governess?"

"No. Madeline got me a part-time job in her office. Three days a week."

"You moved in with Madeline?" Mirko asked.

"No, I have my own place. Not much, but it's cheap. You know where Leavitt Street is? Between Robey and Western?"

"Never heard of Leavitt Street," he replied. "Why did you move out in such a hurry? Why didn't you wait till I came back?"

"You kidding? You think I want Chris to find me in HER home?" Kate told her brother.

"Chris isn't here, she's in Omaha."

"How come?"

"She had to go back home for a while, and find a replacement. You shouldn't have moved out, Kate. You and Chris will get along well. You ought to come back home, and use your own room. The place is too empty with you gone, and nobody using Nick's room." He waited for her reply and when Kate made it clear she had moved out for good, he asked:

"Do you like it there on Leavitt Street? Where about is it?"

"It's near North Avenue. I like it all right," Kate said, and she did not tell her brother that the first week she moved into her furnished room, she had lived through one of the most terrorizing experiences in her young life.

She had never before known what real fear, physical fear, meant. The Yaniches were not a fearful crowd. Like the others, Kate was indifferent to personal danger, because she was unaware of its existence—till she moved to her furnished room, with that elderly couple.

Wishing to maintain an appearance of sophistication and self-sufficiency, she did not ask anyone to take her home that particular late evening when the big unemployed rally at the Ashland Auditorium adjourned. She hadn't realized yet that it was not very smart for a young woman to be walking the streets alone, after getting off the street car.

In the year 1931 Chicago enjoyed a worldwide notoriety—lawlessness, gangster domination, vice, graft and corruption—all were of staggering proportions. The newspapers carried numerous accounts of holdups, robberies, and attacks on women in various parts of the city.

Kate, however, never read that part of the news, and this was, in fact, the very first time in her life that she found herself going home alone at such a late hour. In back of the yards it was different. There was always someone to walk her home. But here, as she got off at the Robey Street stop, she suddenly found herself walking towards her new home on a totally dark block, and just as suddenly she became aware that it was a deserted block, that not a living soul was anywhere in sight, either on the street or in the unlit homes.

The drug store was already closed for the night, and when she automatically turned her head in that direction she noticed a parked car with several occupants in it. She continued walking in her even stride, but soon the car caught up with her, and, like the confident cat that is sure the little mouse is trapped, but still wishing to tease and play a while before making the catch, the car slowed down a few paces and let Kate get ahead. Then it speeded up and raced three or four houses in front of her.

Kate had made the mistake of walking on the wrong side of the street, where the deserted churchyard with the broken-down fence was situated, instead of walking on the side where there were homes, and people inside those homes, and doors and windows, and where a young girl in trouble could scream for help.

At last the car caught up level with her—she was trapped. Maintaining her calm, Kate pretended that she was about to get into their car, but instead—in a flash—she raced across to the other side of the street and with lightning speed ran through a narrow passage to the rear of one of those homes, up a flight of stairs, where she grabbed hold of a knob to a door, ready to bang on the door and to scream for help.

It all happened so fast, and Kate had disappeared from the sight of her pursuers into the dark passage so quickly, that she confused them, making them think that she had entered her own home, and had outsmarted them.

Kate held her breath and waited on that back porch in frozen fear, while she continued gripping the knob in her hand till she heard the car's motor again and heard it drive off. Then, cautiously, on tip toe, she walked down the unfamiliar rear staircase of this strange home, and began to run the remaining distance to her furnished room, a block away.

She told no one about that incident, and attempted to forget it all as one tries to forget a weird nightmare. But now, talking to her brother, answering his questions about her moving out, she thought that if he insisted that she move back home, and if he sounded sincere about it, she might do just that. But Mirko's voice didn't sound right to her. She knew that the tradition of the Yaniches would be continued, and Mirko would have his own home, to himself, when his future wife would join him.

She wasn't going to tell him about her new life, anyway—only that Zal Harris was in Chicago not long ago, looking for him, for Mirko, the very day she was moving out of the Yanich home. Kate gave her brother only a few of the bare details . . . she was alone in the big flat, packing her suitcase, when she heard a knock on the door. Those wonderful few moments now flashed through her mind.

"Come in," she remembered saying without looking up.

Zal walked in and softly closed the door behind him. He was in the same living room where he had been once before, about two years ago; and he now saw the same girl, packing a suitcase.

"Hi, Kate! Remember me?" he asked and waited for her

248

reply without moving away from the door. For a split second Kate thought she saw a vision—the same boy, without cap or hat, his dreamy brown eyes smiling—exactly as she always remembered Zal.

Yet, as she continued to stare at her unexpected visitor, she realized that before her stood not the mischievous boy of so long ago, but a man with a serious face, a little heavier and bigger, with his thick sweater buttoned to his chin to protect himself from the cold bite of Chicago's early frost. She extended her hand and motioned him to be seated.

"Sure I remember you, Zal. I'm glad to see you again; but Mirko isn't home. He won't be back till early next month, when the Hunger Marchers return from Washington."

"I know. Chris wrote that school will be out soon and that most of them are going to Washington before returning home."

"Is that all she said?" Kate asked cautiously.

Zal smiled at the worried girl, but answered seriously: "She told me about Mirko. I'm glad they're planning to get married soon."

"But you don't sound like you're glad," she said softly.

"I don't?" he asked indifferently, and suddenly dropped the subject.

"Say, are you going on a trip, or something?" he asked.

Before receiving an answer, he continued: "I would have recognized you anywhere in a crowd, but there's something . . . say, didn't you . . . of course, you cut off your long braids, but you still have the bangs," and this time he laughed heartily, loud. "How's that for remembering a girl's looks all this time? You must be eighteen now, right?" As he asked that question he realized that he was talking to a mature young woman, and that she probably did not appreciate being teased about her age or looks.

"Yes, I had my eighteenth birthday the same week I lost my governess job. But starting Monday I'll be working again. Remember Madeline? She took me into her office, three days a week. I'll be making almost twice as much as working as a governess."

As she talked on quietly, in a soft, pleasant feminine voice, Zal became even more aware that Mirko's kid sister was pretty, and had a mind of her own, and was able to look after herself. He now wondered if she shared Mirko's views, and whether

249

she knew that there was a very important event taking place in Chicago—radicals from the entire midwest coming together to talk about whom to run for president in the 1932 elections. That's why he had come to Chicago.

She asked him again: "Do you remember Madeline?"

"Sure I remember her. I thought she and Mirko were . . ."

"Were friends?" Kate helped him. "They were very good friends, but Mirko found too much fault with her. He was too critical of her. He'd tell me some things about Madeline that I didn't think were particularly bad, but he . . . I could see that he was building up a case against her. She and I are very good friends."

"Does she know about Chris?"

"Sure! I told her as soon as I received Mirko's letters. I don't think Mirko was ever in love with Madeline, in the first place, and Madeline is kinda glad that Mirko and Chris found each other again at the school."

"What do you mean? Were they looking for each other?" Zal asked.

"In a way I think they were. You know how it is sometimes, when two people meet, for a short time, and they don't know too much about each other but they wish they did. Without thinking about it, or talking to anyone about it, it seems they would like to meet again so badly that somehow they actually meet. That's what happened to Mirko."

"You sound like you believe in fate, that they were bound to meet again."

"Not that way—I don't believe in fate just like that. But take Mirko, for instance. He lost interest in Madeline, but he couldn't tell you why. And he drifted away from her. Madeline knew it all the time, and that's where I agree with my brother: Madeline looks out for Madeline. She wasn't going to sit around and wait till Mirko would get disillusioned with someone else, and come back to her later. She's too practical for that. . . ." But Kate suddenly felt that she had talked too much, and to a stranger at that, because she barely knew this man who had just walked in on her.

"I don't know why all this talk about Madeline and Mirko," she said. "Are you planning to wait for Mirko?"

"I took a chance that he'd be home ahead of the others. But I have to stay over a while anyway and get my teeth fixed. I

250

remembered Mirko telling me that there were some good dentists here who were willing to help out people like me, I mean the full-timers, who can't afford to pay."

"Are you a full-timer?" she asked.

"Haven't been back in the plant since I got kicked out, but I've been plenty busy."

"You're working full-time for the Movement then?" Kate asked.

"Yes, and Chris' leaving us is going to make it tough on us."

"You knew that she was going to leave Omaha?"

"Sure, we knew. She wrote us that when she returns from school she'll be staying in Omaha only a short while because she's planning to get married to a Chicago man. She made a PS to me, asking me if I remembered a guy by the name of Mirko Yanich. She had forgotten that I introduced her to him. I don't see much good in her working in Omaha and Mirko working in Chicago. She won't be good to us there. I know that girl."

"Are you still in love with her?" Kate asked naturally, in a matter-of-fact tone. Yet Zal had noticed that her interest in his answer was not casual. He looked at her this time, with his old twinkle in his eye, which had confused her once before. But now she didn't drop her eyes.

"No, Kate, I'm not in love with Chris. I don't think that I really ever was. Now I can say it, but not two or three years ago. At nineteen or twenty you think differently than at twenty-three."

Kate smiled, and again Zal noticed the big change that had taken place in her: it was the smile of a mature young woman, who understood very much, but, who was not ready to reveal that understanding. She seemed to have a need to keep in reserve her reactions, he thought. Zal liked that. It was so different from Chris' artificial aloofness.

Now he felt that Kate was observing him, studying him, taking mental note of the many things he had said, without pursuing the point. He also recognized that Kate's reserve would some day break down, and perhaps become something else, if it were not abused. He was older than she, experienced with girls, and appreciative of her simple coquettishness.

"Someone going to move you?" Zal asked, after Kate explained the importance of leaving the newlyweds alone.

"No, I was going by street car. This isn't too heavy. I'll have to come back for the other things some other time."

"I can take you to your new place, if you want. Your valise will fit into the rumble seat," Zal said, pointing to the partly packed suitcase. "You can take along some more things in a box, or bag, if you wish."

She hesitated to let him see the "furnished room" she had rented, her new home. It was an old, run-down building, also a cold-water flat; and she wasn't sure that Zal ought to accompany her into this new place the very first time she was bringing in her personal things.

"We won't stay there; we'll just drop off the stuff. Then I, too, have to go to this meeting you mentioned," Kate said.

"See, and you said you didn't believe in fate. I do! Now you can show me how to drive to the place, and then how to get to the meeting."

He helped her pack her books, and urged her to put more things into the suitcase as Kate was emptying her closet and stuffing things so tight that both of them had to tie up the suitcase and boxes with strings.

"We can't eat here," Kate said after a while. "I got everything cleaned up and fixed for Mirko and Chris, in case she came back with him. And there isn't a crumb in the house."

She was cheerful now, having forgotten that only about an hour ago she was sitting there alone, reminiscing, and even trying to work up some tears over leaving her home—for good.

"I know where we can have a full-course meal for 40 cents, the whole works. It's not too far from the Ashland," she added.

"That suits me fine, but what are we going to use for money? I came here looking for a meal, not for Mirko. I knew he was still in New York," Zal said laughing guiltily, and yet seriously telling her that he was broke.

"Don't worry. I couldn't steal anything really worthwhile from that rich family, but I saved every penny I could, and I have a few dollars left after paying rent for the month. Tonight let's celebrate Mirko's engagement to Chris, and it's on me!"

"I don't object, gal! I'll eat everything they give me on that dinner!" Zal said, and he picked up the heavy suitcase in one hand, and a box of books in the other, and started towards the door.

"Wait a minute. Just another minute. I want to show you

what I TOOK home," Kate said, emphasizing the word TOOK to make it clear that in her own mind those things belonged in the Yanich home as much as in her former employer's home. When she opened the door to her parents' bedroom, Zal stood back and asked:

"Won't those flowers wilt by the time they come here from Washington?"

"Nope! They're artificial, and that's the most expensive perfume on the market that you're smelling now. I have a few more drops left which I'll spray a day or two before Chris comes here."

Then they hurried out of the house, and towards Kate's furnished room, where they threw her things in, and hurried again towards the Ashland Auditorium. But as they crossed Division Street the old jalopy conked out, and they had to abandon it temporarily.

They boarded a Robey Street car that was still in motion, holding hands and laughing; Zal went ahead as Kate paid the fourteen cents and asked for two transfers.

"You shouldn't have paid," he said after they sat down.

"Well, I didn't see you pay, and we need transfers on the Van Buren car."

"In Omaha we ride the street cars, and some of the buses, without paying. Sometimes the conductor, or driver, doesn't want to bother calling the police to throw us off, so they leave us alone. We get away with it most of the time. If they call the police, we disappear, to avoid arrest."

"They've been doing this here for some time, too. I've been in a couple of those 'free trips' but we can't do it when there's only two of us. We need a large group to make it effective."

"It doesn't hurt trying it in pairs, or even alone, like we do at home, and we tell the conductor to collect the fare from the mayor. That's what we say in Nebraska."

"We say 'charge it to the governor!' I wonder why the governor?" Kate asked.

"Sometimes we, too, tell the conductor to charge it to the governor. The main thing is to refuse to pay the fare, on a large scale, all over the city and state," Zal added.

They sat snuggled close, discussing the benefits of those free rides, and Kate was questioning whether the people really learned anything from such actions, whether that wasn't anarchy, learning nothing important; but they reached no conclusions by the time they got off to make the transfer.

"Let's get that supper you promised me, before we go inside the hall," Zal said, expecting to eat his first meal of the day.

"But we'll be late. Shouldn't we go in first and see if we have time?"

"No, we shouldn't! We'll eat first," Zal replied firmly, and Kate understood by his tone that the meal was more important than anything else.

Mirko was drawn into the raging storm of the new year immediately after his return from Washington. Wherever he turned DEATH was scrawled in large letters: new millions were added to the ranks of unemployed, thousands more were seeking crumbs in the ashcans: middle-class families were pauperized; wages were cut drastically for most workers—but strikes against further cuts had spread.

Equipped with a deeper analytical grasp of the events, and reinforced now with new ideas, Mirko called upon the people to continue pushing the fight for relief and for unemployment insurance. The chain of Unemployed Councils had grown, speakers were exchanged, experiences were shared: Mirko and Willie were in high demand and often went together to large rallies.

"The government is trying to demoralize the unemployed and to take the initiative out of our hands by offering us crumbs, and by telling us that the charity relief will do," Mirko shouted to his thousands of listeners. "This is a fraud and sheer propaganda. The private charities will not suffice; the gimmicks used to quiet us down will not feed the hungry famiiles!"

All over the city he, and the others, reported in detail the results of the Hunger March, and urged the people not to be discouraged just because their demand for unemployment insurance was yet unheeded.

"We will have to learn to fight better—that's all there is to it. Unemployment insurance is on the agenda for these United States of America. If we don't get it in 1932, we'll get it in 1933, or the next year, but we'll have to get it! Until then we have to squeeze more out of the city and state governments; until the federal government assumes responsibility to the people, we must not allow them to starve us to death, or to demoralize us!"

He kept reminding his audiences that pressure upon the City Fathers, and upon the others in government leadership, was bringing results. "So what happened to those 20,000 jobless men who are now living in the municipal lodgings? You all know what happened: there was that big march of five thousand Unemployed Council members which forced some changes, some important improvements of conditions for these men. Without that march, without us fighting for these homeless men, many of them would have died—maybe most of them would have died, who knows? But pressure of the Unemployed Council members avoided a disaster for these homeless men. This pressure we're putting on is a necessity if we're to survive; it's a necessity if we're to make another winter, and another winter, until we'll receive unemployment insurance, and other help."

Mirko was now a more seasoned leader, having grown in self-assurance, and thinking more often as a man soon to be married, a man with new responsibilities to a family of his own in the near future.

Willie often followed him on the platform, pointing out the irony of the latest campaign conducted by the William Randolph Hearst chain of newspapers. "Hearst tells us that we'll get out of this mess if we listen to him and take his advice and BUY AMERICAN, and SPEND AMERICAN, and SEE AMERICA FIRST. But I'd like to ask this great American patriot: BUY AMERICAN with what? He's not talking to me or to my people. We have nothing to buy with, American or otherwise. I can tell Mr. Hearst that I SEE AMERICA FIRST all the time, and I don't like what I see! I don't like what I see happening to my people and to all of us! I'm going to tell you something, Mr. Hearst: For almost fifteen years your papers all over the country have been saying that socialism can't survive in the Soviet Union; but I'm beginning to wonder if capitalism can survive in this country if this keeps up much longer."

Since the death of Isaac, Willie had been studying with great care the international events, and always seemed to have with him clippings of important data and statistics, just as Isaac used to have. He believed that Isaac's unfinished message had to be told and retold; that to honor the memory of the gentle Isaac, Willie had to always remind his audiences about the danger of another war.

"Maybe Mr. Hearst should be a little more outspoken and

tell us that he goes along with his German pal, Adolph Hitler, in blaming the Jews and the laboring people and militants, and that another war would take care of all that. The smell of war is already in the air. All of Manchuria has become a puppet state of Japan, and already Japan is attacking China proper at Shanghai. Mr. Hearst and his pal Hitler are very pleased with that, and he'd like to see us get involved; and we'll get involved as sure as my name's Willie Rivers if Japan is allowed to continue with her aggression. Hearst and his pal Hitler may want another war, but I sure don't look to a war to pull me out of this mess, 'cause then I'll be in a worse mess."

Willie hadn't recovered fully from the beating he took during the eviction fight. He tired easily, and had to depend on Mirko for rides to and from meetings. The two friends were thrown together a great deal and Willie had noticed that a big change had taken place in Mirko since his return from New York and Washington. On the way home he told him half seriously: "You're beginning to sound like a college man, or a professor, the way you talk."

"You haven't heard nothing," Mirko replied, deliberately using the two negatives. "They want me to teach a class on dialectical-materialism, that's philosophy, you know, Marxist philosophy. Me teaching philosophy!"

"Are you going to do that?" Willie asked.

"I will if you'll help me."

"I think something really must have happened to you, man. You sound a little off your rocker."

"You bet something happened," Mirko replied. "All this noise about philosophy and dialectical-materialism, it isn't half as complicated as it sounds. You just got to dig into this stuff, read it—and here's where you come in. You got to talk it out, discuss it with somebody, hear what it sounds like, after you've understood it. I want to rehearse things with you before I take on a class on Marxist philosophy. We read this material and have a bull session before I take it to the class."

"You got some more ideas like these?" Willie asked. "That gal Chris must have had something to do with this."

"You leave her out, Willie. Everything I say or do, people tell me is on account of Chris. It just ain't so! Chris is smart, that's true, she made a good Group Leader, but she ain't going to have a monopoly on the brain trust in the Yanich family."

"Oh, brother!" is all Willie said, as Mirko stopped his car and let him out.

"Can I bring Hattie to your rehearsals? She catches on fast."

"She sure does. She caught on to you all right. You set a date yet?"

"Not yet. We don't have to be married to come to your rehearsals on philosophy, or do we? Is it only for married couples?"

"Why don't you jump in the lake? You know you're not fooling me. I expect you and Hattie will be studying the books I gave you, and then you'll both try to make a fool of me. If you do that, I'm going to recommend that you teach instead of me," Mirko said with a broad grin, and pulled away in his noisy Ford.

CHAPTER IX
Escape From a Hyena

The presidential elections already loom high as the new year opens with a multitude of promises, and panaceas, for recovery, by all the candidates. But the waves of panic continue everywhere. In Chicago only fifty-one banks remain open out of the two hundred twenty-eight;* while thousands of small-town banks also close their doors, adding further to the suffering of the ruined farmers.

The Dunhill farm, too, is wiped out and its members scattered to various parts of Southern Illinois, having forced Betty Dunhill to seek refuge in Chicago.

To escape the fury of the unabated storm sweeping throughout the country, two million people, mostly youths, drift into the big cities and merge with the millions of other homeless and jobless sufferers. Chicago, crossroads of the continent, is host to tens of thousands who left their homes. These hungry men and women fight with others for edible wastes left by the city's food processing at the garbage dump, as the city hospitals continue to report a sharp increase in the number of deaths from starvation.

Looting is on: groups of forty to fifty people are seen entering large grocery stores—they load up with packages of food and quietly walk out. It's hushed up for fear it would spread still more. Helen Kanofsky is among them.

After a brief reunion, Helen realized that she could not remain in the old Kanofsky home. The gap between her and her aging parents had become too great. The Chicago of 1932,

---

* September, 1932.

its streets, its people—everything had undergone a profound change—including Helen herself.

The bleakness was everywhere; the unrelenting threat of death from hunger would soon engulf her, too, unless she ran from the Kanofsky home, from her neighborhood where she had grown up; unless she did what so many others were doing —looting for survival.

Helen moved in with Betty Dunhill, in the cold-water flat which Sylvia had found for the farm girl, but she refused to eat Betty's food without replacing it somehow.

"I've never been in such a bad situation," she confided to Chuck Lamson one evening when he walked her home.

They were seen together a lot since her return from the south. Some members of the club said that Chuck was so much in love with Helen that he had accepted her even on the rebound. But few knew how happy Helen was made to feel now by Chuck's attention and care. It was not like before—she was so much more mature, so much more understanding, that she began to see Chuck Lamson in an entirely different light. He was no longer "the old man" to her, in contrast to the dashing Art Walton. She could talk to him now about everything, and about herself, her sister Sylvia, and even about Art Walton, and what had happened between them to break them up. She talked to him about her new home, and her new room-mate, and Helen knew that he would understand her well.

"Betty is very generous, and she wants to make up to Sylvia for having helped her when she was driven off the farm, but she has no work herself, and she is eating up her last few pennies. I must do something about it, I just must! I have to get food into the house, or soon move elsewhere."

Chuck had never been as protective of anyone in his entire life, as he was now of Helen. It seemed to him that it was inevitable for Helen to return to Chicago, to his club, and to him. How could it have been otherwise? Art Walton could never have understood and appreciated this true daughter of the people, because he was not one of the people himself, Chuck often thought. Helen's return—to him—was welcomed with great joy, and soon he found himself again spending much of his time with her, planning the meetings and demonstrations, and the free rides on street cars and buses; but he was unable to offer Helen material assistance. He had gone hungry more often than he was willing to admit. He acquiesced to the looting of groceries by the hungry groups, and to Helen's participation in the raids.

Betty Dunhill, however, felt altogether differently about such actions. Upon learning how Helen had obtained her bags of groceries, she showed disapproval, and urged her to make more effort to find employment.

"You know a lot about sewing, why don't you try getting work in one of the Sopkin Dress Shops, where Hattie Green is working. She says there are over a thousand women in there, most of them Negroes, and if she knew the operators she could do something about setting up a union in there. The operators are the key people . . . "

"Say, who's been working on you? Has Mirko been bothering you while I was away?" Helen asked and looked straight at the farm girl.

"What do you mean by 'bothering' me?" Betty laughed, a faint blush covering her face. "All he did was tell me how to go about getting a job in one of the packing houses. Sylvia said that he was the only guy who could help me find some way of getting a job in there. That's what he came to see me about. And he's been telling me about Willie's girl friend, Hattie. He thought if I knew how to sew, if I was an operator like you, this Hattie could help me get work in her shop, in case I failed to get in at Swift's."

That peculiar pang in Helen's heart, as she listened to Betty, had returned. She had felt it many times before, when Art had failed to come home. Is it possible that this Mirko Yanich is another Art, she thought to herself. Is he, too, carrying on with others, with Betty Dunhill, while his wife was getting settled here? Helen had already met the newlyweds. Chuck introduced them to her, and she knew instinctively, by the embarrassment caused to Betty when Mirko's name was mentioned, that she was not telling the full story.

It was a fact, of course, that upon Sylvia's insistence Mirko had agreed to help Betty find work in a packing house. Some of the plants were working only one or two days a week, and the Employment Offices were practically shut down. There was no hiring of new hands anywhere at the time Sylvia first approached Mirko with her plea to help her locate some work for Betty.

He ran into Sylvia several times during the new year, at a

Midwest conference of activists, and at a large public rally attended by people from Gary and other nearby communities; and it was Sylvia who prevailed upon Mirko to meet Betty and try to get her into packing.

"It's true what you're saying, Sylvia. There are a lot of women still working in packing. It would be very good for us to have a few more girls in there, our group is made up almost entirely of men, and . . ." Mirko began to calculate aloud. He had never separated himself mentally, or emotionally, from the problems and activities inside the packing plant. He was still as much a part of everything going on in the stockyards as if he were actually working there yet. He had been meeting regularly with the militants and radicals on the inside; on several occasions he brought Willie Rivers with him to group meetings because he wanted Willie's help when they made their plans to extend the union-organizing work to departments with large Negro representations.

Mirko suggested that a big campaign be started to "Remove the Stars." The company had followed an old practice of putting a star on the time cards of the Negro workers, thus identifying them on sight, and when the time for layoffs came, the foreman selected a higher portion of cards with stars. "Remove the Stars" became a rallying slogan for some time. The militants inside the plant improved their relations with the Negroes, but their contact with departments that had large groups of women was very weak.

Mirko thus kept calculating to himself, at first, that it would be quite an asset to have a girl from the outside, one who was under no suspicion by the company of being a radical . . . "Yes, if we could get a few more girls in there, to strengthen our group, it would mean a lot," he continued, spelling out his intentions.

"Wait a minute, Mirko. Betty isn't one of us. She knows she can still get me mad every time she uses her favorite phrase, 'you gonna make a revolution, Sylvia?' "

"Then why are you knocking yourself out for her? You helped her get that flat, she's not sitting on the street; and now you have your sister living there with her. But you've been pestering me all evening about helping Betty find work, as if I had jobs in my little vest pocket. I'd take one myself if I knew how to get work somewhere. But I kept thinking to myself that if we had another one of our girls inside there, unknown yet to the stoolpigeons, then she could do some good working among the women."

"Now I can see that it's true what some people say about guys like you," Sylvia said, having decided to shame him into a different position. "You got a one-track mind. All you think about is organizing packing, and to hell with everything else."

Mirko burst out laughing and could be heard all over the auditorium. He was genuinely amused by Sylvia's comment. "Look who's talking! You've been in Gary—how long is it now —two or three years? and when you had a chance to come back to Chicago, after the Hunger March, you refused, telling everybody that the Big Mill has to be organized. That's all we ever hear from you; and you've never even worked inside that joint. But no one can get you out of Gary, and I bet you won't leave until something happens in that steel mill."

"Oh, come off it, Mirko. This has nothing to do with me. I'm talking about Betty. She came to Chicago on account of me; she knew her cousin Molly and the other Dunhills weren't in Chicago any longer, and when she wrote to me that their farm went bankrupt, and all that, she asked if she could stay with me until she found some work. What could I have done? I couldn't tell her not to come to Chicago just because I was in Gary, could I? What's wrong with helping an old friend?"

"And you still insist that she's husky, and beautiful, and that someone might hire her just because of that?" Mirko asked, laughing softly in ridicule of the young Kanofsky girl, who had been dubbed "Ma Connors", and who, at twenty years of age, hadn't yet had a date, and didn't look favorably upon people who, in the midst of this great economic catastrophe, were getting married and raising children.

"Why didn't you bring your Betty with you tonight?" he asked.

"She doesn't like to go to meetings and meet new people," Sylvia explained, already feeling better because she could tell that Mirko was beginning to consider seriously her urgings to do something for Betty.

"She'll have to meet me if I'm going to help her find work in packing," Mirko said joshingly.

"You're different—I hope! She knows you're a married man, and she heard me and Helen say nice things about Chris."

"Oh, you mean she doesn't want to meet single men?" Mirko asked. Being in a good humor that entire evening, he opened his wallet, and took out a picture of an infant, and asked Sylvia to guess who it was.

"You," Sylvia said.

"Try again, two more guesses."

"I don't know any other Yaniches," Sylvia said with some irritation.

"Yes, you do! You sure do!" Mirko insisted.

"You don't mean this is Chris when she was . . . "

"None other. This is Chris and she tells me it's been like that for several generations in the Wesly family. All girls are born redheads and they remain redheads, while the boys are dark. She says our baby is going to be just like her, just like Chris, because she knows it's going to be a girl."

Although not interested in that discussion, Sylvia pretended that she, too, would prefer that the newlyweds had a girl instead of a boy. She wanted most of all to keep Mirko in that mood, so she could continue with her pressure for help. Soon she reminded Mirko again that they had been talking about Betty and what it would mean to help her now.

"I think, I think . . ." Mirko said, snapping his fingers with some decision. "I think your girl friend, your Betty, ought to go next Wednesday, about eleven in the morning, to the gut shanty," and again he snapped his fingers. He explained to Sylvia that one of the girls from the sausage department was quitting next week, and if Betty got there a few hours later, and applied for work, she might just be lucky enough to be hired for that job. Tell her to answer 'yes' to all those silly questions: that she knows how to steel a knife, and how to butcher a pig, and the other stupid things they ask, just to make sure that the girls they interview aren't lying when they say they just came off a farm."

"But it's true, she is just off the farm. She won't have to lie about anything. She knows how to butcher a pig."

"How do you know what Betty has been doing on that farm?" Mirko teased her. "You ought to tell her that if she gets that job in the sausage department she'll be paid $32\frac{1}{2}$ cents an hour, a dime less than the men doing the same work, and that she better keep her mouth shut about it, or out she'll go. Our group in there is trying to get rid of that differential in pay,

263

but they'll think she's a Red if she shoots off her mouth about that dime difference."

"Don't worry about that. Betty isn't a talker."

"That's good. We need someone inside who could keep quiet for a while. We think we know one of the stoolpigeons, but we need someone working inside whom he doesn't know yet as one of us . . ."

"But Betty isn't interested in stoolpigeons, or unions or anything else."

"Or men?" Mirko asked.

"Or men. She needs a job, and that's all there is to it," Sylvia said with some impatience. "She wants to get some work, any kind of work, and I thought that through you, maybe she could get something in packing, even two days work would be better than doing nothing."

"Do I have to get an OK from you to talk to Betty about this stoolpigeon, or can I go see her on my own?" Mirko asked.

"If she gets that job next Wednesday, you can do what you darn please."

"You mean it?" he asked kiddingly.

"Oh, you can go to hell, Mirko! I wouldn't even talk to you again, if Betty gets work in there, or some other place."

And that is how it happened that Mirko Yanich began to visit Betty, a few weeks after she had been hired in the sausage department. And Betty was so very grateful to him when he came up to find out how she was getting along, and how she was being treated by the foreman.

He explained to her that the work in the gut shanty was about the lowest grade of work one could get, but that later she might be moved elsewhere, to another department. That would depend on the foreman, and his moods.

"We have a group of girls at Swift's—they're all in the movement."

"Wait a minute, Mirko, I don't want to have anything to do with this thing you call 'the movement'."

"I know you don't want to get mixed up with the movement, but you should know that we have about a dozen girls in your department, they're all about your own age, and are doing all kinds of things to get a foothold for unionism. They're not preaching communism, they're not talking about how great the Soviet Union is; they're talking about conditions inside that

264

plant and what to do to improve those conditions. You can become part of that group, and I might be able to help you . . ."

"Why you? You ain't even working yourself there."

Mirko liked the way she put it: she mixed good English with the "ain'ts" like it was part of her. While she appeared like a rough girl, yet she went out of her way to tell him that she knew how to typewrite pretty well having practiced on the farm during all her spare time. She'd sure like to get work in an office, but she was grateful to Mirko for helping her get that Swift job, she said.

Mirko knew exactly what work was like in the gut department, and he showed understanding of her complaints about the smells. "I know also that those boots to your knees are heavy, and the rubber aprons you have to wear while cleaning and measuring the casings in which you stuff the sausages smell like hell. It isn't anything like on the farm, or in an office, but you'll get used to that stink from the guts. In time you won't even know the difference between the smells of the sheep casings and the hog casings."

He warned her that the girl who had quit that Wednesday when Betty was hired couldn't take it any longer. He knew from the days when he had been working as a cooper, near the gut department, that many women and young girls, off the farms, wouldn't show up for work a day after being hired. Those who did show up, and those who remained, had to stand all day on their feet, on a wooden platform, in front of a big washtub, and on a metal pipe they'd string the casings, and after making careful adjustment, the water would come in and they had to make sure that there were no holes in those guts.

"The foreman likes to have Polish, Croation, and Lithuanian girls around him who will cater to him. That foreman of yours, whom they call 'the hyena', will soon ask you what your religion is. Tell him you're Catholic. During the religious holidays he expects gifts from the girls, and you better appear to him like one of the others. If he likes someone in a special way, he transfers her to the bacon department."

Betty was a good listener. She didn't interrupt.

"If you stay there a while, you'll be invited by one of our girls to go with them to the Settlement House, where they have set up a club, just a social club. They also go to dances once in a while. You might be interested in that."

"I don't dance. Don't care about that," she said.

"Last month a woman lost two fingers in the sausage machine, and about fifty-five workers walked out—a protest walk-out—and they made them put guards on that machine, so women's fingers don't get ground up with the sausage meat."

"Why are you telling me all this?" Betty asked, completely discouraged, and almost wishing she was back on the farm, or with her sister Lucy in East St. Louis.

"Those women don't just walk out like that," Mirko answered, snapping his fingers. "Two of our girls started it and the others followed, and while everybody knows who these two girls are, the foreman doesn't dare do anything against them because the women would protect them."

But Mirko soon realized that he was wasting his time talking to this farm girl about labor problems that didn't interest her.

Betty was on the night shift, and when Mirko visited her the second time it was close to lunchtime. She was wide awake and fully rested, and dressed in a colorful, flowered house coat, wrapped snugly around her thin waist, which made her look taller than her natural five eight. The blue in the housecoat brought out sharply the blue of her eyes. She probably had washed her hair like in the olden days on their farm, because the sheen on her long blond bob was high, something that Mirko had never seen before on any woman's hair; a natural blond halo, he thought to himself. And when she asked him to please sit down and have a bite of lunch with her she didn't show any of the reserve or dislike for men that Sylvia had spoken about. She appeared fully relaxed, and smiled often, and Mirko couldn't help notice that he had never before seen such beautiful teeth. He found himself staring at Betty several times because her natural beauty, and her unassuming farm manners and refreshing outdoor skin color that clung to her despite confinement in the gut shanty, just made him feel good inside, especially when she told him not to be in such a hurry, that she had plenty of time before going to work.

When he tried to make conversation about the labor conditions inside, or what his friends were doing to change things, Betty again indicated that she was not interested.

"I'm very thankful to you for that tip about the girl quitting, and me coming in at just the right time to get her job. I don't

266

know what I would have done if I didn't get work soon. But don't count on me getting mixed up with the Reds. I just ain't interested in any of that stuff," Betty said, standing up and stretching herself to her full height, as if telling him that she had nothing more to add, and no other business with him.

She was a big farm girl, Mirko thought, and he had guessed right in the first place, that the "laughing hyena" was bound to notice it, too; and that he wasn't going to pass up an opportunity to have this beautiful young girl under his thumb, obligated to him.

As Mirko traveled back to the south side he became angry with himself for having wasted so much time. He should have listened to Sylvia's warnings about Betty's lack of interest in unionism. But he really wasn't angry about that so much, as he soon realized. He had become intrigued with that pretty girl, and he knew that he would have to see her again, presumably for organizing purposes, even after having received such a rebuff from her.

Mirko was angry with himself because Betty Dunhill didn't pay any attention to him, and just like Sylvia said, Betty Dunhill didn't seem to be interested in men, and she wasn't in the least responding to the compliments and the mild flirtation he had ventured cautiously. Yet somehow he knew that there would be another opportunity for him to see her, that he would return.

He did, several weeks later. Then there were other visits to Betty's flat, when Helen was away.

But Mirko was confused by Betty's conduct: she never actually closed the door so tight that the subject of cooperating with the militants inside the plant could not be raised again with her. At first he concluded that her hesitations stemmed from lack of experience in the labor movement, and that she was beset by fears of losing her job if she became involved in the plant activities. Yet she also seemed to have new misgivings about her rapid involvement with the other side, with management.

As anticipated by Mirko, the foreman had already spoken to Betty about transferring her to the bacon department, where the work was considerably cleaner and the pay among the highest of any department.

"I sure can use that extra money," she told the "hyena."

"You're doing all right, Betty. I hear you're minding your own business and turning in the daily norm, like a good girl."

She thanked the man for moving her out of the smeary, bloody shanty, where she thought she smelled so foul that people on the El moved far away from her as soon as she entered a car. But on the way home, as she reconstructed that brief interview with the foreman, she kept seeing that imbecilic smile on the man's face when he repeated with emphasis the words "like a good girl." It made her slightly nauseous, but she attributed that ill feeling to the long ride on the elevated and street cars.

She had walked through the sliced bacon department several times and knew that it meant quite a lot to a girl who was depending on her own earnings to get such a promotion. Through the glass windows visitors would look down and see women in clean white frocks, and white caps, packing the bacon that was "not touched by human hands"—a motto that the company made famous everywhere. There was in that department only one black woman, who had been placed far off to one side, behind a high structure so that she could not be seen through the show window by the visiting groups.

The bacon was picked up with prongs and turned over on the scale and measured and the weight adjusted with the same prongs—but as soon as the visitors left, and the foreman was not looking, the girls would pick up the bacon with their fingers so that they could turn in 140 packages an hour—making them among the highest paid—seventeen dollars a week plus a bonus of seven dollars.

While Betty was working up some excitement about her good luck, she also became concerned about this new thing that had happened to her. There was no one home to talk to about that "hyena." Having been warned once by Mirko, she now felt that she had gotten herself trapped with that transfer, and that she would be expected to be "a good girl" for other things, when other requests would be made of her later. Tired from work and from travel, and from the extra burden of this new, ominous development, this pending threat from the foreman, she walked up the flight of steps in the dark hall, put the key into the door and was startled by the loud ringing of her telephone. In an unnatural, almost mannish voice, she shouted:

"Hello, hello!"

"What's the matter, Betty? Has something happened to you?"

"Oh, Mirko! Am I glad you're calling!" she said, letting out a strong pent-up sigh of relief. "I just walked in when I heard the ringing . . . say, why are you calling so late? Where are you calling from?"

"I'm at the Finnish Hall, a few blocks away from you; I knew you'd be coming home about this time, and if you're not too tired, I'd like to stop off for just a few minutes, if you don't mind."

"Honest to God, you must have read my mind. I have something to tell you, something that happened tonight when I came to work . . . You're on your way over? Good!" and she heard a click.

Hurriedly she rushed into the bedroom and removed all her clothes, which smelled of meat and blood and stockyards; she threw everything on the floor of her closet and rushed to the bathroom, where she began scrubbing her face and hands and neck, with soap and water, and brushed her hair briskly as if expecting that with those movements she would get rid of those dreadful smells that she had brought all along from the south side, that had permeated her entire body and the flat and the dirty clothes. By the time she put on her housecoat, and house slippers, there was a knock on the door.

Mirko said nothing as Betty opened the door to him, smelling fresh of the perfumed soap and looking clean and happy, and more beautiful than he had ever seen her before. For several seconds he kept staring at her before crossing the threshold, and slowly closing the door behind him, without taking his eyes off her, while she moved a few steps away, to make room for him to come through the narrow foyer.

He whispered almost like in prayer: "You can throw me out if you want, but I must kiss you, Betty: I've never seen anyone look so beautiful in my whole life."

Turning her cheek to him, and holding her hand between them, she let him kiss her, and then took a couple more steps backwards, towards the living room, where she proceeded immediately to tell him:

"You have no idea how good it is to see you. But what are you doing this late in the neighborhood?" she asked sincerely.

"That's why I called you from the hall as soon as we adjourned our meeting. I knew you wouldn't be asleep yet. There's

269

a group formed out here, the "Neighbors for F.D.R.", that's Franklin Delano Roosevelt, the New York Governor, who's going to run for President. This group is looking for someone who knows how to typewrite, to start work for them right away, maybe tomorrow morning, and I thought you might want it before someone else gets it."

"Why me? I got a job, and I was transferred to the bacon department today, that's what I wanted to tell you."

"Did that hyena call you in already?" Mirko asked.

"How did you know? One of the girls told you already?" Betty asked.

"No one has to tell me; I knew it would happen as soon as I heard you were hired the same day you applied. But I didn't expect it this fast. You must rate high with him," Mirko said with genuine concern. "This opening for a typist might be just in time, just the thing. You won't stay long in the bacon department either, unless you want to play ball with that foreman."

He was not looking at Betty now, but neither was he through yet, and he was still thinking aloud about this new situation. "You refused to get mixed up with our people inside, but now you're all mixed up with the management. I know it's not your fault, it's not of your doing, but you've made it tough for us to do something about this; and we missed a good opportunity to get the goods on at least one stoolie."

"I don't know what you're talking about. What could you have done about that hyena if I had gotten myself involved with your people?" she asked.

"Nothing, nothing. We can't do a damn thing now if that guy asks you next for a date, can we? So you'll string him along for a while. Then out you'll go. Oh, he'll transfer you again, and he might even give you another promotion of some kind, so he can have his eye on you. But he wants you isolated, working by yourself, and talking to nobody, meeting nobody. He's got you where he wants you because he knows that there are no jobs sitting around and waiting even for a girl like you. He knows that. But he might have left you alone, at least for a while longer, if you had been going out with the girls to the Settlement House, or if you had come along to those Friday night dances—that's what our girls are doing, mixing well with the others, making contacts with the honest-to-goodness militants inside. They visit them at home, they socialize with them, and talk unionism to them. Some listen and like the idea, and those will be on the ground floor when they get a genuine union going in there."

"Look here, Mirko. it's too late for you to lecture me about unions. I just didn't want to get mixed up with anything until I could buy some city clothes, and pay the rent for a couple of months in advance. But don't get any ideas that I like working there nine hours a day, six days of the week, and when they get real busy they work seventy hours, like I did last week. Don't think I like that. Today I was told not to come to work for the next three days—it's slowing down; to come to work instead next Monday, and I don't like that business any more than the other girls."

"But don't you see, Betty, there's nothing we can do to protect you from this foreman; he's gonna go after you now, and none of our people, or these girls even met you yet, I mean outside your own department. We can't issue a leaflet, or a bulletin and say 'Betty Dunhill was fired because she refused to go to bed with the laughing hyena.' They don't know who Betty Dunhill is, and they don't care."

There was a long silence as the two remained sitting at the kitchen table, where Betty had put out some bread and was making hot milk for herself. Since working on the night shift she had been drinking hot milk, to relax before going to sleep. Mirko declined to eat anything, telling her that he had to hurry home, that Chris was alone, waiting up for him. "She's getting pretty big, but she don't give up. She thinks like so many others do, that with the election of Roosevelt, things will begin to change in the country."

"Well, don't you think so?" Betty asked, as if everybody could see that it was true.

"I didn't know you were interested in politics. Maybe you should think about that opening in the neighborhood, and get in there and help them set up the headquarters for F.D.R. I took a chance and threw your name into the hopper when they asked if we knew anybody who could typewrite."

Mirko gave her other details about this grass roots movement that was mushrooming in favor of F.D.R. He explained to her that millions of people were taking the election of the next president more seriously than anything he had seen before.

He urged her to drop in at the new headquarters anyway, as long as she was laid off for a few days, and look around.

Betty thanked him again for proposing her name, and when he left, and she heard the downstairs door to the street close, she began to go over in her mind all the new things that were happening to her. Mirko . . . Mirko . . . His ideas, sure he's right . . . I know there'll have to be a union inside over there some day; how else can one get protection on the job? But why does he come up here to see me? Does he tell Chris about these visits? Will he tell her that he was here tonight, after his meeting at the Finnish Hall? I wonder! But he's a good man; has good ideas. The man and his ideas: they're one and the same; Mirko and his ideas, one and the same—they're both good. No, no! That's not so. He belongs with Chris . . . I must meet her soon, I must talk with her and tell her what a good husband she has.

It was near dawn when Betty fell into a peaceful sleep.

II

Late the next afternoon, rested and refreshed, Betty decided to walk over to the new headquarters of the "Neighbors for F.D.R." and look around. She welcomed the idea of filling in her free time with something she believed in—electing this New York Governor as the next President was something she thought would be good for the country. She knew the Hoover administration was ruining the small and middle farmer; and she saw new hope in the forthcoming elections.

She walked into this noisy store front of chaos and total disarray; a man was talking on the phone with nervous gestures, the young couple standing near him were motioning him to cut his conversation—they were in a hurry to get instructions from him. Several others were moving a desk out of the way, pushing it against a wall and making room for rows of folding chairs. On the floor was spread a long streamer with freshly painted *WE NEED F.D.R.* being touched up by the volunteer painter. There was activity and confusion all over the place. A tall, balding man shouted. "Anybody here know how to type-write?" and when Betty waved her hand he motioned her to come forward, and, handing her several sheets of paper and carbons, asked her to put them into the typewriter as he began to dictate.

She had been typing for several minutes before she looked up, directly into the bright blue eyes of a young man, with a velvet-trimmed jacket and matching corduroy slacks—a camera focussed on her, on her hands, and on the man who was dictating —clicking off rapidly shots from various angles.

He did not ask her permission to use her as a model; he continued to snap pictures of the man who was still working on the huge F.D.R. sign, and soon after he went for several shots of the others who were carrying chairs and pushing furniture around.

Betty became curious now about this man and his activities. He was well dressed, yet he did not appear to be a professional photographer. His equipment, however, she could tell was expensive. Soon the man who was dictating to her explained that Neil Hartwig was preparing a pictorial study of the grass roots movement for F.D.R., and this new headquarters was of great interest to him, to follow it through from the very outset. Later, she was told, this material would be collated with other pictorials for a large brochure on F.D.R. Betty was now even more intrigued by this young man's camera work, and she returned his smile several times.

In her silent monologues Betty was formulating letters she would like to write to Sylvia about this fellow. Only with Sylvia did she feel comfortable to exchange her intimate thoughts. When later in the week she began to write her lengthy letters about Neil, Sylvia encouraged her to return to poetry writing, and commended her talents. The letter written *August 6, 1932,* just two weeks after Betty's first date with the attractive Neil Hartwig, Sylvia folded carefully and tucked away in her pocketbook. She was reading it now for the second time:

. . . then this fellow with the camera asked me where I lived and said, "I'll drop you off." When we came to the house he asked, "How about going to a concert with me tonight?" I thanked him but said that I was already dated for that evening. I didn't like the idea of going out with this fellow the very first time I met him. So I lied to him.

But about 11:00 p.m., when I was already in bed, I heard someone walk up the steps and slip something under the door. It was a note which said, IF YOU GET HOME BEFORE MIDNIGHT, PLEASE COME TO 1800 HALSTED. Real excitement caught hold of me, Syl, and I got dressed quickly and proceeded to that address. When

I walked through that tavern door, there was Blue Eyes watching for me. He held out his arms and I walked into them. I felt at home for the first time since I got off the farm. The next two weeks became the most important ones in my whole life. He encouraged me to quit the bacon department, and to give all my time to the NEIGHBORS FOR F.D.R., which I did. That's where I'm now typewriting this. It's very late and I'm waiting for Neil to pick me up.

For over three weeks Sylvia heard no more from Betty. Then arrived the confusing letter, dated *August 29th,* also written from the F.D.R. headquarters.

Neil comes from a very rich family, and I'm always aware that he's somewhat ashamed of me—but it doesn't bother me. My involvement with Mirko, as I explained to you, was mostly because of the new ideas he brought to me—when I began to like the new ideas I also began to like the man, but why did Mirko do the same thing my Dad did? I could see it coming: he was in his own mind already betraying his wife Chris, and I knew that in the long run he'd reject me also. But with Neil I feel that someone loves me, and that I'm capable of loving him. But I also know that there's no hope for marriage to him. Maybe I don't need marriage, maybe I'm not capable of a lifetime involvement with a man.

You'll understand this, Syl: Neil too seems to be floundering, and is lost, just like me. His need for another human being is as desperate as mine. His need for reassurance in the female is as desperate as my need for reassurance in the male. Although coming out of a very rich home, having had everything he ever wanted, he was rejected—perhaps for the first time in his life—by a female. I've been rejected all my life: by Dad, by our twin brothers, by the school teacher when I first came to Chicago (remember how heartbroken I was).

Neil and I are like two lost souls, hurt, not knowing really why, not even able to understand what had happened to us. I fell in love, Sylvia. An odd word for me to use. There are so many different kinds of love. Except for you and Grandma, I always felt I was unloved, and was myself an unloving piece of humanity. You know how reserved I've been all my life, but now there isn't the slightest doubt in my mind: I love this guy, this Neil, and for the first time in my life I told a man that I love him. I say it every day, many times a day. Neil meets every emotional need I ever had. He aroused needs I never had before—as you know sex had always played a minor need in my life. I had never felt feminine, or thought feminine, except for outward appearance. I had never dealt in feminine wiles. But with Neil I feel loved, wanted, needed very much as a woman.

274

Betty enclosed several pictures of herself taken by Neil, and other material used during the election campaign. She wrote again later in the month, but only briefly, telling Sylvia that she was too busy to go into detail, but people all around her were sure that F.D.R. would win the elections, and that all the reports coming in were very encouraging.

The other letter which Sylvia saved was dated almost two months later. It, too, was typewritten at the F.D.R. headquarters.

You are mistaken, Syl. When Neil moved on, to some other part of the country, I was not left dreary, hurt, or bitter. He had healed a lifetime of wounds with his devotion to me. He found a lonely person and he left a woman behind. I missed him, I grieved for him, I had never really thought of marrying him; no expectations were dashed. I knew him so well that I knew all along of my embarrassment to him, socially and otherwise. I knew that no matter how great his love for me might have been, he was not capable at that time of helping me bridge the gap between us. I hold no rancor. I loved him and understood him.

I knew from the beginning that it would be over soon. My soul touched another human being's soul once in my life—that is often enough. I will always love Neil, the young fellow with the sharp blue eyes. The tears I shed over him were healing tears that nurtured the woman within me that he had unearthed.

Sylvia did not respond to the last few letters from Betty. She was planning to come into the city for a week-end visit with her parents, and with Betty. When at last the two friends faced each other, Betty complained to her.

"You hardly said anything to me about this whole situation. I don't even know what you think about it. You were busy, I know, like everybody else, but you could have written a few lines in answer to my last letters."

"Sure I was busy. Everybody is busy trying to get F.D.R. elected. But that isn't the reason why I didn't write sooner. Your letters are too contradictory and it would have taken me hours of writing to unscramble your confused reasoning."

"Oh, oh! If it was so confusing why did you let it wait so long?" Betty asked sincerely. She had been making demands on Sylvia more than on anybody else; she trusted her judgment and her objectivity.

"I don't think there was any confusion about you and Neil

falling in love. That part looks simple to me. It's your own personal conclusions that bother me. That business about embarrassing him, about not being able to bridge the gap. I can't follow that kind of logic," Sylvia told her.

"You and your logic. You have to have everything fit into a pattern, everything must have a place . . ." Betty began but Sylvia cut her off.

"That's true. Things must be seen with some kind of sequence; they must be seen in motion and not in a static form, or you'll get nowhere. One has to understand the process of development. You can't go around explaining things away, like you've been doing all your life, with your notions about good and bad males determining everything, and that males have been hurting you all your life, like your Dad and your twin brothers, and now Neil came on the scene and healed everything for you, because he's a good male. According to what you've told me, Neil too was hurt, hurt by some bad female, and when you met you were able to heal each other. The way you put it the whole world can be studied from the viewpoint of good and bad males. And don't go telling me that I know nothing about these matters because I've never been in love. If you feel that way then why are you so anxious to receive answers from me to all your letters? But to shut you up for the time being: I'll tell you now that there's a guy in the Big Mill—I don't know if I'm in love or not. I guess you'll be telling me that if I was in love with him I'd know it. All right, so I'll know some other time, but right now don't let me get away from what we started talking about," Sylvia held her ground and insisted on pursuing her point.

"Keep going—I can see you up there on the platform lecturing. Why don't you skip over to Neil."

"Neil, Neil. He wasn't ashamed of you or anything. After a while Neil just lost interest in you. You said yourself that he healed your wounds. Well, maybe you healed his wounds. He picked you up on the rebound. He was in love with some beautiful dame who evidently turned him down, so he started up with you and let time do the trick of healing for him. But he doesn't belong with a farm girl, or a stockyard girl. He was true to himself and he went back to his class. Where is he now? You don't even know! But I know. I saw his picture in a Hollywood magazine—he was to some big party with an attractive actress

276

on his arm, and it said he was sponsoring this gal, and you'll probably see her soon as a new Hollywood star. So don't go building stories or fantasies about him."

The two girls were alone in the flat for that entire week-end. They took their time, both being in good form, in a good talking mood.

"Start from the beginning and try to see it my way, then you'll come out with different results. So Mirko was infatuated with you, all right. Maybe you led him on; maybe he's having trouble with Chris, and he doesn't say anything about it to anybody, and in this way he was testing himself. You said yourself that he's a good man. He flirted but he never really made the kind of advance to you that would have betrayed Chris."

"Who knows how far he would have gone if I had let him," Betty added.

"Oh, let's skip it. Let's get to this character Neil Hartwig, whom you keep glorifying. You have a way of seeing things in the extreme: your Dad turned against you, your brothers turned against you; I don't think anybody turned against you. Your Dad knew that your mother was incurably ill and he began to prepare the basis for this upstairs girl becoming his future wife. What's wrong with that? And your Dad didn't desert the farm, the farm collapsed, like so many other farms that went bankrupt. Everybody had to get off that farm, but you refused, you thought you could shoot it out with your gun, like some other farmers were doing. Well, that didn't help save the Dunhill farm, and your Dad was smarter than you on that one point."

Sylvia was trying to veer Betty away from a discussion on Neil; she was anxious to get more information about farm life, how the people in the country were managing their life during this great upheaval. She asked Betty many questions, and at last Betty began to answer some of them.

"When things started going bad for us, last fall, we dug holes in the ground, lined them with straw and began to bury turnips, cabbage, apples and sweet and Irish potatoes in them. Then we covered them with straw and dirt. But someone must have seen us do that, because Dad has been telling us that someone out there has been digging in those hills, getting the food out. Dad pretended that he didn't see or hear it. Things are getting so bad there that not a day or night passed that someone didn't come to our door asking us for food."

Sylvia had never been on a farm, or outside Chicago, except Gary and on that Washington Hunger March. She was interested in all details, and encouraged Betty to go on.

"If you saw this family of sharecroppers, Syl, with five half-grown boys, none in school, coming to our house every morning about ten o'clock, you'd understand why we couldn't sit down and enjoy our meal. Dad took those boys with him rabbit hunting, and after they cleaned their catch and cut them up, Dad put in some pork and then they ground up all that stuff together and made sausages. It seems to me that everybody in our neighborhood was eating the Dunhill sausages, no one refused them. But we got low in that, too."

At first it seemed that Betty resented all that questioning by Sylvia, and even kidded her with her old saying, "you gonna make a revolution on the farm, too?" But she continued talking; she trusted Sylvia and saw how pained her friend's face became when she described what went on in the one-room school near the Dunhill farm, where all grades up to eight were taught in that one room.

"The county nurses and doctors come in and give all those kids shots and some of the parents object, calling it government interference. Some of the kids had lice, and most of them were half-starved. Soon Dad started taking hundred-pound bags of beans to the school, and every morning the teachers would put a big pot of beans on the top of the potbellied stove, to cook. With those beans the kids would get corn bread which some school board members brought in.

"On the way up here, on the bus, I saw people living in tents, mostly made of old blankets and quilts. They were living in ditches along the road sides. I can still see their weather-beaten faces, as the men stood outside their home-made tents, envying the bus that was getting away from that place."

Sylvia was pushing for more details; she wanted to know why Betty and the other Dunhills couldn't get enough food with all the land her Dad owned.

"We had lots of watermelons and cantaloupes, and when Dad shipped them to St. Louis, he couldn't make enough to pay for the railroad cars; so my father either let them rot in the fields or he would take truck loads to Cairo, or Marion, to peddle them. He sold those cantaloupes for one penny, and the melons for five cents each."

278

Some time back Sylvia had already noticed how much easier it was for Betty to express herself. She seemed to have lost that reserve that she had when she first came to Chicago. She answered Sylvia's questions without waiting to think, or to formulate her ideas with some care. Once, during their reunion, she talked, as if to herself.

"You cannot murder a human being without murdering something inside yourself; you cannot abandon a child, without abandoning something of yourself. You cannot hate without hating yourself before it is over. All things done to the black man, the white man did to himself; it is the unusual man, black or white, that escaped this fate, where I come from. 'Truth crushed to the earth shall rise again,' says the minister. If it does it will rise through the efforts of the southern woman, black and white."

Sylvia listened closely, but looked with surprise at her old school chum, and wondered whether the fight for the freedom of the Nine Scottsboro Boys had reached Southern Illinois, and had influenced her. But she did not want to interrupt. She let Betty continue.

"There was a large family not far from our farm. His name was Newman, and his claim to fame was that he had killed two 'niggers' when he lived in Mississippi. This was talked about by others as an accomplishment, but with all of his big doings, nobody was his friend. Everyone pitied his family and when his wife got a broken arm there was no one that didn't believe that he broke it. Nobody wanted to be considered a friend of his. Mrs. Newman was Mississippi-born, and came of a fine family. But she could not take the stigma—even in Mississippi—of her husband being a murderer, though supposedly it was all right to kill Negroes. I was terrified of that man my whole life; I remember calling on his daughters, hoping I wouldn't see him, and if he was there, I watched him every minute. I didn't trust him, he had killed. And I still wonder what happened to his children, the children of a man who had killed two black men."

Betty's political maturing was a natural process. Working in the very center of the grass roots movement for the election of F.D.R. enabled her to perfect not only the technical skills required in the headquarters. Her interests broadened, her involvement stretched beyond the day's working hours as Office Manager and Coordinator. Soon Betty Dunhill was drawn into activities that called for personal initiative and ingenuity. Both her name and picture began to make frequent appearance on the pages of the newspapers as a knowledgeable woman, and important activist for F.D.R.

As the election campaign was pushed into high gear, Sylvia, too, began to lean on Betty for advice and for specific bits of information. The two were seen on occasion together at political rallies, both speaking on subjects most familiar to them: Sylvia Connors on what the new president must do for the relief of the suffering of the industrial workers, and Betty Dunhill on the failures of the Hoover administration's policies in the countryside.

Betty, now a long distance removed from the pursuing "hyena," was especially effective when she described to the attentive audiences the details of the suffering among the farmers. "It is impossible for the farmers to continue to live under the present conditions. The banks and the insurance companies are foreclosing on mortgages because the farmers' income is now less than half it was, and they can't meet the payments. But they can't go on like this. Already over a million farmers have lost their property. Here in the cities the people get a little relief, but the farmers get nothing, absolutely nothing."

She explained that this was the reason why the farmers in Illinois, and practically all over the midwest, were conducting strikes against the cut prices on their crops.

"There are hundreds of barricades and road blocks leading to the markets. With shotguns and pitchforks the farmers are fighting for their survival."

She told them how milk was being dumped in the ditches, vegetables and grain were being scattered to the road sides and the drivers of the trucks were being beaten whenever they attempted to run through the barricades to sell their products on the cheap market.

But the thing that pleased most the destitute city unemployed was when Betty told them about the "penny sales" that had developed throughout the farm communities.

"When a foreclosed farm is about to be put up for auction, some friendly neighbor always shows up to bid a penny for that farm. The others who assemble make sure that nobody bids above that penny."

CHAPTER X

Mendel Goes to County Jail

Betty Dunhill's rapid and uneven development during the third year of the Great Crisis had often brought her to the very verge of deep despair, and gave her moments of total confusion from which she could not extricate herself without outside assistance. The short-lived affair with the exciting Neil Hartwig, which had thrown her into a complete emotional tailspin, tended to confirm her earlier erroneous theories that good and bad males decided everything in contemporary society, and had left her even more confused. The sweeping social movements all around her were developing with great rapidity, but her ability to understand their essence had not kept apace.

Sylvia often succeeded in getting through to her with her own interpretations of the dynamics of the modern world, and as her trips to the Windy City increased so did Betty's dependence upon her former school chum. But in that process Betty had also become the link between the two Kanofsky sisters. At her typewriter in the F.D.R. Headquarters, Betty would automatically make brief reports on Helen Kanofsky's whereabouts and doings, and mail those notes to the grateful Sylvia. The very last bit of information was that Helen was serving a month's sentence in the County Jail, but was in good health and spirits, and that it would be best for Sylvia to inform their parents about this latest arrest, so they would not worry about it unnecessarily.

Sylvia telephoned her parents.

"Pa, Pa, can you hear me? It's Sylvia. I'm calling from Gary. How are you? How is Ma?" She didn't wait for him to answer each question separately before she threw others at him. "Where's Ma? How come you're answering the telephone?" After a brief pause: "Is Ma all right?"

Mendel hardly ever spoke on the telephone. He usually shied away from it. It was Frimma who played the role of the modern

281

woman, talking calmly, taking messages for their daughters and son, when they lived at home. Everybody expected that of Frimma, just as they expected Mendel to be indifferent, and unresponsive to new ideas or new gadgets in the kitchen. To him the telephone was something he had no personal need for, preferring to transact whatever had to be done in person, face to face.

In Mendel's simple life, most of the modern innovations, including the telephone, seemed to be cluttering up and complicating life for everybody. He personally had never made a telephone call himself, and now he answered, after the third ring, only because Frimma was not home. Suddenly this familiar voice on the telephone was asking him a string of questions, and was insisting on getting answers from him.

"Who is this?" he asked, holding the telephone a little distance from his ear, as if it would be sinful to let it touch his bearded face.

"Pa, it's me, Sylvia. Can you hear me?"

"Now I can hear you, yes. But why are you shouting like this? Talk in Yiddish." Whenever Mendel had some trouble, he would forget all he had ever learned in the English language, and automatically revert to his "old country Yiddish," exactly as it was spoken fifty or a hundred years ago. Sylvia, realizing that her father had asked her to speak in Jewish, and that there was some trouble at home, became somewhat panicked and shouted again into the telephone: "Why doesn't Ma answer? Is she sick? Where's Ma?"

"Ma went to the store. She'll be back right away. You want to wait until she comes back?" Mendel asked calmly.

"No, no, Pa! I'm calling from Gary, and it costs more calling from here than when I telephone you from Chicago. But I'm glad you answered, Pa, because I want to tell you something very important. Can you hear me?"

"Yes, now I hear you better."

"I want to tell you that Helen is in jail, in the County Jail. She'll be there for about a month. Betty, Betty Dunhill, with whom Helen lives, wrote to me and said not to worry if we don't hear from Helen for a while. Betty visited her this week and says that Helen feels fine."

"But why are you telephoning, Sylvia? Are you all right?"

"I'm all right, Pa, only I'm busy and can't come to Chicago

for some time to visit Helen and you and Ma; we're too busy with this election campaign, but I thought I'd let you know so you won't worry about us."

"That's good. I'll tell Ma what you said, Sylvia. Good-by."

"Good-by, Pa," Sylvia said and hung up. She originally had in mind to say a lot more, but somehow the conversation had come to a natural conclusion after Mendel told her that he would relate everything to Frimma. After all, weren't all phone calls meant for her?

Now Mendel was trying hard not to forget the name of the jail, as he repeated to himself several times "County Jail, County Jail," instinctively sensing that remembering the name of the jail where Helen was locked up would be of some importance to him later. Just why it would be important he hadn't figured out yet.

With his mind still heavily attached to that telephone conversation with his youngest daughter, he walked into his "factory" and mechanically began to roll the cigars, and to put them into the empty molds. "Why would Sylvia telephone all the way from Gary just to tell me that Helen was in jail?" he mumbled to himself. Both Helen and Sylvia had been in jail before—this was not something new any more to the elder Kanofskys. They were never ashamed of it either; if their daughters had to go to jail, they had to go to jail. "But Sylvia must have wanted something from the way she repeated several times that Helen was in the County Jail, like she wanted me to know exactly where Helen was this time."

"Maybe she wants me to go see her?" he said to himself with some surprise. "That's what it is!" he decided resolutely. "Sylvia said she was glad that I answered the phone instead of Frimma—that means that she wanted to talk to me about this important matter; that could mean that there was some reason why Sylvia wanted me to see Helen in jail; some reason that she could not speak about on the telephone."

This entire matter now looked differently to Mendel. A new phase of life had unfolded to the quiet, reticent Mendel, with that one telephone conversation, which had moved him deeply. "My Helen is in trouble, and somebody should be near her when in trouble," he whispered half-aloud.

The pride that he always felt about the things his daughters were doing for humanity suddenly vanished; the many "mitzvahs" that he could recount which Helen and Sylvia had performed since they left their own nest, the Kanofsky home, had somehow lost their meaning in his present assessment. "My oldest daughter needs me—I must go to her, and tell her that both Frimma and I will do all we can to help her . . ." he said softly, without realizing that a tear had rolled down his cheek, as he was repeating in silence a prayer for Helen's safety. He now recalled her every gesture, her beautiful smiling face; he almost felt the physical impact of her two arms, embracing him from the back and mockingly asking him "Guess Who?" when instead he realized it was Frimma talking to him.

"What are you mumbling to yourself for?" she asked as she walked into the cramped "factory" and began to label the cigars that Mendel had ready for her to put the finishing touches on. "You haven't heard me open the door, or come in here. Are you sick, Mendel? Maybe you should go outside on the porch and get yourself a little fresh air? It's too dusty here. Too much tobacco dust isn't good for anybody."

"Don't bother me, Frimma. I got to finish these boxes. Mr. Tuckerman is coming for three boxes of cigars, and you haven't even started the first one."

By the way he said "don't bother me," Frimma knew that he was not angry with her, but that he wanted to be left alone—maybe to think about something to himself.

"Anybody telephone?" she asked casually.

"Yes, Sylvia just telephoned. From Gary, she said. She'll be busy and she said she won't be able to come to see us, but she was feeling fine and said not to worry about her," Mendel answered, but he knew what was coming next, and he hadn't made up his mind yet what to tell her. They never had any secrets between them—they had learned, in their long marriage, that life was easier by not keeping things from each other. He knew that he'd tell her the truth if she asked.

"Did she say anything about Helen?"

"Helen is in the County Jail, but that farm girl, Betty, who lives with her, wrote to Sylvia and told her that she was all right, too."

"Who's all right, too? I'm not asking you now about Betty," Frimma said slowly. She understood the message her husband was giving her only too well; and she knew now that Helen was in jail, and that according to Betty, Helen was all right. But

Frimma was deliberately stalling: she felt that Mendel wasn't telling her everything, and she hoped that by pretending that he was confused, he would begin all over again, and would tell her more about that telephone call from Sylvia. But it had the very opposite effect; for Mendel turned around in his straight chair, and, facing his wife, said sharply:

"Sylvia said that Helen is all right. Will you stop bothering me now? Mr. Tuckerman is coming for lunch and for the cigars, and you sit there talking and asking me a lot of questions."

Now Frimma became even more concerned about that telephone call—something did happen to make Mendel talk like that to her, when he could easily see that she was labeling the cigars as fast as she could, that she was putting them into the box in even rows, and Mendel knew very well that all three boxes would be ready in time. She kept silent and continued working and thinking, and wondering.

Mendel, too, continued working and thinking. He couldn't shake the total impression he had received from his daughter's telephone call that she wanted him to visit Helen in jail, and ever since he hung up the receiver he had been occupied with that single thought. Now he had begun the process of asking and answering himself numerous questions: Where is the County Jail? Do they let Jews in there, for a visit? They must, he decided, because there are Jews sitting in jail, like other people. Mendel knew that there were many places where Jews were excluded, and this bothered him quite a bit, because he had just about made up his mind to visit his daughter, but he didn't want to go there if he'd be unwelcome.

The biggest problem, however, that he was occupied with now, was the matter of telling or not telling Frimma about his decision to visit the County Jail. If only he could share this whole idea with her, life would again become so simple for him; she would know how to find the location of the jail, and how to go about finding out the best time to arrive there, and maybe if she went along with him, it would be best for all of them.

That was the reason he suddenly turned sharply on his wife: he was in the process of thinking through all these complicated, new problems, that had arisen in the last few minutes—all because he answered the telephone instead of his wife—and his wife wasn't giving him the opportunity to come to some decent, sensible conclusions on these important matters.

But that wasn't entirely true; Frimma was giving him all the opportunity he needed to think. They both continued working in silence for quite some time, Mendel having returned to his original big question—should he tell Frimma that he had decided to go to the County Jail to visit their daughter, or shouldn't he?—and Frimma, believing that by keeping quiet, like Mendel requested, he would eventually volunteer what was really bothering him. Yet, nothing happened. The silence remained in that tiny, boarded, so-called porch factory; the three boxes were labelled and packed and sealed by Frimma's nimble fingers; and Mendel's molds filled up with the rolled cigars at a good pace.

"I'll have lunch ready soon," Frimma said, and left the "factory."

Mendel sighed in relief. He knew now what he ought to do. If he hadn't told Frimma during that dreadful silence between them, he won't tell her now, or later. "I'll find out how to get there, and if everything is all right with Helen, I'll tell Frimma when I come back home that I've been to the County Jail. Why make her worry about all these things? It can all wait till I come back," he said to himself.

Mendel didn't waste much time before carrying out his decision. Casually, without drawing any attention to himself, or his activities, he managed to brush his large, black hat, which he used during the holidays. In the privacy of the bathroom, he trimmed his goatee beard just a little bit here and there—so that the total result wouldn't be noticeable—yet the stray hairs under the chin, and in his nose, were removed, and he felt better already.

He had some misgivings about being able to walk out of the house in his long, black coat which he wore only on special occasions. But that, too, somehow fell into line, and when Frimma said that she was going to the basement to straighten out some things there he quickly donned his hat and coat, dusted his shoes with the towel from the clothes bin, and softly walked out of the house.

About an hour later Mendel was sitting in the Waiting Room, next to another man—whose face was faintly familiar. He dared not ask any questions or make conversation with this stranger; he decided to just sit there on the bench, like he was told to do by the guard, until his Helen would be brought out for their visit. He knew that never, never in his remaining life, would he tell Frimma that during those few long minutes his heart felt very peculiar, like beating too fast, and that his breath was a little short. He would never tell her that he felt like he was himself a prisoner now, being watched by a guard, and some screened windows were in front of him, and a locked door in back of him. Never having been to a jail before, he actually believed that all visitors had been locked up for the duration of their visit. And somehow he began to feel terribly sorry for his daughter, Helen, terribly sad that she had to be treated like an animal, instead of a good human being, that she really was, and just as he was going into a little more silent review of that whole situation, Helen Kanofsky walked through the barred doors, into the arms of the man next to Mendel—before she became aware that her father was there also.

"Pa, Pa!" is all she could think of saying, embracing him, and kissing him; tears already beginning to gather in her eyes. "Pa, how did you know I was here? Oh, Pa, you never met Chuck—Charles Lamson . . ." Chuck extended his hand to Mendel, and with a broad smile told him: "We have a jail bird in the family," and Helen, sitting down between the two men she loved most in the entire world, now pieced together the story about Betty Dunhill's call to Sylvia, and Sylvia telephoning while Frimma was not home.

"Does Ma know?" Helen asked.

"Ma knows you're here, till the end of this month. But she doesn't know that I'm here," and all three laughed, and Chuck reminded Mendel that about three years ago he came to fetch Helen to a meeting, and now it all came back to Mendel why that face of his was faintly familiar. Mendel's eyes were asking Helen all kinds of questions, which he and Frimma would want to know, and wanted to know three years ago—about this very nice young man.

"You heard Chuck say 'we have a jail bird in the family,' Pa. I was going to tell you later, after coming out of here, that Chuck and I are planning to get married as soon as the elections are over. He's too busy electioneering, and I'm too busy here mending the torn linens of this jail, you know what I mean?"

But Helen noticed the disturbed, pained look in her father's

287

eyes, and she knew that he would never ask the question that was still bothering him most. "No, Pa, this isn't the man I eloped with to the South. This is Charles Lamson, and he's Jewish, Pa." Helen explained and waited. Chuck Lamson also said nothing, as Mendel was studying the clean shaven man, without the hat, with an open shirt collar.

"Mazl Tov!" Mendel said at last, "this will make Ma very happy! I should have taken her with me for this happy occasion. Mazl Tov!" he said again, and shook Chuck's hand. He then bent over and kissed his daughter again.

CHAPTER XI

Willie Rivers—a Buryat Citizen

As the third year of the devastating crisis pushed closer to the presidential nominating conventions, it seemed also that all contending forces were thrown into sharper confrontations. Tens of thousands were depending entirely on public or private charities for their existence, and were at the mercy of local politicians, like Mayor Cermak. Although he admitted publicly that "the situation is desperate, the Federal Government must come to our relief," yet the people were suddenly threatened with the greatest disaster yet encountered by them. Without previous warnings, the announcement was made that relief would be cut by half for 160,000 family men.

"Impossible! It must not happen!" went up the cry of the destitute. They began to prepare to battle for their survival: to prepare a march through the Loop to Grant Park, where they would shout their defiance to this destruction of human life. In Grant Park they would demand the withdrawal of the cut; there they would demand, instead, an increase in the original allowances for the third winter of suffering.

The atmosphere throughout the Windy City became more charged, more tense, with each passing hour. The Mayor and the police department were hostile; a permit to march was refused, the newspapers and radio stations predicted a bloody battle as they kept up a barrage of details of police preparations to prevent the demonstration from taking place.

Hurried meetings of the unemployed organizations were held in all parts of the city; the leaders prepared to meet the threats of an attack upon them by calling on still larger numbers to respond, and to fill the Loop with Hunger Marchers.

"We must march with or without a permit," Willie told Mirko, late that night, as the two walked out of the Unemployed Council Headquarters. He was repeating the decision of the activists to reassure himself, and to hear his friend's reassurance.

289

Casually, inconspicuously, Willie touched his head, feeling the scars left there from a previous battle against an eviction in Reverend Green's block. In silence he asked himself, "What right have I to ask the others to walk into a police trap, into a bloody massacre?"

Mirko, too, was thinking the same thoughts, in his own silence. He knew it would be impossible to survive on a cut budget, on half the allowances received by those thousands of families. The pale, drawn face of his starved mother kept coming back to him, as if admonishing him not to permit others to starve the slow, agonizing death that was hers.

"What else can we do?" Mirko said aloud to his friend. "All the participating organizations have voted to march to Grant Park, with or without a permit. They all know it might mean broken heads, and arrests, but they all said it won't be as bad as going through another winter with half the allowance for relief." He felt responsible for the thousands whom he, Willie, and Chuck Lamson, and others would soon be leading.

"If they attack us, after letting us into the Loop, we'll be badly cornered," Willie said grimly. "There won't be any opening for us to break ranks and disperse. The blows will fall heavy, if we can't get away from them—that is, in case they decide to attack us."

"I know, I know; that's the chance we have to take. Like Chuck said at the meeting, this is an election year, with Roosevelt challenging the guy in the White House and telling the country that he's for the forgotten man, and for a New Deal. Maybe they won't crack heads. The Mayor and the machine want the votes of these forgotten men that we'll be leading tomorrow into the Loop. We have to take advantage of this, and force them to rescind the cut," Mirko said, and repeated his argument for the hundredth time, believing strongly that the Chicagoans would respond in large numbers, and would force the police to retreat.

Fifty thousand grim-faced men and women, black and white, responded and fell in line, and started Chicago's Hunger March as scheduled by the leaders of the unemployed movement. They marched without a permit—Willie Rivers flanked on one side by Mirko Yanich, and on the other by Chuck Lamson—all at the head of the great throng of hungry humanity. Closely behind marched the fifty men and women selected by the participating organizations.

Hattie Green, Chris Wesly-Yanich and Helen Kanofsky held hands tightly, eyes on their loved ones in the front line, as the march turned east on Randolph Street.

"Will they get him again? Will they beat him again?" Hattie asked herself, and kept her eyes glued on Willie Rivers—fear spreading in her heart; another blow, another beating over the old wounds would mean the end. She prayed softly that he be spared, that all be spared. She prayed that God allow her to marry this man, as they had planned, soon, very soon. "Please dear God, we waited so long for each other." She squeezed Helen's hand but continued to stare with her glazed, tense eyes at the three men in the front rank.

Helen leaned over and whispered: "I think they'll let us through," repeating Chuck's words. Only last week she had come out of jail, where she had served time for "looting," and this was her first big public demonstration since returning home.

Somehow her mind drifted at this moment to Art Walton— she wondered where he was during that particular dangerous time in her life. "Must I lose Chuck, too? Will they beat him? Will they blind him like they did Isaac? Oh, Chuck, don't let them!" she said to herself, and continued to watch him. He looked back, and their eyes met.

His curly, dark hair had begun to recede rapidly, and made his forehead look big, and the top of his head appeared heavier than the rest of his face. But his eyes, his smiling, youthful eyes, remained ageless—she thought—and kind.

Helen now recalled his confidential discussion with her about Sylvia, when he told her that Sylvia had romantic notions about this big movement that had developed throughout the country, and that she looked upon herself as some kind of a heroine who had to prove herself in some dramatic way.

"Yes, I thought so, too," Helen replied then. "She makes people feel a little uncomfortable on account of that concept of hers." But now she thought that Chuck was doing the same thing himself—he seemed to be testing himself, up there in the front lines, as if trying to prove himself.

Helen didn't see the others around him; she was prepared to run to Chuck in case he was attacked. She imagined herself pulling him away from the policeman's clubs and saving him, saving Chuck—he must be saved! "I won't let them take him away from me, I won't let them!" she repeated to herself.

There was no conversation, no singing of patriotic or labor songs. They all march in deathly silence, in grim silence—all eyes on their front line, on the three men leading the Chicago Hunger Marchers. To Chris Wesly-Yanich it seems as if she had walked already a thousand miles, an eternity; with her lips tight, teeth touching, repeating in her mind: "I should have listened to Mirko, I should not have come, should not have come, should not have risked our child's life. It's wrong, wrong, wrong!"

The sidewalks are now jammed with thousands of new arrivals, many waiting their turn to enter the marching ranks, to join the demonstrators, as the throng continues to swell and to march fourteen abreast, and to watch each gesture of their leaders, each movement of the three men, and each breeze on their banner in front of them.

Then suddenly, from nowhere, like an apparition, they see the solid wall of uniformed police, blocking the three leaders with their outstretched clubs—they hear Willie's clear voice commanding the marchers to halt . . . they hear the Police Captain's words: "It's against the law to march in the Loop without a permit!" An ominous silence hangs momentarily between the two camps, as Willie steps forward and turns towards the thousands behind him:

"This is a peaceful demonstration of the unemployed. If there's bloodshed and violence we'll hold you, the police, responsible for it!" He looks at Mirko, and, in that split second laden with the courage of his black people, their eyes meet in agreement to proceed with the march. Willie, Mirko, and Chuck raise their hands and signal the thousands to follow them, to go forward, to ignore the cordon of uniformed men . . . the thousands move forward, the police retreat to both sides of the street, and the Chicago Hunger Marchers cross the full width of the Loop and pour into Grant Park. Hattie and Helen let go their sweaty, tight hand-grip; Chris smiles, and with eyes filled with grateful tears embraces and kisses the other two women; singing breaks out spontaneously from many parts of the marching thousands and they continue swelling the grounds near the waterfront.

Loud, joyous laughter and singing continue, and Willie Rivers mounts a speaker's stand and shouts clear across Lake Michigan:

"We've just won a great victory, a victory for all the people of our city. It's a victory for the fourteen million unemployed in our country, who won't be silenced. We won't be intimidated by the police or by the mayor. Your elected delegates will now proceed to the County Building with our petition and our demands. Remain here till we return with the mayor's answer . . ." and the single file, led by Willie Rivers, Mirko Yanich, and Chuck Lamson, marches out of Grant Park, to the wild, tumultuous applause of the thousands.

Other leaders wait their turn to speak; they listen to the familiar, young militant mother: "In these past few years millions of our homes were laid waste as if an invader had swept through our country. Millions of our families were broken up, as was mine, and many of us are reduced to beggary. Our children are starving, and will be freezing this winter, and will be dying by the thousands, unless we stop this now!" She waits for the applause to subside to add: "I'd rather die in this fight for food and shelter than to let my children die this winter of hunger and cold."

Quickly others follow with brief speeches, and when the Reverend Green begins, there's a hush, for he speaks softly, calmly: "We've seen every enemy of this big movement try to disrupt it. These enemies tell us that we must first rid ourselves of the communists before the federal government will agree to grant us unemployment insurance. But that is not so! During these hungry years we've learned that if we give in to that kind of rubbish, then we'll be told next to exclude the Catholics, and then the Jews, and next my people, the Negroes, and others. This movement is strong and powerful, as we've seen only minutes ago, because we refused to bite that poison . . ." and the rest gets lost in the loud applause and cheering.

Suddenly all heads turn towards the entrance to Grant Park, and the huge crowd sprawled over the grounds quiets down as the delegates to the mayor's office file back towards the platform. The ripple of applause becomes loud and strong, and the clapping of hands is beat out in unison, in rhythm, as Mirko takes the microphone and says angrily: "Nothing satisfactory came from our visit with the mayor. He refuses to . . ." and the

293

crowd curses and pledges to come back again, in still greater numbers. More speakers follow; disappointment is replaced with anger; they leave the park seething, bitter, with threats to return ten times as large in numbers, with their families and their children.

They return to their Unemployed Council Headquarters, to the union offices, to their gathering places in back of the stockyards, in the churches—they return to make plans for a bigger demonstration on the morrow.

On the morrow Chicago awakens to the announcement over the radio and in the newspapers that the mayor's office is withdrawing the fifty percent cut in relief.

II

"I'm going to leave you soon, Mirko. You won't see me around for a couple of months," Willie said.

"Doctor's orders, ah? Your head bothering you again?"

"No, on the contrary. Doc said it's okay for me to go traveling now," Willie answered.

"You mean . . . you ain't kidding?" Mirko asked and looked at Willie with a joyful smile.

That is how Willie Rivers made his first announcement about his delayed trip abroad. He had been chosen by the International Labor Defense to go to the Soviet Union for the May Day celebration, with the request, however, that he arrange to remain there for several weeks.

The now-famous case of the Nine Scottsboro Boys had reached a high stage of confrontation. Blacks and whites fought desperately for the release of the innocent youths. The issues of racism, legal frameups, and exclusion of Negroes from jury service were being discussed nationally and internationally. The General Secretary of the International Labor Defense, J.Louis Engdahl, was already in Europe, traveling together with Mrs. Ada Wright, mother of two defendants of the Nine Scottsboro Boys, and scheduled to appear in almost thirty countries.

Willie was invited to tour the major cities of the U.S.S.R., to personally acquaint the Soviet people with the full meaning of this extraordinary case. He accepted, and within a few days departed for distant lands, and for the Moscow May Day festivities. He then travelled clear across the full breadth of the Soviet Union, to Lake Baikal and Irkutsk, where he was to spend several weeks with the Buryat Mongolians.

Together with hundreds of Russians and a small American delegation, he traveled for days and days without end, it seemed. The Trans-Siberian train took him beyond the Ural Mountains, into the vastness of space which relaxed his mind and body, and allowed him to look back at his homeland in retrospect, with objectivity. The other four Americans with him also seemed affected in similar manner. They talked freely among themselves, sometimes opening up their hearts, and laying bare to each other their deep concern for their country and what was happening to it. Vicki, the young textile delegate from Gastonia, had missed the May Day celebration in Moscow. In London, England, she somehow became disconnected from the rest of the American delegates, and only by getting on an American boat headed for Leningrad was she able to rejoin the group a week later. Now on the train to Siberia, sitting next to Willie, she spewed her anger at the wealthy owners of that boat, which was making a world cruise, and indulging in luxuries which Vicki had never believed existed.

"I knew that we have a wealthy class in the United States, that was living very well all during these depression years. The word 'millionaire' was something abstract to me; it had no meaning until I reduced that word to 'rich' or 'very rich.' But never, never in my life could I even imagine that while people all over the country were living on scraps from the breadlines and soup kitchens . . . I never imagined that there were others enjoying at the same time the luxuries that I had seen on that cruiser. It's like seeing some kind of barbarism practiced before your own eyes."

"Barbarism? Why do you say that?" Willie asked her, surprised to hear the girl use that word. That was a term he had used once, when he described to Mirko the southern racist who showed him a human souvenir, a piece of a lynched Negro.

"Well, for some people to be starving, I mean literally starving, and freezing to death, and at the same time other people gorging themselves with all kinds of foods, and wines, and desserts, until they get sick and have to call the doctor to give them something, so they would be ready again the next day for more of the same! It's just unbelievable! Do you know that everybody on that boat who works for the owner and his family had to be a college graduate, and had to come from some well-recommended, respectable family, meaning a family of means? And they all acted like flunkeys to this owner and his family. Do you realize how many people could be fed with the food that I saw them waste over there? I mean just the food they leave uneaten on the tables? I'll bet all the families of my mill, where I used to work, could be taken care of for a whole year on the money this one family of eleven people spends on its world cruise."

"But that isn't it," Vicki continued meditatively, more calmly, now that she knew the others were listening to her, "it's the sadism, the barbarism! Surely they all know that people are hungry in the U.S.A., that children are starving and dying from malnutrition! How can they enjoy living like that? And the owner, and his family—forever surrounded by some flunkeys, who would jump up at their slightest little whimper or belch, to serve them, to take care of their needs. I've never seen anything like this, even in the movies; and if you told me all this, I wouldn't have believed you, if I hadn't seen it all with my own eyes."

There was no stopping her. "Only eleven people in the family, but they had over sixty college men and women serving them. Even in the engine room, in the beauty parlor, in the bar, in the theater—they had college or university people waiting on them. You know what happened the last day I was with them on that world cruiser, I mean the last night? They gave a farewell masquerade ball—it seems every other night they have something like that. They found out that there was a stranger in their midst who had gotten on in London, for the ride to Leningrad. That became the big talk aboard, that broke some of their boredom, and they decided to bill my last night on their cruiser as a Farewell Ball to me! Honestly! Then I knew I was in real trouble because their masquerade balls are only an excuse for wearing their expensive jewelry, and their fabulous evening clothes, and for the women—God! You should see those fantastic hairdos! Don't think that I'm off my mind and that I'm sitting here on a Soviet train going to Irkutsk, and telling you stories that I'm making up on the spur of the moment. Some of the women's tiaras with the expensive array of diamonds would blind you; others have earrings or bracelets that are priced in the hundreds of thousands of dollars."

"How do you know all that? These women didn't come to you and tell you all this?" Willie asked.

"Of course they didn't," Vicki replied with a slightly twisted smile. "They didn't even greet me on deck. I was an outcast in their midst, even when I wore the French woman's clothes, which fitted me pretty good. Oh, I should tell you that they put me up in a cabin with one of the French maids, and her clothes fitted me beautifully. The owner wanted his two young brats to speak only French on this world trip, so he got himself this woman to look after them. But this Mrs. Dannielle Taix, this so-called maid, somehow was bored with that crowd, and with all that show of wealth, I imagine, and she found me a relief from her own boredom. Whenever she had an opportunity to spend time with me, without making herself conspicuously absent from the others, she'd answer all the questions that I asked her, because I told her that if the surgery on my hip were successful, then I'd like to write a book about my trip, later on."

"You going to have surgery on your hip?" Willie asked with a sad expression. "Something serious?"

"Oh, that was the story I gave the purser so I could get on that boat; there's nothing wrong with me, except the nightmarish experiences with that crowd. They aren't real, I tell you; they all seem to be living like in a dream world—trying to entertain themselves twenty-four hours a day with eating, drinking, and whoring. They are degenerates—that entire class is a degenerate class of people," and it appeared as if Vicki was about to take off on that track, when Willie reminded her where she was in her story.

"What happened at this Farewell Ball for you?" he asked.

"Well, you know I had no clothes for that kind of a deal, and if I had worn Mrs. Taix' evening clothes and her jewelry, I would have looked pretty stupid in it all. I'm not cut out for that kind of stuff. So I was going to play it differently, pretend I was too sick, 'my hip is beginning to bother me again' I said to Mrs. Taix. 'I'm not sure I'll be able to make it tonight.' But she's a shrewd gal—maybe they're all shrewd in their own way. I don't really know; how else did they get all that wealth? Not by working with their nice little manicured hands. They had to get it by cheating, or stealing. Right?"

"What did you wear for the ball?" Willie asked, and smiled.

"I decided to wear my own clothes, the dress I had on when I boarded their cruiser, and my own shoes, and my own Five-and-Ten-Cent Store jewelry, and see what happens. I tried this idea on Mrs. Taix and you know what she said?"

"No, I wasn't there to hear what Mrs. Taix said to you," Willie answered.

"Come on, guess! Take a crack at it anyway," she urged her listeners.

"How would we know? We've never been around those crackers. Why don't you tell us," another of the delegates said.

"She said: 'This is the best idea we have yet had on this trip. We've been away from home more than ten weeks already and it'll be a real treat for all of us to have a girl tonight dressed like you are, at our masquerade ball.' So I began to think: I'll be on display, they'll probably be making fun of me anyway. Why not go all the way? There's nothing they can do to me any more—we were docking early in the morning, and they wouldn't throw me overboard, so I got some cardboards, and crayons, and a piece of cord, and made myself a sandwich sign, and just as they were all lining up—they give prizes at those balls—I joined them in the march, with my sandwich sign reading BUY AN APPLE, PLEASE! and as I walked along, with the others, in a circle-like, I shouted BUY AN APPLE, PLEASE! Now don't ask me why I did it, but that won me the booby prize!" And Willie and the others burst out laughing so loud that they were heard all over the car.

"What did they give you as a prize? A roll of toilet paper?" someone asked.

"I'll show you what. If someone offered to pay one hundred smackers this very minute, I wouldn't take it," Vicki said, and from her pocketbook pulled out a tiny Cellini snuff box, made of pure gold, and decorated with an original painting by some famous Italian painter, whose name she had forgotten. "Mrs. Taix explained to me all this about the box, and about Cellini, and all the rest."

"What are you going to do with it? Buy yourself some snuff and use it at big meetings, where you'll be reporting about your trip?" Willie asked and again all Americans laughed at such a possibility.

"Then you'll take the little snuff box around to the ladies, and you'll tell them, 'please, madame, a very fine snuff,' " and again they laughed.

"But I intend to do something with this anyway," Vicki told them.

She had thought about this before, and she knew exactly what she wanted to do with that very expensive gold snuff box. "We're going to run a raffle on this. I bet we can raise a lot of money, if we do it right, and tell the people something about Cellini—he was supposed to have been the greatest in that field of work—and we'll find out something about the painter and tell the people a little about him, too. We can raise enough money to pay for at least one leaflet for our shop caucus."

"How much is that?"

"About thirty dollars," Vicki said.

"Well, you might at that. I can just see the chairman opening up a meeting, and pausing long enough for all to see him display this little gold Cellini snuff box, as he takes out a pinch of snuff, and pushes it up his nostrils," Willie said reflectively. "I bet you'll consider this a high point of your trip to Europe, ah? I mean this experience of traveling with the top cream of American society."

"I sure will. You can bet your, your . . . snuff box on that."

In Siberia the Americans split into two groups—Vicki stayed with Willie, where both addressed small, and sometimes large, groups of farmers, or workers inside their factories, and once a group of students in their school. On one occasion a mass reception for the Americans was arranged in a distant city, which took some more traveling. When they arrived, the large dining room was filled to capacity with "udarniks," shockworkers—men and women who were selected from various plants and educational institutions for their exemplary work.

Softly, but joyously, Willie greeted these shockworkers in the name of the International Labor Defense, and thanked the Russian equivalent, the M.O.P.R., for inviting him as its guest. But suddenly Willie broke into his natural, oratorical platform style:

My life isn't worth a penny if they string up the Nine Scottsboro Boys on the usual and familiar frameup charge of rape. Saving these boys from a legal lynching will be our first big breakthrough, not only for black America, but for all America.

Your protests in this country, and the protests all over the rest of the world, are helping us in our fight, and I'm here to thank you in person. A victory in this fight could open the door to many other victories and to still greater unity between the black and white people. A victory that will clear these young boys could bring closer the day when blacks and poor whites will be sent to Washington to represent America, in Congress.

The applause and cheers were deafening. Willie proceeded to give the details of the frameup of the nine young boys. At the end of the festivities the guests swarmed around him and Vicki, many requesting autographs of the Americans, and, in turn, giving them souvenirs of their personal belongings—handkerchiefs, cigarette holders, pins and rings.

The response was the same wherever Willie Rivers made his appearance: promises of protests against the threatened execution of the Nine Scottsboro Boys, and promises of continued support until all were set free. Willie's tour brought the young Chicago "Orator" in close contact with thousands of Soviet citizens. Many of those who were hosting Willie explained to him how they operated their plants and collective farms, and assured him that it was only the beginning, only the foundation for the building of their socialist society. Willie's enthusiasm was matched only by his strong desire to see more of the new land, to study more of the new society, to collect more information so that upon return home he would be able to report back about the land where there was no color line.

His return to Chicago's South Side was widely announced. Hundreds crowded into all available space. A feeling of great interest, and anticipation, prevailed among the people—they expected Willie Rivers to tell them something truly unusual. They were familiar with his ways, and with his twinkle in the eye, and understood it to mean—just wait a little longer and I'll tell you all.

In a semi-mysterious voice, the chairman of the South Side Unemployed Council, said: "I give you now the world traveler from Washington Park, and the citizen from Buryat Mongolia."

Slowly Willie rose and looked upon the many familiar faces;

some he greeted with a wave of his hand, others with a silent movement of his lips, as if calling their names. When at last he began his report on his travels abroad, Willie Rivers did what he had done before: he played with his audience, he teased it, and aroused the people's curiosity.

"I speak to you as a citizen of Buryat Mongolia," he said evenly, and a hush fell over the audience, many of them wondering if they would soon lose him for good, to another country.

"The people of Buryat Mongolia have asked me to bring you hearty greetings. Both young and old, and even some of their lamas, begged me to tell you that they will help free the Nine Scottsboro Boys." More bewilderment: who are those lamas? Will some of them come here and help personally?

But Willie was a master of timing. Sensing that it was necessary to talk plainly, and to tell them where he had been, he began to describe the receptions given him in Moscow, and in distant cities in Asia. "They treated me like an American emissary, like I was the Ambassador of the United States, and in the factories and farms and educational institutions we learned that those Russians know very much about the American Negroes; they know very much about the southern tenant farmers and sharecroppers; they asked me questions about the Chicago stockyards that put me to shame, because I didn't know how to answer some of those questions. They asked me why the packinghouses haven't installed showers for the men and women who get covered with blood; they asked me why our men and women aren't getting their aprons and their gloves free, as they do over in their Russian packinghouses. And what about the fifteen-minute rest period they take every two hours —do we have that here? I met them face to face, and saw a dream come true; the people had full control of their natural resources, of their natural wealth, and of all industry, and they're using it all for the benefit of the people. At the Narodny plant, their union leader explained to us how each plant is owned by the people themselves, and how they distribute the results of their labor for improvements of their life by building hospitals and schools and creches and libraries, as they go along."

Willie pulled out a small notebook from his jacket pocket, and began to follow some of the notes he had taken on his trip. For nearly two hours he spoke about what he had seen and heard, and when during the question period a man asked him, "Now that you're a Mongolian citizen, are you going back there?" Willie laughed as they had seen him laugh before, and they were waiting again, in a hushed hall, for a straight answer.

"When we arrived in the capital of Buryat Mongolia, in Siberia, almost the other end of the country, not far from the world's deepest and biggest lake, Lake Baikal, the mayor of the city gave a dinner in our honor, and told us that he had been authorized by the City Soviet, that's like our City Council, here in Chicago, to give us all full citizenship in their Republic. He told us that any time we come there, or if any time one of us wishes to come to them permanently, he would be treated with full equality, like one of their own people." When the cheering and applause subsided, someone shouted: "Are you going back to Mongolia?" and Willie replied, "Hell, no! They don't need me over there!"

Studying the small pages of his notebook, Willie cited numerous facts he had collected on his trip: Buryat Mongolians were dying of hunger and disease. Thousands of their very young perished during their revolution, the older boys and girls joined the Red Army, and went far away from their homes. But the central government of Moscow began pouring in help to this dying republic: they sent them doctors and teachers and food. They gave them grants for building up their schools and hospitals; they took care of the children first, and gave everything they needed for growth and good health; within five years the country of Buryat Mongolia began to change, and began to catch up with the other republics."

Without saying much more, Willie and his black audience, many of whom had come out of the decaying Black Belt, were thinking together, and envisioning together, how much simpler it would be to rebuild their own southern homelands, if the federal government were to do for them what Moscow had done for Buryat Mongolia.

The Buryat Mongolian citizen of Chicago's south side and dozens of others stayed on till past midnight, and examined the souvenirs Willie Rivers had brought back from his European and Asian trip, and felt part of a big event—having linked themselves spiritually with peoples across the oceans.

No resource of mind or heart or organization can be excluded in the fight against
what is, after all, our real enemy. Our
real enemies are hunger, want, insecurity,
poverty and fear.

—*Franklin Delano Roosevelt*

CHAPTER XII

A Separation and a Wedding

I

Like an incurable malignancy on the body of American society,
the ranks of the jobless multiply and grow to the gigantic size
of fifteen million. Hunger and poverty continue to spread without letup, forcing hundreds of thousands of young children
out of their homes, into the streets and highways, wandering
across the country, in search of food.

Families born or reared during the height of this Great Storm
break up, separating husband from wife, and parents from their
offspring. Chris and Mirko Yanich, caught in this web of near-
devastation, now argue continuously.

"And how do you expect me to get the milk for her?" she
asks accusingly, pointing to their redhead infant in the crib.
"I can't leave the house; stuck here, sitting here, and waiting for
you to show up, to come in like a stranger to both of us."

Chris never actually blamed her husband for the lack of food
in their home, or for the cold they had suffered during the
months when they were confined to the kitchen and bedroom,
having closed up the rest of their home. It was her inability to
do something about their condition that drove the former unemployed leader to fits of anger and sharp quarreling. Her
frustrations deepened with Mirko's long absences, and the arguments between them became more frequent.

"You have time for everything, and for everybody," she
almost shouted at Mirko when he returned that late evening,
completely exhausted from his day's activities.

"You haven't been out this late to a meeting, Mirko, and I'm
telling you right now that I'm taking Mara with me back home,

and then you can have all the freedom you want; you can even bring Betty right here, into your sacred Yanich home, the day I'm out of it!"

Mirko turned pale at the mention of Betty's name, and became thoroughly confused. How did Chris know that he had seen Betty that very afternoon? It had not occurred to this busy organizer and leader of thousands of unemployed, that Chris was only guessing, only surmising, that he had been spending time with Betty. Chris had been suspicious from the very first time she had seen the pretty farm girl, that her husband was more than casually fond of her. But Chris' threat to take their daughter away with her, and to hike back to Nebraska, infuriated the tired and harassed Mirko.

"What do you think I do all day? Where do you think I go? I saw Betty this afternoon about getting her office to issue a special bulletin to the Swift packinghouse workers. What's wrong with that? What's wrong with asking the Swift workers to back F.D.R. in the coming elections?"

Still on his feet, Mirko's anger mounted as he looked at his sleeping infant daughter. "And don't you dare, don't you ever dare take her away from here!" he said, in a harsh whisper between his tight lips.

There were other times when their arguments ended with a conciliatory compromise by one or the other. Mirko was not unmindful of the desperate situation that Chris had been forced into ever since her arrival in Chicago. First were weeks of confinement, then months of care of their first-born, their Mara, or Margarita, after Ma Yanich. But it was impossible for Mirko to break his pattern of life, to change his routine, and snatch time from the mounting responsibilities he had carried during those sharp battles of the unemployed.

There were, of course, many mornings during which Mirko and Willie, and several other leaders, had to meet to plan their strategy for the day's or week's activities. The Yanich home was frequently used for such purposes; but that did not free Chris, nor allow her to go away during those hours and leave Mirko in care of their child. He was completely helpless and clumsy when left alone with their daughter.

Tonight, however, as Mirko looked at his haggard, young wife, and again noticed the sad expression on her thinning face,

304

which somehow gave her the appearance of a trapped person, with no way out—he felt deeply sorry at having been so sharp with her, and for having neglected her so much, and for having permitted their life to deteriorate so rapidly.

"You must understand, Chris, that things have changed since I came back from the New York School. The demands made on me are different now. I don't know myself what to do to help you get into the activities again, in our own neighborhood, and in the city. I think about it many times; I thought about it only this evening before coming home, when Willie and I arranged to meet here in the morning. I told him to come here so you could go out, or do whatever you have to do, until noon. I'll try to take care of Mara. You don't have to take her with you this time." His voice became soft and appeasing, and Chris knew that he was as helpless about his home situation as millions of others throughout the country whose families were breaking up. She knew that he was not able to act differently; that he had to continue to give leadership to a movement that involved thousands of families.

Their quarreling dwindled, and the harshness between them disappeared completely this evening. When at last Mirko fell asleep, Chris noticed how nervously he was tossing and turning, and at one time his entire body shook, as if experiencing something dreadful in a dream. She leaned over and asked him softly:

"What's the matter, Mirko? Were you dreaming?"

He opened his eyes, and looked at his wife confusedly. Then he mumbled, "I fell all the way down to the basement."

"Did you get hurt?"

"No," he answered, and smiled appreciatively at his wife's humor.

"Then go back to sleep."

"All right," Mirko said and kissed her before turning over and pulling the blanket over his ears.

But other times, many times, the seed of dissent between the two Yaniches grew into sharp clashes, each accusing the other of opportunism, or of lack of concern for the people's plight. Such was the case when the great South Side fire took place, a few blocks from their home, which had driven many of the ghetto families into the chilly streets. Mirko and Willie were at the State Capitol, in Springfield, with a large delegation of unemployed men and women, pleading with the governor not to cut off the seventeen million dollars from his current budget.

The fire was seen great distances away. Chris had grabbed her infant, and blankets for both of them, and run outside. Later she returned to her block and persuaded several neighbors to take in the families who were completely burned out; others agreed to donate or lend blankets for the shivering residents who were compelled to spend the rest of the night on the street.

Mirko, victorious in the fight with the governor, returned home hours after the fire had been extinguished, to find his wife and child still on the street; Chris still arranging shelter for the remaining families, and personally helping those for whom shelter could not be obtained.

"You'd make a good social worker in this neighborhood," he told his wife sarcastically when he caught up with her.

"Social worker? What would you have done for those people, let them sit there, or would you and Willie have taken them to the City Hall, with a petition, demanding that the mayor find shelter for them?"

"That's exactly what we would have done! All these homes are fire traps; this might happen again tomorrow—then you'll go out again to collect blankets and to find homes for the homeless?"

"Yes, I'll do it again, if there's another fire. I'll do just that!" she answered with anger, exhausted from her night's activities and annoyed at the disapproving remarks of her own husband.

"Patching the system isn't going to make revolutionaries of these people; it'll only quiet them down. You might just as well move over to Madison and Halsted Streets, and do your missionary work there, among the lumpenproletarians!"

Chris was shocked at his callousness. They quarrelled all the way home: Mirko angry at his wife for having kept their infant daughter out most of the night, but also angry at himself for not admitting to Chris that helping those people during that dreadful fire was the most important thing she could have done.

With the passing of time their differences sharpened still more. Mirko became a fluent speaker, and a welcome teacher of current events among hundreds of unemployed. He was pleased with himself after his first attempt to teach a class on philosophy, with Willie and Hattie in attendance. He was now in high demand in other parts of the city, and he continued to stay away from his home and his family till late at night.

Chris, however, was unable to break out of her confining, narrow world. She was unable to find ways of involving herself in the still rising movement. She became depressed and grouchy, and even less communicative with her rarely seen husband. Her burdens of holding the Yanich home together became heavier and, at last, unbearable.

She knew that the street battles of the hungry millions were temporarily merged with the battles inside the halls, where all contending presidential candidates vied for the conscience of America. But Chris Yanich was left too far behind to be part of it all.

With her daughter in her arms, she was at that moment hiking to the Wesly home, on the outskirts of Omaha, where food and shelter was promised for the two Yaniches.

Chris was hundreds of miles away from Chicago, where the man with the cigarette holder at a jaunty angle rose to tell the nation that he, Franklin Delano Roosevelt, if elected president of these United States of America, would heed the cry of the forgotten man.

I pledge you, I pledge myself, to a new deal for the American people. Let us all here assembled constitute ourselves prophets of a new order of competence and of courage.

Defying the old traditions that presidential candidates should remain in professed ignorance of what was happening at the nominating conventions, Roosevelt flies to the Democratic Party convention to receive the nomination and to shatter all precedent. He gives the country a foretaste of his gifts for drama, and *HAPPY DAYS ARE HERE AGAIN* resounds throughout the vast hall, and throughout the nation.

In that same month of June, another precedent gets shattered in another hall: the first Negro candidate for the position of vice president is nominated, since Frederick Douglas's nomination for that office by the Equal Rights Party, in 1872. *JAMES W. FORD,* the grandson of a black slave, is nominated as the vice presidential candidate on the Communist Party ticket, headed by William Z. Foster. *FORD* tells his cheering audience:

In this so-called democratic United States, which is at the peak of capitalist culture, the white ruling classes now use the most shameless oppression of twelve million Negroes—Jimcrow and persecute them; Negroes are existing as a nation of "social outcasts" in this country.

He is soon followed by the famous strike leader, William Z. Foster, the presidential candidate, who in accepting the nomination for this high post, tells the people:

The Communist Party never forgets that its task is to organize the workers for their revolutionary goal . . . such measures as we propose now constitute only relief, not cure for the ills from which the toilers suffer . . . capitalism must be overthrown, the industries and land socialized, exploitation abolished, and socialism established . . . that's the only cure for poverty, and unemployment, economic crises, and fascism, war, and the rest of the miseries of capitalism.

Mirko Yanich cheers and applauds, and merges with the thousands assembled at the Chicago Coliseum as they pour into the aisles and begin to carry the two top candidates on their shoulders, shouting in unison, *BLACK AND WHITE UNITE AND FIGHT.* His pale face, however, betrays his loneliness and sadness for his wife and daughter. In his ears still ring Chris' accusation that he was not capable of understanding the suffering of his own family, including his own mother. His regrets are too late; he continues to march with the others, and in silence pledges himself to restore his family when the millions of other Americans are restored to a normal life.

Frequently his eyes fill with tears as he waves to a friend, and now to Sylvia Connors, who is marching with her youthful Gary delegation; and to other out-of-town visitors whom he recognizes. He sees Zal Harris, under a Nebraska state banner, with his sister, Kate, on his arm, but he cannot hear Zal when he asks her: "Will you wait for me until Labor Day week-end, when I come back to Chicago? Will you return with me then, Kata, as my wife?" Mirko sees his sister lean over and kiss the smiling, happy Zal, on the cheek, and tighten her hold on his arm.

II

The economic blizzard continues throughout the land: the school system is often threatened with collapse and total destruction, even as teachers take pay cuts several times. The banks continue to close their doors in many states, and the central nervous system of the wealthiest country in the world soon ceases to function altogether. Libraries stop purchasing books, hospitals operate with inadequate staffs and supplies, wages fall from thirty to fifteen dollars a week in the Pittsburgh steel community—in this year of presidential election.

Pressures continue to mount; unemployed World War I veterans journey from all parts of the country to Washington, to petition Congress for the immediate payment of funds still due them on veterans' bonus certificates.[9]

Americans everywhere greet the war heroes with public demonstrations and provide them with food, clothing and lodgings. 50,000 Cleveland citizens gather to back the demands of the Bonus Marchers; 5,000 townspeople of Cheyenne, Wyoming, sit up to midnight to meet arriving groups of veterans and stage a torchlight parade; in East St. Louis, Bonus Marchers board trains as a crowd of several thousand along the B&O tracks yells and cheers the former soldiers. More than 20,000 Bonus Marchers pour into Washington, but President Hoover refuses to grant them an audience.

At a stretch of ground near the Potomac River, at the Anacostia Flats, an encampment springs up with tents and dugouts and becomes the new home for most of the war veterans arriving in the national capital. But soon sickness begins to spread, intestinal disorders and malnutrition take the lives of several veterans' children—and terror sets in as the leaders of the encampment are threatened with their lives. Several are kidnapped and brutally beaten; then the battered bodies of two veterans are found floating in the Potomac, galvanizing the war heroes' resistance and preparing them for the battle of July 28, *BLOODY THURSDAY*.

A large police contingent attempts to evict hundreds of veterans from two abandoned government buildings, but the veterans refuse to leave. The police charge and hurl tear gas bombs at the occupants, as the veterans fight back. Police draw their guns and fire, wounding several, two mortally.

On this *BLOODY THURSDAY,* President Hoover gives his order for the military to drive the veterans from their encampment. General Douglas MacArthur, aided by Major Dwight D. Eisenhower, orders eight companies of cavalry and infantry to go into action, with bayonets and tear gas. The army of bonus seekers is driven from the shanty village near Pennsylvania Avenue as the troops set fire to the veterans' shacks.

III

The turbulence proceeds unabated throughout the land. Battles for survival often take on the character of mass rebellions. New giants appear on the horizon, and suddenly rise to lead the seething throngs. The people recognize them as one of their own. Such was the young Tennessee coal miner, Angelo Herndon, who found himself dumped on the slag heap without work, without relief, without hope of escaping hunger and death from starvation.

Angelo drifts on the highway, and at last arrives in Atlanta, Georgia, where he picks up a leaflet on the street which says that the government must assume responsibility to provide work, or provide bread. He thinks deeply about this; he studies and reads more about the kind of a world he was thrown into, and when thousands of Atlanta white and Negro citizens are dropped from the relief rolls, leaving them desperate and hopeless, Angelo Herndon, the black youth, leads them into the fight for government help.

They follow the youth to the City Hall with a petition demanding work or relief, but Angelo is arrested—charged with incitement to insurrection, under a law passed in 1861—and is sentenced to 18-20 years in prison.*

In Chicago's Washington Park, in New York's Union Square, all over the country are repeated Angelo Herndon's words, spoken calmly, and with assurance, to the face of the judge and to the face of the prosecutor:

Your Honor, you may do what you will with Angelo Herndon. You may indict him. You may put him in jail. But there will come other thousands of Angelo Herndons. If you really want to do anything about the case, you must go out and indict the social system. But you

* He was freed in 1937.

will not do that, for your role is to defend the system under which the toiling masses are robbed and oppressed. You may succeed in killing one, two, even a score of working class organizers. But you cannot kill the working class.

This modern Hercules seems to take on the only world he had ever known, the southern world, and lifts it off its base, and holds it in his hands, as he tells everybody to look at it, and see what it really is like. Whites and blacks of the South, and of the North, break out of their color barriers and listen to Angelo's voice: they merge with the others in the long trek to save Angelo Herndon from a living death, and before the world unfolds one of America's greatest legal battles, often merging with the famous case of the Nine Scottsboro Boys. The upsurge swells as the election campaign for a new president rises to high gear, and for many thousands the demand for federal relief from the ravages of the Great Catastrophe is joined with the demand to free Angelo Herndon and the nine innocent black Scottsboro youths.

There is no end in sight to the spiral of decline; but President Herbert Hoover, the Republican candidate who promises a continuation of the same for another four years, stands firmly by his doctrine of local responsibility for relief. He is often laughed at by the men on the bread lines and soup kitchens when he tells the nation that "the only real and lasting remedy for unemployment is employment."

This is said by the Chief Executive in the face of a continued sharp decline in industrial production, and a drop in the national income by more than half. It is said at a time when the New York Governor, with the magic Roosevelt name, takes his battle to the country, shows himself to the electors, and presents the nation with his power of phrase-making, in his matchless, appealing radio voice.

He promises federal aid for the relief of the distressed; he promises to save and restore America. He pledges himself against the Four Horsemen: destruction, delay, deceit and despair, and nearly twenty-three million voters choose the prophet of the New Deal as their next president.

November 7, the day before the American electorate gives its largest vote ever cast for a presidential candidate, Willie

Rivers mounts the box in Washington Park and announces to thousands of south side residents that the Supreme Court has reversed the conviction of the defendants in the Scottsboro case.

IV

A strange, momentary calm seems to have set in, and to prevail everywhere. It is the calm of anticipation, and of hope. The people have been heard, and have made themselves felt. Evictions have almost come to a standstill after restoring tens of thousands of families to their premises; Unemployed Councils everywhere are now on guard, looking after the most needy cases—and death from hunger has been reduced temporarily, in the big cities. Relief, of sorts, has been wrung from city and state governments, frequently supplemented by private charities. Joint actions of blacks and whites had reached their highest as reports of the reversal of the Scottsboro case conviction reached out to every corner of the land. Lynching, the press is reporting, has practically been done away with. Talk of Workers Unemployment Insurance, financed by the federal government, is now on the lips of millions, as they look to the new President of the United States to help them make it a reality.

This peculiar, momentary calm, following the elections of the New Deal President, seems to be waiting for the answer on people's minds: where to? what next?

Attention shifts now to other lands: the stirrings overseas have barely reached the American shores, but now people, faintly familiar with the name Adolph Hitler, are beginning to read his *MEIN KAMPF*, the bible of the German fascists and wondering: where to? what next?

Preparations for Willie's and Hattie's wedding—postponed until the end of the year—are proceeding calmly as Hattie meets Helen Kanofsky at the store to select a pattern and materials for Hattie's wedding dress.

"We'll have to be very careful, Helen. Dad talks big but I have no idea where he'll get the money for all the things he wants for my wedding," Hattie cautioned her friend.

"Why worry about 'all the things'? You and I are here for

one thing only, for your dress, right? We can go up to $6 you said, all right? Then leave the rest to me."

Like two school girls out on their first big adventure, they finger the fine silks, and toy with the expensive brocades and appliques. Both pretend to be casual and indifferent about the delicate materials, and the high priced goods. Soon they had to make an important decision. In the Ladies Lounge they sat down for their conference. Many times before, they had conferred in the Sopkin Dress Shop washroom, where Helen, too, was working as an operator; and now, sitting comfortably in this store's restroom, they began to figure carefully how much material they would need for the pattern they had selected; and how to stretch Hattie's allowance so they could purchase the blue applique which had caught Hattie's attention.

"If you leave it all to me, Hattie, and let me have it my way, I'd get that blue silk you liked so much, for a tight-fitting blouse; that won't take much material. And let them cut us a quarter of a yard extra, for something I'll fix up for you as a headgear. Then we'll get something that will blend with this applique for the widest skirt ever worn by anybody—wedding or no wedding."

Hattie agreed.

Two full weekends were spent at the Green's sprawling home, cutting, fitting, and sewing Hattie's wedding garments. Sylvia came in from Gary the second weekend, and joined in with the hemming of the "widest thing ever worn."

Now the two sisters and Hattie, sitting on the living room floor, over which Hattie's mother had spread a large, clean cloth, were finishing the fine stitching on the silk blouse, and hemming the skirt with a lock stitch, so that Hattie wouldn't catch her heel in it, and trip.

Like millions of other young people throughout the country, Hattie had matured very rapidly—she seemed to have blossomed during the hectic weeks and months since Willie's return to her. Soon after Willie's recovery, she began to attend classes at the Unemployed Council headquarters, and, more than any other student, read the assignments made by the volunteer teachers as religiously as she had studied the Bible in her earlier days. She was one of the most serious students, and when, at one time, she and Willie attended a class on dialectical materialism, taught by Mirko Yanich, she had put so many questions to the inexperienced teacher that he threatened to turn the class over to Willie.

Now, as all three girls were finishing up the wedding garment, it was Hattie who started the conversation between them in a hushed monotone. "You talked about male supremacy, or male chauvinism, as you like to call it. The last time you were here, Sylvia, I had trouble following you. I wasn't sure I knew what you meant then; but I know now."

"How come?" Sylvia asked.

"I think Willie is a male supremacist," Hattie replied.

"That's a very serious accusation you're making, Hattie," Sylvia said.

"Don't worry, she isn't going to change her mind about marrying Willie," Helen said with a motherly smile and continued with her stitching.

"How do you know so much what Hattie is driving at, and whether she will or won't change her mind?" Sylvia asked.

"She better not! She won't get another wedding dress from the Reverend Green again; besides I have no intentions of seeing Hattie waste all my work on this garment. You better go through with your wedding plans, and tell us next month, or next year, about Willie's male supremacy."

"He isn't the only one. I don't even know if there are any men whom you wouldn't call male supremacists," Hattie continued in the same voice.

They were worried about her tone of complaint.

"Dad has never accepted Mom as an equal; Willie doesn't treat me as an equal; and I bet Helen can tell us the same about Chuck—if she's honest about it. All men are that way."

"Say, what goes on here? Are you looking for some excuse to back out? In another week it'll be too late—when you're Mrs. Willie Rivers you won't be talking like this."

"I know I won't," Hattie answered in her hushed, soft voice, looking up now, into the face of the older sister. "After our wedding, I'll be telling these things only to Willie."

"But that won't do you any good," Sylvia interjected. "One doesn't overcome white supremacy, or male supremacy, through private little talks between husband and wife. I think pressure by the group is more effective. When you expose a male for male supremacist behavior in public, he's bound to act differently the next time. It's the same thing with the white chauvin-

314

ists. We all have it, it's bred into us; we're almost born with ideas of white supremacy. But it's getting weeded out a lot when it's put under a strong light, and shown what it really means. When it's done on a large scale, like we're doing now all over the country, showing the people that being white didn't protect them from this crisis—and that they're no different from the millions of Negroes—then white chauvinism takes a real beating. If you want Willie to free himself of his male supremacy nonsense you'll have to put him to shame in public."

"If Hattie listened to you, my dear sister, she'd be getting a divorce before she even got married," Helen stopped her.

They continued with their sewing, and talking, and at last were ready for the final fitting and adjustment. The little cap of blue applique, covered artistically with a short, trailing veil, made Hattie the prettiest bride the two Kanofsky sisters ever saw, and the more approving comments they made, the happier became Hattie's smiling face.

Their discussion on male supremacy was cut off abruptly as Hattie began her modeling and posing. But at the wedding reception, where several hundred black and white guests had gathered, the subject somehow came up again, when Sylvia introduced her escort—the Gary steel worker, Peter Edgehill—who had only recently returned from an extended stay at the TB Sanitarium. Hattie, during a rare free moment with Sylvia, whispered to her: "He's probably the only man in this entire crowd who's not a male supremacist. You wouldn't be seen with any other kind in public."

Sylvia agreed heartily, her face reflecting, from then on, a newfound happiness, as she rejoined the throng of wedding guests.

V

For Betty Dunhill and Sylvia Connors the excitement generated by the wedding had spilled over into the New Year, and continued in high gear for the first several weeks of 1933. It was at the wedding party, when many telegrams and letters of congratulations from various parts of the country were being read, that the two girls first learned—to their amazement and disbelief—that Cousin Molly was on her way back to Chicago, returning from Europe, after a three year absence. The Master of Ceremonies had just been handed another Postal Telegraph envelope, which he opened and read slowly over the microphone of the spacious South Side Ballroom: ARRIVING CHICAGO JANUARY FOURTEENTH WITHOUT BERNARD WILL WIRE FROM NEW YORK, signed Molly Goldstein.

From the rear of the hall Betty and Sylvia rushed forward to claim the message, which had confused the M.C. and the guests assembled at Willie and Hattie's wedding. Sylvia explained that there was an error, that the telegram was not meant for the newlyweds, but for her. Privately she continued to explain to her friends what had happened, and soon she unscrambled the mystery of the cable from abroad. It appeared that Sylvia's mother refused to accept the cable delivered to her home, and advised the messenger boy that Sylvia Connors could be found that evening at the South Side Ballroom.

The Kanofsky home had remained, during the three years of crisis and turmoil, the one stable address through which communication was exchanged between the two Dunhill cousins and Sylvia. Frimma Kanofsky had developed good techniques as a Postmaster, and helped keep the communications flowing smoothly. Cousin Molly, who had traveled with her newspaper husband, Bernard Goldstein, to many parts of Europe, occasionally sent startling clippings from various capitals. One such newspaper cutout was mailed to Sylvia, and bore a British dateline:

When the German government lifted the ban on the Hitler Storm Troops, on June 18, 1932, the signal for armed conflict against the various existing organizations was given. The Nazis have carried on armed warfare against the Marxists and particularly against the Communists; in less than six weeks 183 were killed and 200 were wounded in battles between workers and Nazi gangs.

Molly wrote a brief note with her enclosure: "I'm heading for home. Bernard will follow soon. Will tell you personally more about new developments here which make it impossible for us to remain in Germany."

Molly's husband had wound up his work in Berlin, and had arranged to return to the United States, but was delayed. She proceeded without him to London, from where she took off to

316

the United States. It was from England that she first cabled Sylvia about her return home. That cable was soon followed by another one stating that her schedule was changed, and there would be a brief delay.

But now, at last, as the train was pulling into the Chicago depot, Molly was once again wondering how Betty would be dressed, what she'd look like; whether Sylvia would be there, too, to welcome her home. She clung to her memories of the two girls as they appeared three years ago, during their graduation. But suddenly the three were reunited in a tearful and joyous embrace, all talking at once, all asking each other many questions without waiting for answers, until they arrived at Betty's Halsted Street flat.

Molly kept staring at Sylvia, and smiling to herself, without saying anything.

"Well, what is it, Molly?" Sylvia asked.

"I don't know myself. There's something so different about you; you've changed somehow, but I don't know exactly how myself."

"Why don't you ask, and I'll tell you. It's my speech, no lisp any more."

"How did you accomplish that?" Molly asked with a smile.

"Simple. I listened to Dr. Brown and pulled out the two teeth that were crowding all the others, and tripping my tongue," Sylvia said, and opened her mouth to show Molly where she had the teeth removed. "I'm not trying to compete with Betty —but you know yourself how ugly those upper teeth of mine used to look."

"It isn't the looks—sure you've changed that way too," Molly said admiringly. "But your speech is really different. I kinda miss that lisp of yours. It was cute."

"Well, I can have Dr. Brown put them back in; he's good that way," Sylvia said and all three laughed.

"Your Mom and Dad—are they all right? You just made me think of your mother. You still sound like her with or without those extra teeth in your mouth," Molly added.

They drew on their memories in an attempt to recapture their past, but they also realized how much each one of them had grown and matured during those years of crisis.

"Betty is back on her poetry beat," Sylvia volunteered. "Look at her—not the same Betty you left behind, ah? Dreamy, moody, romantic—and confused," Sylvia said, putting a protective arm around Betty.

"Sylvia is right.

> In the night, and overhead a shovel of stars
> for keeps, the people march;
> Where to? What next?

I feel just like Carl Sandburg: I don't know where to from here, or what next. Only Sylvia knows all the answers," she added, freeing herself from Sylvia's arm.

"Just like the good old times," Molly observed in silence.

"Sylvia looks like she's ready to make a speech but hesitates. Why don't you go ahead, Sylvia. Say what's on your mind. You know you're gonna make a revolution yet, aren't you? Tell it to Molly," and she smiled disarmingly.

Molly continued studying the two girls, sensing that there was some kind of inexplicable bond between them; they understood each other well; both had matured so much that she felt somewhat left behind despite her travels and associations with people from the newspaper world.

"No, I'm not gonna make a revolution, but some people say that Franklin Delano Roosevelt is. And I don't believe he will either. Even if he could he wouldn't. Just because he says that he's going to recognize the Soviet Union doesn't make him a revolutionary," Sylvia said in her usual serious tone. But Betty was listening attentively, showing visibly the respect she held for her. "I don't like to go around telling people 'You see, I told you so'. I told you in 1929 that we were heading for a crisis but you all made fun of me, and now it's not too hard to see where this country is heading," Sylvia continued.

"All right, Sylvia, what's your prediction now?" Molly asked.

"I don't make predictions, I just read the signs."

"Isn't that the same? Because you can read the signs you have a right to make predictions," Molly said, and again noted in silence that Sylvia was the same argumentative girl, but sincere, dedicated.

"Well, you were there; you, too, can read the signs. You ought to know that what I'm saying is right—that unless Hitler, and all he stands for, is licked, the world will be heading right into another war," Sylvia said.

"I'm not in a hurry. We'll have plenty of time to talk about these things after Bernard comes back from Berlin. But what are your own personal plans, Sylvia?" Molly asked.

"Tomorrow, when I return to Gary, I'll begin a jail sentence of sixteen days. We now refuse to pay the fines they dish out to us: it's either sixteen dollars cash, or sixteen days in jail. We decided to go to jail because it's getting to be a habit with the Gary police to pick us up and fine us on any excuse, and because we're so busy with the movement, we've been raising the money and paying the fines—and it seems like we're practically financing the police with the fines we've been paying them. So we decided to put a stop to this: we'll serve the sentences instead. That'll cut down on some of the arrests, too, when they have to feed us and spend money on us, instead of getting money from us."

"That's smart," Molly commented. "Why did it take you so long to make this decision? In one of your letters to me you said that you had been arrested about a dozen times and had to pay a big fine. Why did you wait?"

"We had to do that in the beginning. They were going to behead our movement, by locking us all up. But we understood what they were up to, so we paid the fines whenever there was a choice of a jail sentence or a fine. But now it's different. The movement is big; there are many people to step in and take the place of those that are locked up, and we're not going to give them the people's money any more. We'd rather serve time. So I won't see you for a couple of weeks, and you better tell us a little more today in case you forget later."

"Forget? Are you kidding? Anyone going through Europe now can't forget some of the sights—especially if you're Jewish, or happen to be married to a Jewish man, like me."

Both Sylvia and Betty wanted an explanation about the confusion in Molly's schedule, her two cables, her follow-up letter, and why she had gone to Hamburg, Germany, from London, instead of coming home directly, like she told them she had planned to do.

"How did you happen to get to Hamburg?" Betty asked.

"That's just it, I wasn't going to go back to Germany with a passport carrying the name of Molly Goldstein. I knew better than that. I took a plane from London to Paris, and there I was to get on a train and connect with an American steamer at

319

Le Havre. I had it all figured out so I'd be able to get on that steamer all right. Bernard was delayed in Berlin again and told me to proceed home by myself. But when I looked out of the window of that plane, I suddenly saw a huge swastika below us, covering the full area of the grounds below within our sight. I nudged the English woman sitting next to me, and she showed real fear on her face when she caught sight of that swastika. All passengers soon got out of the plane and were told in French, German, and English that this was an emergency landing due to a leak of oil, and that this was Hamburg, Germany, and that those who wished to stay over night could do so and continue the following morning on another plane. The others who wished could leave within about half an hour on a train. I asked the English woman what she was going to do and she didn't have to think twice it seemed to me. 'I'm getting out of here right away; I'd rather be on a train than stay here a whole night in some hotel.' I later learned that she was the famous British Shakesperian actress, who was known all over the continent, and she expected that courtesy would be extended to her on the train through Germany, going towards France. Then all of a sudden she asked me: 'What nationality are you, Miss?' When I told her that I was an American, but that my husband was Jewish, she added quickly: 'Tell me your name on your passport, and where you were born, and where you're going from here, I mean from France. I'll claim you as my personal friend, and they'll leave you alone.' I told her I was born in Chicago, returning home, my passport name is Molly Goldstein. She repeated it all twice, to make sure she had the name straight, then she took my hand and put it through her arm, and began talking to me, and laughing, and pretending that she was telling me some jokes, and when we got on the train she explained to me quietly: 'I knew they would leave you alone if they'd see that you were with me, my companion.' She also told me that once we got to Paris I'd be able to continue traveling to Le Havre without any trouble. But in the meantime I saw something on that German train that I'll never forget the rest of my life."

She began detailing the gruesome scene she and the British actress had witnessed when a group of Storm Troopers boarded their train at one of the small-town stations. "Going from car to car, half-crazed with power, they shouted: 'Heil Hitler! Heil

Hitler!' And only a few seats away from where I and this British actress were sitting, we saw them grab an elderly gentleman with a white beard, and pull him out into the aisle, and almost tearing off his beard as they swung him, and kicked him, crying 'Jude! Jude!' and as soon as the whistle of the train was sounded, they left this gentleman lying there in the aisle, in a faint, and disappeared. When we pulled into the Paris depot, this elderly man with the white beard barely dragged his feet off the floor, and was helped by another passenger into the waiting area. I walked over to him and asked him if he'd care to give me his name, because being married to a Jew I know how he felt, and I'd like him to know that anything I could do for him, after I returned to Chicago, I'd be glad to do. 'But I'm not Jewish, my dear girl. I'm a German of the Greek-Orthodox religion. I'm a theologian, on my way to a conference in Paris,' he said softly, and limped away, thanking me for being so kind."

Molly somehow seemed to have turned pale and worried, as she finished talking, and then blurted out: "I wonder if there'll be someone over there to help Bernard. It's almost two weeks since I've heard from him."

Now all three were wondering—What Next?

Historical Footnotes

1. *Nicola Sacco,* the shoemaker, and *Bartolomeo Vanzetti,* a fish peddler, two Italian radicals, were arrested on May 5, 1920 in the wake of the notorious Palmer "Red Raids." They were charged with committing a $15,000 payroll robbery in South Braintree, Mass., during which a guard was killed. Both were convicted and sentenced to the electric chair. For the next seven years gigantic demonstrations, strikes, and protests against this frameup, took place here and abroad, and almost saved them. They were finally executed in Charlestown, Mass., midnight of August 22, 1927.

2. The *International Labor Defense* (I.L.D.) was formed in Chicago, June 23, 1925 and became one of the most influential defense organizations. Its main purpose was the development of mass political and legal defense against frame-ups, devoting much of its attention to labor cases. It played a leading part in the unsuccessful attempt to save Sacco and Vanzetti. The I.L.D. concerned itself especially with the legal and extra-legal attacks upon the Negro people, and in later years led the historic fights to save the Nine Scottsboro Boys and Angelo Herndon, having made these celebrated cases known all over the world.

3. The *Trade Union Education League* was organized in 1920 in Chicago, by *William Z. Foster* (1881-1961), and was the most vocal body favoring industrial unionism, amalgamation of craft unions, organization of the unorganized with full equality to Negro workers; it crusaded for unemployment insurance, peace, and recognition of the U.S.S.R. It placed its main stress, however, upon the work within the conservative trade unions. In September, 1929, it was reorganized into the *Trade Union Unity League,* with its main emphasis upon the organization of the unorganized into industrial trade unions, stressing the need of organizing new unions in the unorganized and semi-organized industries. William Z. Foster was elected its general secretary.

Foster, considered the "father of modern left-wing—progressive—unionism," led the great 1919 steel strike, which dramatized that industrial unionism was an effective weapon even though that strike was broken. In 1921 Foster joined the American Communist Party, and because of his gifts as an organizer, political leader and Marxist theoretician, held the position of chairman of the party continuously for over 30 years.

4. *March 6, 1930* has become a landmark in the fight for unemployment insurance; it was the first major nationwide demonstration for government aid to the victims of the Great Crisis. The leaders of the unemployed were filling the jails and were denounced as a menace to Law and Order. Two hundred were arrested in Chicago, seventy in Milwaukee, hundreds throughout the country. In New York City some 25,000 police and firemen concentrated at Union Square and when the spokesmen of the hungry throng attempted to present the mayor with their grievances, they arrested William Z. Foster, Robert Minor, Israel Amter and Harry Raymond—all well-known Communists—and sentenced them to three years' imprisonment.

5. *Scottsboro Case:* On April 7, 1933, Ruby Bates reversed her previous testimony and appeared in court for the defense. She then joined *William L. Patterson,* the revered black attorney and Executive Secretary of the I.L.D., in a mass delegation to Washington with a petition signed by 200,000 demanding the freedom of the boys.

Said Mr. Patterson (*Freedomways,* 3rd Quarter, 1969): "It was a political

322

frameup, a conspiracy of government against the Constitution, black citizenry and as well, whites. . . . The Communists and the leadership of the I.L.D. . . . introduced the art of mass struggle, of defense demonstrations in the streets. . . . Blacks and politically conscious white men, women and youth, fought together desperately in that case to expose the roots of racism and to mobilize against it the millions, white and black alike, who are so disastrously affected by it."

Between July 24, 1937, and June 16, 1947, eight of the Nine Scottsboro Boys were paroled; July 17, 1948, Haywood Patterson escaped Kilby Prison.

6. *The American Federation of Labor Committee for Unemployment Insurance and Relief,* a rank-and-file committee headed by Louis Weinstock of the Painters' Union, together with Harry Bridges representing the International Longshoremen's Association, and Elmer Brown representing the International Typographical Union, Local #6, was heard throughout the country. It successfully initiated and led the fight within the A.F.L. for unemployment insurance, and won support not only from 3,000 local unions, but also from 35 city central labor councils, 6 state federations, and 5 international unions, and was a major factor in compelling the A.F.L. to reverse itself (in 1935) on the matter of unemployment insurance.

7. Early in 1931, the American Communist Party formulated a *draft law* for a system of unemployment insurance, which later became known as the *Workers' Unemployment and Social Insurance Bill,* and was placed formally before the 73rd Congress, 2nd Session, as H.R. 7598. It was introduced by Representative Ernest Lundeen (Farm-Labor) of Minnesota, on *February 2, 1934.*

It was the only federal bill proposed for the purpose of paying workers and farmers insurance for loss of wages because of unemployment, part-time work, sickness, accident, old age or maternity. It was the only bill to propose that such insurance shall be administered by workers' commissions composed of rank-and-file members of workers' and farmers' organizations. It stipulated that funds for such insurance should be provided at the expense of the government and the employers, and that no contribution should be levied on the workers.

8. *Unemployment Insurance Bill,* presented to Congress during the first Hunger March, December 7, 1931, in Washington, D.C., read as follows:

To the Congress of the United States:
We, the undersigned, demand of the United States Senate and House of Representatives, the enactment of a bill establishing government unemployment insurance which shall be based upon the following measures:

Immediate Unemployment Insurance at Full Wages. 1. That a system of Federal government unemployment insurance be immediately established by an Act of Congress and made immediately effective, guaranteeing full wages to all workers wholly or partly unemployed, through no fault of their own, for the entire period of unemployment.

For All Workers—No Discrimination. 2. That unemployment insurance be paid to every unemployed worker, adult and youth, whether industrial or agricultural, office employees, and all other categories of wage labor, native or foreign born, citizen or non-citizen, white and Negro, men and women, and without discrimination against any race, color, age or political opinion. No worker shall be deprived of unemployment insurance because of refusal to take the place of strikers or to work for less than union rates of pay.

Insurance at the Expense of the Employers and the Government. 3. That full funds for unemployment insurance shall be raised by the government from funds now set aside for war preparations and by taxation upon the capital and profits of corporations and trusts and also by sharply upward taxation upon all incomes over $5,000.00. In no instance shall there be any contributions levied upon the workers in any form whatsoever for this insurance.

ADMINISTRATION BY THE WORKERS. 4. That the unemployment insurance fund shall be administered and controlled by the workers, through committees elected by the workers themselves.

FOR OTHER FORMS OF SOCIAL INSURANCE. 5. That social insurance be paid to workers to the amount of full wages to compensate for loss of wages through sickness, accident, old age, maternity, etc.

9. *Veterans Bonus Certificates,* officially called Adjusted Service Certificates; the Bonus was an additional payment to veterans of $1 for every day served in the armed forces at home; and $1.25 for every day spent overseas. The 1932 Bonus Marchers sought to obtain the right to borrow money on the payments due the veterans.